GORGIAS DISSERTATIONS

EARLY CHRISTIAN STUDIES

Volume 1

John Rufus

and the World Vision of
Anti-Chalcedonian Culture

John Rufus

and
The World Vision of
Anti-Chalcedonian Culture

JAN-ERIC STEPPA

GORGIAS PRESS
2002

First Gorgias Press Edition, 2002.

Copyright © 2002 by Gorgias Press LLC.

All rights reserved under International and Pan-American Copyright Conventions. Published in the United States of America by Gorgias Press LLC, New Jersey.

ISBN 1-931956-09-X

GORGIAS PRESS
46 Orris Ave., Piscataway, NJ 08854 USA
www.gorgiaspress.com

Printed in the United States of America

To Jessica

PREFACE AND ACKNOWLEDGMENTS

Looking at the whole of modern scholarly work on Syriac literature, we find hardly any publication on the concept of spiritual sickness and healing.

My first encounter with the anti-Chalcedonian movement took place on a beautiful day in the late summer of 1994 when, as a member of *Collegium Patristicum Lundense*, I had the great pleasure to be a guest when Lars Rydbeck, my teacher in Greek and Latin, celebrated his sixtieth birthday with a garden party. Since I was at that time finishing my work with an undergraduate paper on Origen's exegesis of Romans, I spent a lovely afternoon, discussing my future with my mentor Samuel Rubenson. When I asked him to suggest a suitable subject for a Master's thesis he immediately began to describe his current work on the Egyptian influences on Palestinian monasticism in the fourth and fifth centuries. In the course of this conversation I heard for the very first time the names of the great ascetic heroes of the anti-Chalcedonian movement: Peter, the remarkable son of King Bosmarius of Iberia, and Abba Isaiah, the Egyptian monk who settled in the wilderness of southern Palestine and became one of the most popular spiritual leaders in the region of Gaza. At once I accepted the challenge of tracing the historical and ideological motives behind their hostility against the Council of Chalcedon 451. From that point a journey began into the world of anti-Chalcedonianism that has continually forced me to reconsider and reshape not only my assumptions about the Christological controversies in the fifth and sixth century, but also my views on the history of Christianity in general.

Many are those who have accompanied me on this journey, and hopefully will continue to do so in the future. I am especially indebted to Samuel Rubenson, my thesis advisor, for his enthusiasm and creative support during the whole process. Through his unfailing participation in the project he has once more proved himself to be a true *abba* for his disciples. My gratitude is beyond measure.

The generous support and encouragement given by my friends in the Patristic Seminar Group in Lund cannot be exaggerated. I wish to express my thanks to them all, especially Kristina Alveteg, Sten Hidal, Gösta Hallonsten, Anna Näppi and Lars Rydbeck. I must also express my deepest gratitude to Ann Heberlein and Henric Johnsén for heroically having read the manuscript and contributed numerous suggestions to improve the text.

I wish to thank Lillian Larsen (Columbia University) for reading my drafts, and helping me to clarify my thoughts during many probing discussions in pubs and coffeehouses in Lund and New York. I would also like to thank Philip Rousseau (Catholic University of America) and Witold Witakowski (Uppsala University), for reading my Licentiate Thesis and providing me with important suggestions for my work with the present study.

I am very grateful to Bengt Ellenberger, who has patiently read the entire manuscript and corrected countless mistakes in the text. It goes without saying that the remaining mistakes are completely my own.

I wish to thank all other friends and colleagues at the Department of Theology and Religious Studies, University of Lund, especially Dan-Erik Andersson, Maria Ericson, Blazenka Scheuer, and James Starr, for their immense patience when I have bothered them with all kinds of practical questions in the final stage of the thesis phase. I also wish to thank Johan Eriksson, who through the whole process has supported me with the joys of friendship in hope and despair.

I also wish to express my sincere appreciation and gratitude to Susan Ashbrook Harvey (Brown University), who served as the faculty opponent at my ThD defense in April 2001, and the members of the examination board: Ezra Gebremedhin (Uppsala University), Bo Holmberg (Lund University) and Reinhart Staats (Kiel University). Their suggestions and recommendations have been extremely helpful in the process of turning my doctoral thesis into the present publication. Finally, I thank George Kiraz and Gorgias Press for thoughtful support and guidance through the publishing process.

CONTENTS

ABBREVIATIONS

AB	*Analecta Bollandiana.*
ABAW	*Abhandlungen der Bayerischen Akademie der Wissenschaften.* Phil.-Hist. Klasse.
ACW	Ancient Christian Writers.
ACO	*Acta Conciliorum Oecumenicorum.*
AHC	*Annuarium Historia Conciliorum.*
AKWG	*Abhandlungen der Königlichen Gesellschaft der Wissenschaften zu Göttingen.* Phil.-Hist. Klasse.
AP	Apophthegmata patrum, Collectio Graeca alphabetica.
ARB	*Académie Royale de Belgique.*
CS	Cistercian Studies.
CSCO	Corpus Scriptorum Christianorum Orientalium.
CSEL	Corpus Scriptorum Ecclesiasticorum Latinorum.
CSHB	Corpus Scriptores Historiae Byzantinae.
DOP	*Dumbarton Oaks Papers.*
GCS	Die griechischen christlichen Schriftsteller der ersten drei Jahrhunderte.
HE	*Historia ecclesiastica.*
HL	*Historia Lausiaca.*
HM	*Historia Monachorum.*
HR	*Historia Religiosa.*
HTR	*Harvard Theological Review.*
JA	*Journal Asiatique.*
JECS	*Journal of Early Christian Studies.*
JEH	*Journal of Ecclesiastical History.*
JRS	*Journal of Roman Studies.*
JTS	*Journal of Theological Studies.*
KvCh	*Das Konzil von Chalkedon.*
LA	*Liber Annuus.*
LCL	Loeb Classical Library.
OC	Oriens Christianus.
OCP	Orientalia Christiana Periodica.
PG	Patrologia Graeca.

PL	Patrologia Latina.
Pleroph.	*Plerophories*
PO	*Patrologia Orientalis.*
POC	*Proche-Orient Chrétien.*
RAM	*Revue d'ascétique et de mystique.*
RHR	*Revue de l'histoire des religions.*
ROC	*Revue de l'Orient Chretien.*
SC	Sources Chrétiennes.
Script. syri.	Scriptores syri.
SHAW	*Sitzungsberichte der Heidelberger Akademie der Wissenshaften.* Phil.-Hist. Klasse
SP	*Studia Patristica.*
StRiOC	*Studi e richerche sull' oriente cristiano.*
Sub. Hag	Subsidia Hagiographica.
SVTQ	*St Vladimir's Theological Quarterly*
TH	*Théologie Historique.*
TU	Texte und Untersuchungen.
V. Ant	*Vita Antonii.*
V. Petr. Ib.	Vita Petri Iberi

Introduction

The motives for the Insurrection

It was with an ambivalent mind that, in early 452, Pope Leo I received the reports from his legates on what had taken place at the Council of Chalcedon Indignant about the twenty-eighth canon, which confirmed the equal dignity of the patriarchal sees of Rome and Constantinople, he held Patriarch Anatolius of Constantinople personally responsible for this act of defiance of the apostolic authority of Old Rome and accused him of being motivated by a spirit of self-seeking.[1] Yet Leo made it known to Emperor Marcian that he was delighted that the bishops at the Council of Chalcedon had finally vindicated the truth and, sustained by the right hand of God, dispelled the last shadows of the Eutychian heresy. In spite of his displeasure about what he regarded as unlawful claims by the patriarchate of Constantinople, Leo was convinced that his personal crusade against the Christology of Eutyches had now reached a point of complete triumph.[2]

In the same year Leo received disturbing news from his confidential agent in the East, Bishop Julian of Kios, news that dampened his hopes for ecumenical recognition of the Chalcedonian definition of faith, which proclaimed Christ to be in his incarnate state of both divine and human nature. The information Leo received from Julian concerned the state in the East, particularly in Palestine, where turbulent resistance to the doctrinal decrees of Chalcedon had broken out in the monastic circles. As a result of this rebellion Bishop Juvenal of Jerusalem had been forced into exile, leaving the control of his see in the hands of monks who fiercely rejected any communion with bishops who had subscribed to the decisions of the Council of Chalcedon. Leo

---

[1] Leo, *Ep. ad Marcianum* (ep. 104), PL 54, 991-998. That Leo otherwise regarded the Council of Chalcedon as a personal victory is emphasized by T. Jalland, *The Life and Times of St. Leo the Great* (London 1941), 338.

[2] Jalland, 338.

did not conceal his fury at the state of affairs in Palestine, pronouncing a harsh verdict over the Palestinian monks in a letter to Julian of Kios, dated November 25.

> The deeds which you Fraternity mentions as being perpetrated by crowds of false monks are serious and to be lamented with no small grief. It is the impious Eutyches who, through the madness of his deceivers, wages war against the evangelical and apostolic teachings, a war which is bound to involve him and his associates in ruin. Through God's patience the coming of the ruin is delayed in order to make clear how much the enemies of Christ's cross are serving the Devil. Heretical depravity now comes out from behind the old veil of pretense and can no longer restrain itself within the limits of hypocrisy. And all the poison which it had kept covered for a long time has now been poured out upon the disciples of truth, not only by the use of the pen but even in manual violence, in order forcibly to extort consent from men either of untutored simplicity or of panic-stricken faith.3

To Leo the rebellious monks in Palestine were nothing but Eutychian troublemakers, prompted by wrong-headed madness. By taking part in the blasphemies of Eutyches and Dioscorus these riotous monks were soldiers of Antichrist, egged on in their simplicity by the ringleaders and pestilential teachers of heresy. If their sedition was tolerated, or if they escaped punishment for their insubordination, they would cause the perdition of many.4

This letter, written in the uttermost rage against what Leo regarded as 'false monks' and 'sons of darkness', ends with a request for continual reports about the Palestinian mutiny. From the next letter that Leo sent to Julian, dated March 11, 453, it appears that his request for further information was not fulfilled in a satisfactory way. Leo simply finds it necessary to repeat his request:

> But with regard to the monks of Palestine, who are said this long time to be in a state of mutiny, I know not by what spirit they are at present moved. Nor has any one yet explained to me what reasons they seem to bring

---

3 Leo, *Ep. ad Julianum* (ep. 109), 1014-1015; tr. by E. Hunt, *St. Leo the Great: Letters*, The Fathers of the Church 34 (Washington 1964), 194.

4 Leo, *Ep. ad Julianum*, 1015-1016.

forward for their discontent: whether for instance, they wish to serve the Eutychian heresy by such madness, or whether they are irreconcilably vexed that their bishop could have been misled into that blasphemy, whereby, in spite of the very associations of the holy spots, from which issued instruction for the whole world, he has alienated himself from the Truth of the Lord's Incarnation, and in their opinion that cannot be venial in him which in others had to be wiped out by absolution. And therefore I desire to be more fully informed about these things that proper means may be taken for their correction; because it is one thing to arm oneself wickedly against the Faith, and another thing to be immoderately disturbed on behalf of it.[5]

Leo's question is simple—why do the monks of Palestine set themselves up against the Chalcedonian definition of faith? Is it because they are Eutychians, or is it because they fear that their bishop Juvenal at Chalcedon had made himself guilty of heresy as he turned his back on Dioscorus, the Alexandrine patriarch, in association with whom he had struggled for so long against Nestorian heretics?[6]

We do not know whether Julian of Kios responded to Leo's question. But in yet another letter, written directly to the monks of Palestine, Leo suggests that the monks were probably misled by an inaccurate translation from Latin into Greek of his letter to Flavian, the so-called *Tome*. This letter, in which he courteously described his addresses as essentially 'greater friends to truth than to falsehood,' turns out to be a rather patronizing exposition of Leo's own Christological view. Having declared that the *Tome* in no way departs from the catholic faith of the holy fathers and that the condemnation of both Nestorius and Eutyches was correct, he accuses them of lack of humility and peacefulness and reproaches them for their violent fury. He ends his letter with an admonition not to deny the true flesh of Christ but to accept the true nature of

---

[5] Leo, *Ep. ad Julianum* (ep. 113), 1026; tr. by C. L. Feltoe, *Letters and Sermons of Leo the Great*, A Select Library of the Nicene and Post-Nicene Fathers of the Christian Church, ser. 2, vol. 12 (Grand Rapids 1983), 83.

[6] See Jalland, 332, including n. 39: 'The point is that Leo could not make up his mind whether the monks were rioting in support of the intruder Theodosius, or because they were dissatisfied with Juvenal's loyalty to the Chalcedonian 'settlement'.

the Incarnation: 'Forswear, my sons, forswear these suggestions of the devil'.[7] In the letter to the Palestinian monks Leo appears to regard the monastic insurrection in Palestine as a result of a zealous devotion to the truth, founded on a severe misinterpretation of the catholic faith as pronounced in the *Tome* as well as by the bishops at Chalcedon. According to Leo, it was an essential lack of knowledge about the truth that made them dispute the faith, while yet believing that they were acting for the faith. If only the misunderstandings were cleared away and the monks humbly joined the body of catholic unity, they would no longer find the Incarnation of the Word a stumbling block to themselves.[8]

Pope Leo's suggestion that the Chalcedonian controversy could be explained in terms of an accidental misunderstanding appears even today to be the most acknowledged way to approach the breach between the Chalcedonian and non-Chalcedonian Churches in the fifth and sixth centuries. But while Leo claimed that it was the opponents of Chalcedon that had misunderstood the truth, it is recognized today that the misunderstandings of the expositions of an essentially shared faith were mutual. For instance, the Joint Commission of the Theological Dialogue Between the Orthodox Church and the Oriental Orthodox Churches in Chambésy, 1990, agreed on the following:

> We have now clearly understood that both families have always loyally maintained the same authentic Orthodox Christological faith, and the unbroken continuity of the apostolic tradition, though they may have used christological terms in different ways. It is this common faith and continuous loyalty to the Apostolic Tradition that should be the basis of our unity and communion.[9]

This was not the first time that a joint commission between the 'Eastern' and the 'Oriental' Orthodox Churches recognized full agreement as regards the Christological dogma.[10] Further, several

---

[7] Leo, *Ep. ad monachos* (ep. 124), 1061-1068.

[8] Leo, *Ep. ad monachos*, 1067-1068.

[9] In C. Chaillot and A. Belopopsky (eds.), *Towards unity: The Theological Dialogue between the Orthodox Church and the Oriental Orthodox Churches* (Geneva 1998), p. 64.

[10] See P. Gregorios, W. H. Lazareth, and N. A. Nissiotis (eds.), *Does Chalcedon Divide or Unite: Towards convergence in Orthodox Christology* (Geneva 1981).

scholarly studies published in the twentieth century, investigating the doctrinal circumstances of the divergence between the Chalcedonian and non-Chalcedonian Churches, have pointed out the absence of any real difference in the views of each tradition on the relationship between the human and divine natures in Christ. At least theoretically, the epithets 'monophysite' and 'monophysitism', polemically indicating the rejection of any human element in the one person of Christ, have been proved inadequate for a valid consideration of non-Chalcedonian Christology.

In 1909 Joseph Lebon published his pioneering study on early non-Chalcedonian theology, focusing his attention on what he labeled 'Severian monophysitism', i.e. the mainstream non-Chalcedonianism that reached a high-water mark with Severus of Antioch, Patriarch of Antioch 512-518.[11] Clarifying Harnack's distinction between real monophysitism (*der Sache nach*) and nominal monophysitism (*nach dem kirchlichen Sprachgebrauch*)[12] Lebon suggested that the ideas that confirmed a confusion or change in the divine and human elements in the person of Christ, or that denied the consubstantiality of Christ with mankind, must be distinguished from what the Chalcedonians themselves regarded as a rejection of the human nature of Christ. The confusion between what is real and what is nominal derives from the term 'monophysitism' itself, denoting the idea of 'one *physis*' but presupposing that '*physis*' refers to the distinct human or divine element in the person of Christ. In this way the use of the epithet 'monophysite' neglects that, in the eyes of the non-Chalcedonians themselves and in accordance with the terminology of Cyril of Alexandria, '*physis*' did not primarily denote the distinct elements in the person of Christ but rather the person itself. As a consequence, the identification made by the non-Chalcedonians between nature (*physis*) and person (*hypostasis*) exposes the inaccuracy of the term 'monophysitism' as regards the principal line of the non-Chalcedonian movement, which forcefully rejected any idea of confusion or transformation of the human and divine properties in

---

[11] J. Lebon, *Le monophysisme sévérien: Étude historique, littéraire et théologique sur la résistance monophysite au concile de Chalcédoine* (Louvain 1909). See also Lebon, 'La Christologie du monophysisme syrien', in A. Grillmeier and H. Bacht (eds.), *KvCh*, vol. 1 (Würzburg 1951), 425-580.

[12] Cf. A. Harnack, *Lehrbuch der Dogmengeschichte*, vol. 2 (Tübingen 1909), 352-353.

Christ. Therefore, according to Lebon, the term 'real monophysitism' can be used properly only when defining the ideas of individual thinkers like Apollinaris and Eutyches, who were rejected not only by the Chalcedonians but, in fact, also by most non-Chalcedonians. Lebon thus reduces the use of the epithet 'monophysite' as regards non-Chalcedonians like Dioscorus, Timothy Aelurus or Severus of Antioch to a matter of scholarly habit in the Western tradition, acknowledging that only circumstances have saved Cyril of Alexandria from being labeled with this epithet.[13]

Lebon, and with him most students of the Christological controversies during the patristic period, thus retained the terms 'monophysitism' and 'monophysite' with reference to the prevailing discourse of dogmatic history. However, in a monograph on the development of the neo-Chalcedonian tradition published in 1979, Patrick Gray pointed out the prejudicial and anachronistic character of these terms, suggesting instead the terms 'pro-Chalcedonian' (or 'Chalcedonian') and 'anti-Chalcedonian' as valid descriptions of the Christological factions in the fifth and sixth centuries. Further, according to Gray, these terms called attention to the real point of controversy, i.e. the question of the reception of Chalcedon, rather than a conflict between two different Christological views, one of Chalcedonian orthodoxy and the other of Monophysite heterodoxy.[14]

Proceeding from the statement that the Chalcedonians and the anti-Chalcedonians essentially taught the same thing, it may seem difficult to find any adequate reason for opposition against Chalcedon in the East. As Johannes Karmiris stated in one of the unofficial theological conversations between the 'Eastern' and the 'Oriental' Orthodox:

> Anyone will be become perplexed who today objectively and unbiasedly investigates the ecclesiastical events of the fifth century a.d. occasioned by Monophysitism. This perplexity is due to the fact that one can find no sufficient dogmatic-ecclesiastical reason for their having detached themselves from the

---

[13] Lebon, *Le monophysisme sévérien*, xxii-xxv.

[14] P. T. R. Gray, *The Defense of Chalcedon in the East (451-553)* (Leiden 1979), 74.

stem of the Orthodox Catholic Church of the East to
which they still organically belong.[15]

We have seen that this vexation about the motives behind the rise
of the anti-Chalcedonian movement was shared by Pope Leo, who
suggested that the reason why the Palestinian monks had set
themselves up against the catholic unity was their misunderstanding
of the *Tome* and the Chalcedonian definition of faith. However,
Leo's suggestion can be regarded as accurate only from a highly
superficial point of view. In fact, to explain the reasons behind the
Christological conflict merely in terms of different usages of the
concepts 'physis' and 'hypostasis' is not a sufficient approach to
elucidate the rage of controversy that shook the Eastern Empire in
the fifth and sixth centuries. It is evident that to the followers of
Chalcedon the acceptance of one nature after the Incarnation
implied approving Eutyches, and that, on the other hand, the non-
Chalcedonians recognized in the confession of two natures after
the Incarnation the Christological view defended by Nestorius.
That each faction linked different contents to the same expressions
probably gave rise to deep frustration, the non-Chalcedonians
realizing that they were accused of being Eutychians, while the
Chalcedonians knew that Chalcedon was believed by many to have
accepted the teaching of Nestorius.[16] But to be content with that is
to trivialize the motives behind the opposition against Chalcedon.
Fundamentally, the Chalcedonian controversy was not a conflict
merely about the semantic connections between certain words and
concepts but about different ways of looking upon reality.

The question, originally posed by Pope Leo to Julian of Kios,
about the cause of the Palestinian rebellion against the *Tome* and
the Council of Chalcedon remains unanswered. Remarkably, only a
very few serious attempts were undertaken during the 19th century

---

[15] J. N. Karmiris, 'The Problem of the Unification of the Non-
Chalcedonian Churches of the East with the Orthodox on the Basis of
Cyril's Formula: Mia Physis tou Theou Logou Sesarkomene', in *Does
Chalcedon Divide or Unite?*, 29.

[16] For instance, Timothy Aelurus intensely rejected rumors that
labeled him Eutychian, mentioning the promoters of such rumors as
'deceivers', in Zacharias Scholasticus, *HE* 4.12, CSCO, Script. syri 3.5,
186. For the Chalcedonian side, see *V. Euthym*, 42-43, TU 49.2, where
Euthymius is reported to have defended the Chalcedonian faith against
accusations of Nestorianism.

Heinrich Bacht - 1st Theory, 'Monastic, Motivation *(1953)*

to bring to light the basic motives behind the anti-Chalcedonian movement. The first important contribution is Heinrich Bacht's lengthy article from 1953 (published in the second volume of the standard work *Das Konzil von Chalkedon*) on the role of the monastic movement for the popular resistance against Chalcedon.[17]

Bacht claims that the key to uncover the motives behind the anti-Chalcedonian movement is to be found in early Eastern monasticism. The political dimension of monasticism, according to Bacht, was established already during the Arian controversy in the fourth century when, in his *Life of Antony*, Athanasius of Alexandria promoted the image of the true monk as a hero for the welfare of the Christian community. But it is only with the Chalcedonian controversy that monks conspicuously entered into the foreground of the theological and ecclesiastical affairs in the Eastern Empire.[18] Bacht points out what Pope Leo apparently already knew, i.e. that it was monks rather than bishops who initiated the resistance against Chalcedon, conceiving as they did the Chalcedonian statement of faith as a revival of Nestorianism.

Drawing a detailed sketch of the ecclesiastical developments from the Council of Ephesus in 431 to the beginning of Emperor Justin's reign, Bacht recognizes the prevalent force of the monastic movement as decisive for the rise and advancement of the Chalcedonian controversy: 'Ohne ihren Beitrag wäre die Bewegung des »Monophysitismus« wohl nie zu einer so gefährlichen Macht geworden'.[19] One major reason was, according to Bacht, the intimate connection between Egyptian monasticism and the Patriarchs of Alexandria. Through the expansion of monasticism in the fourth century into a veritable mass movement, the monastic population became a valuable instrument in the hands of the patriarchs, as well as an important force to consider in an efficient administration. But the expansion of monasticism also promoted 'scandalous conditions', which can be explained within the framework of mass psychology. Many monks received the monastic habit solely for the sake of appearance, and were not immediately motivated by the ideals of asceticism. According to

---

[17] H. Bacht, 'Die Rolle des orientalische Mönchtums in den kirchenpolitischen Auseinandersetzungen um Chalcedon (431-519)', in *KvCh*, vol. 2 (Würzburg 1953), 193-314.

[18] Bacht, 194-195.

[19] Bacht, 292.

[handwritten: William Frend - Pushes this same theory - (1972) see below for added emphases]

Bacht it was the close connection between the monastic movement and the Patriarchs of Alexandria that motivated the monks to oppose the imperial authorities. Prompted by what Bacht designated as the 'subjectivism' of Eastern monasticism they were at the same time sturdily loyal to the Alexandrine Patriarchs, something that made them a particularly violent force.[20] Having emphasized the role of monastic authorities standing in the front-line of the monastic crowds,[21] Bacht concludes his argument by drawing attention to the ecclesiastic aspect of the aim of the monastic life, i.e. the idea of active participation in the life of the Church as an ascetic commitment. In this way the personal struggle against demons in the desert is linked to this aim not only for personal salvation but also for the salvation of the entire Church.[22]

Bacht seems to consider monasticism as the source of a fanatic conservatism that provided the opponents of Chalcedon with a spiritual motivation to meddle in matters in which they had no reason to be involved in the first place. But even if his assessments leave much to be desired, there is no doubt that, according to him, the essential motivation and identity of the anti-Chalcedonian movement was based on an uncompromising attitude possible only in a monastic setting. This argument is followed up by William Frend, who in his survey on the emergence of the non-Chalcedonian movement published in 1972, regarded the monks, representing 'the swelling tide of public opinion', as the main force behind the resistance against Chalcedon.[23] On the question why the one-nature formula attracted the monastic population in the East, Frend suggests the contribution of a range of motives, among them the loyalty to the Alexandrine Patriarchs and the appeal of the one-nature Christology to those simple-minded monks who saw salvation as dependent on the undivided incarnation of God. He also draws attention to the emphasis within Egyptian monasticism on the Bible and the Council of Nicaea without, however, sufficiently elucidating his argument.[24]

---

[20] Bacht, 295-296.

[21] Bacht, 297.

[22] Bacht, 312-314.

[23] W. H. C. Frend, *The Rise of the Monophysite Movement: Chapters in the History of the Church in the Fifth and Sixth Centuries* (Cambridge 1979), 136.

[24] Frend, *The Rise of the Monophysite Movement*, 136-137.

One of the most recent contributions to the seemingly elusive relationship between anti-Chalcedonianism and Eastern monasticism is included in Johannes Roldanus' study of 1997 on the monastic involvement in the Chalcedonian controversy.[25] In his attempt to solve the question why certain monks chose to reject the Christology of Chalcedon, Roldanus begins with a presentation of the views of Carl Mönnich on the one hand, and Francis Murphy and Polycarp Sherwood on the other.[26] As Roldanus observes, Mönnich does not recognize any essential difference between Chalcedonian and non-Chalcedonian Christology, and rejects Christology as the main point of controversy. According to Mönnich, the problem for the anti-Chalcedonian monks was rather that the authority of Chalcedon had been defiled, as a result of the deep involvement of the imperial authority. The widely spread affection towards monastic authority was, in Mönnich's opinion, the main source for a fundamental distrust in the Emperor's claim for ecclesiastical leadership, particularly when effectuated through evident despotic measures.[27] Roldanus then proceeds to the views of Murphy and Sherwood, who also emphasize piety rather than theology as the basic motive for the opposition against Chalcedon. Since in the two-nature formula the anti-Chalcedonian monks recognized a reduction of Christ's divinity, they feared that the possibility of the human soul to unite with Christ in the final process of divinification was lost. But in the end, according to Murphy and Sherwood, it was not piety, mysticism or ascetic values that caused the secession of the non-Chalcedonians from the

---

[25] Roldanus, 'Stützen und Störenfriede: Mönchische Einmischung in die doktrinäre und kirchenpolitische Rezeption von Chalkedon', in J. van Oort und J. Roldanus (eds.), *Chalkedon: Geschichte und Aktualität: Studien zur Rezeption der christologischen Formel von Chalkedon* (Louvain 1997).

[26] Cf. C. W. Mönnich, *Geding der Vrijheid, De betrekkingen der oosterse en westerse kerken tot de val van Constantinopel (1453)* (Zwolle 1976), 180-182; F. X. Murphy and P. Sherwood, *Konstantinopel II und III*, in G. Dumeige and H. Bacht (eds.), *Geschichte der ökumenischen Konzilien*, III (Mainz 1990), 49-50.

[27] Roldanus, 'Stützen und Störenfriede', 139-140. Cf. Mönnich, *Geding der Vrijheid*, 180.

[handwritten: Murphy and Sherwood's theory]

imperial Church, but simply the lack of political support from the emperors.[28]

Roldanus remains skeptical to both these conclusions—that the resistance against Chalcedon was caused by suspicion towards the influence of worldly authorities in the establishment of Orthodoxy, as well as that the cause can be found in the view that the Chalcedonian dogma implied a danger to monastic piety. Criticizing Mönnich's simplistic view on the relation between monastic values and worldly authorities he remarks that some emperors clearly followed anti-Chalcedonian sentiments in their policy. Further, he refutes the opinion of Murphy and Sherwood, bringing in the hagiographic works of Cyril of Scythopolis as evidence that even in ascetic circles the two-nature formula of Chalcedon could easily be accepted without fear of jeopardizing the worship of Christ's divinity.[29] *[handwritten: Roldanus' refutation of them.]*

In the following discussion Roldanus builds his argument entirely on Bacht's opinions from 1953, and fails to present any new insights on the essential motives behind the anti-Chalcedonian movement. He touches upon the close connection in the monastic concept between ascetic retreat and involvement in the ecclesiastic affairs that had been established by Athanasius in his *Life of Antony*. This connection had made monks regard themselves as responsible for not only their own salvation but for the salvation of the whole Church. He also emphasizes the role of ascetic authorities as an important force behind the emergence of the diverging factions within the Eastern Church as these ascetic authorities directed the attitudes towards Chalcedon from their opinions whether Chalcedon was in accordance with the Council of Nicaea or not.[30]

[handwritten: Roldanus shares Bacht's theory.]

[handwritten: His emphasis]

The preceding survey of various approaches to the causes of the anti-Chalcedonian movement reveals a prevalent state of confusion and a remarkable lack of sufficient and penetrating investigations into the problem. Since Leo posed his question to Julian of Kios fifteen hundred years ago, no scholar—neither Bacht, Frend nor Roldanus—has yet succeeded in providing a completely convincing and satisfactory answer to why the monks of the East furiously opposed the Council of Chalcedon. Except

---

[28] Roldanus, 140. Cf. Murphy and Sherwood, *Konstantinopel II und III*, 49.

[29] Roldanus, 140-141.

[30] Roldanus, 142-146.

for some important remarks already put forth by Bacht, including the monks' loyalty towards the Patriarchs of Alexandria, the role of the ascetic authority, and the involvement in ecclesiastic affairs as a monastic theme, the problem remains unsolved.

Hagiography and Culture

There seem to be at least two reasons behind the insufficient results in earlier investigations on the emergence of anti-Chalcedonianism. The first reason is that the inquiries, explicit or not, still to a large extent follow confessional boundaries. The underlying obligation—most evident in Bacht but present also in Roldanus—to defend Chalcedon leads to a perception of the non-Chalcedonians as obstinate enemies of orthodoxy, thus obstructing any intentional attempt to understand the world of anti-Chalcedonianism.

The second reason, which is in some respects associated with the first, is found in the sources for our knowledge of the Chalcedonian controversy. Some of the most important of these sources belong to the literary *genre* of hagiography.[31] For the situation in Palestine scholars have mainly relied on the series of hagiographies written by the Chalcedonian monk Cyril of Scythopolis in the sixth century, which describes the lives and acts of monastic authorities such as Euthymius and Sabas.[32] But even within anti-Chalcedonian circles hagiographic writings were produced that are today indispensable for any balanced consideration of the monastic resistance against Chalcedon in Palestine. To this group of hagiographic writings belong the works of Zacharias Scholasticus and John Rufus. Recently, in the most fruitful contribution of the last few years to our knowledge of anti-Chalcedonian literature, Bernard Flusin remarks that anti-Chalcedonian hagiography has consistently been forced to the periphery in studies of Palestinian monasticism, in a way that has

---

[31] For a pioneer study of hagiography, see H. Delehaye, *Cinq leçons sur la méthode hagiographique*, Sub. Hag. 21 (Bruxelles 1934). For one of the most important contributions for the contemporary study of hagiography, see P. Cox, *Biography in Late Antiquity* (Berkeley 1983).

[32] *Vitae*, ed. by E. Schwartz, TU 49.2 (Leipzig 1939).

led to an 'error of perspective'.[33] One symptom of this error of perspective, caused either by confessional considerations or by unwillingness to take into account texts not preserved in Greek, is the tendency to regard the Chalcedonian hagiography of Cyril of Scythopolis as a mainstream representative of Palestinian hagiography. Such a view is based on a disregard for the complexity and discontinuity of the history of Palestinian hagiography, a disregard that does not correspond with our present knowledge of that literature in the fifth and sixth centuries. Throughout his discussion of Palestinian hagiography Flusin makes it clear that the Chalcedonian controversy in Palestine was essentially a struggle about history. In this struggle hagiography was a forceful weapon, since it had the power to reconstruct as well as rewrite history. In Palestine, Chalcedonians and anti-Chalcedonians alike based their own ideological preferences on the past, while discrediting their opponents with accusations of novelty, innovation and change. In using hagiography as a method of reconstructing history each faction established its own 'facts', in order to identify the unbroken line between the ancient fathers in the past and the champions of orthodoxy in the present. In this way, by means of individual selection and organization of these 'facts,' Chalcedonians and anti-Chalcedonians created their own separate forms of cultural identity.[34]

It is evident that the anti-Chalcedonian movement was deeply motivated by concerns fundamentally associated with monasticism. This view has been undisputed since 1912, when Eduard Schwartz, in his pioneering study on John Rufus, declared anti-Chalcedonianism to be a 'Mönchreligion'.[35] The ideological rhetoric of anti-Chalcedonian literature, as presented by such authors as John of Ephesus, Zacharias Scholasticus, and John Rufus, rests entirely on the notion of monastic life as the ultimate way to reach

---

[33] B. Flusin, 'L'hagiographie palestinienne et la réception du concile de Chalcédoine', in J.-O. Rosenquist (ed.), ΛΕΙΜΩΝ: *Studies Presented to Lennart Rydén on His Sixthy-Fifth Birthday* (Uppsala 1996), 26.

[34] See for instance Flusin's discussion about the idea of unbroken continuity between the holy fathers of the Egyptian desert and the Chalcedonian monks in Judaea; Flusin, 'L'hagiographie palestinienne', 46-47.

[35] Schwartz, 'Johannes Rufus: ein monophysitischer Schriftsteller', in *SHAW* 3.16 (Heidelberg 1912), 13.

spiritual knowledge, and certainty about the faith of the fathers. In
this way, anti-Chalcedonian literature was an integral part of the
hagiographic tradition of Eastern asceticism.

The Christian discourse of Late Antiquity included a variety of
forms of verbal communication and rhetorical expression. But
among the variety of textual genres and subgenres biographical
narrative, as Averil Cameron has pointed out, enjoyed a special
preference. As a literary form, sprung from the ancient lives of
pagan philosophers, sages, and statesmen, the biographical
narrative succeeded in building up a social identity and a viable
Christian worldview.[36] According to Cameron, the biographic
narrative was an integral part of the Christian discourse. In the
early history of Christianity this was manifested in at least three
different stages. The first stage represents the composing of the
Gospels and the Acts of the Apostles. The second stage coincided
with the periods of persecution and the writing of the passions of
the martyrs. The third stage, finally, represents the emergence of
the lives of Christian holy men, as a result of the development of
the ascetic movement in the fourth century. In this stage we find
the first expressions of Christian hagiography in the proper sense
of the word. These texts, with their constant emphasis on the
importance of the ascetic way of life, quickly proved to be the most
popular form of Christian discourse.

Hagiography is closely associated with the cultural climate in
the world of Late Antiquity. As a device common to pagans, Jews,
and Christians, it was born out of the meeting of various literary
and rhetorical expressions with the reality of the Late Hellenistic
world.[37] A formal definition of hagiography as a specific literary
genre is not possible. Rather, it is to be regarded as an all-
embracing code-system for the articulation within a literary context
of the meeting between heaven and earth through such human
beings as were commonly recognized as 'holy men'. The definition
of hagiography in Late Antiquity, therefore, presupposes a proper
definition of the Late Antique notion of the holy man.

At the heart of Late Antique hagiography rests the notion of
the holy man as a mediator between heaven and the material world.

---

[36] A. Cameron, *Christianity and the Rhetoric of Empire* (Berkeley and Los
Angeles 1991), 91-93.

[37] M. van Uytfanghe, 'L'Hagiographie: un 'genre' chrétien ou antique
tardif', *AB* 111 (1993), 147-149.

The holy man was not a mere oracle, mediating such knowledge of the future of ordinary men as he had received through some kind of ecstatic experience. Instead, the holy man was an expression of the Late Antique hope for a staircase between this world and the other, based on the hope that there were individuals who, in their own person, had been transformed into *loci* for the direct encounter with divine providence.[38] The holy man was the voice of God, a position received through years of ascetic wrestling with the powers of materiality. He was an active force in society, a living idea of the interplay between the divine and material realities founded on the *paideia* of early Christian asceticism. But he was also a man cocooned in stories that helped preserve his post-mortal memory. These stories were not only a device for remembrance of the holy men but also a device for imitation.[39] In their lives holy men had showed the way for the personal realization of holiness for everyone. Thus hagiography showed the way for every human to reach divinification, to be a man of God.] - *Definition of a Holy Man.* [1]

To write and to mediate stories of holy men was one of the features of ascetic life. It was a labor not reserved for learned and sophisticated men gifted with literary articulation (in spite of the humble remarks on their lack of every talent and knowledge in the prefaces of their works). It was a labor that involved every member in the monastic community. Hagiography was more than edifying stories, written by a few for the entertainment of the many. Above all, as in the case of folklore, it was an instrument for organizing the collective memory of monastic culture.[40]

---

[38] P. Brown, 'The Rise and Function of the Holy Man in Late Antiquity', *JRS* 61 (1971), 80-85.

[39] See Cameron, *Christianity and the Rhetoric of Empire*, 56: 'written *Lives* provided the guidelines for the construction of a Christian life, and the ascetic model (...) provided the guidelines for the construction of a specifically Christian self. (...) Written *Lives* were mimetic; real ascetic discipline in turn imitated the written *Lives*'.

[40] There are surprisingly few studies on Christian hagiography as a discourse for the preservation of ideological and cultural structures. P. Rousseau comes particularly close to a consideration of this perspective, see *Ascetics, Authority and the Church: In the Age of Jerome and Cassian* (Oxford 1978), 68-76, and *Pachomius: The Making of a Community in Fourth-Century Egypt* (Berkeley 1985), 44-55. For the relation between hagiography and ideology in the Western tradition, see R. Van Dam, *Saints and their Miracles*

The need within the monastic communities to maintain the idea of discipleship even when the great ascetic masters had long since departed, was the immediate motive behind the production of hagiographic writing. In order to give meaning to the yearly remembrances of the holy men's deaths and to preserve their memory for coming generations of monks, their deeds and words had to be recounted. The memories of holy men were preserved through literary devices commonly recognized all over the late Roman Empire as adequate ways to describe them as historical facts. It was essential that the stories of the saints were based on events that were considered to have occurred in historic times and therefore true. Thus, hagiography was closely connected with history and truth. In hagiography, where the claim for truth was put in the context of a historical narrative, the interaction between truth and narrative was essential for any report of the life and actions of a holy man.[41]

Closely connected to this interaction between truth and narrative, hagiography was also a communal report, reflecting the views of the local Christian community. Hagiography presented itself as a genre of monastic discourse implicitly directed towards the conservation of the traditional structures and ideals of a proper ascetic conduct. Often motivated by disputes with other communities and beliefs, the lives of holy men served as written or orally transmitted manifestations of a culture considered spiritually superior to that of the men of the world. In the lives of the holy men the controversies of the days were considered according to well-tried rhetorical strategies and solved against the background of fixed ideological conventions. In early monasticism these strategies and conventions were assumed as ways of contemplating ancient ideas of ascetic purity. Thus, they functioned as normative

---

in Late Antique Gaul (Princeton 1993), and T. Head, *Hagiography and the Cult of Saints: The Diocese of Orléans, 800-1200* (Cambridge 1990).

[41] See Cameron, *Christianity and the Rhetoric of Empire*, 93. For the relationship between fiction and history in Late Antique biography, see Cox, *Biography in Late Antiquity*, xi-xiv. Late Antique biography, according to Cox, implied a constant 'play' between history and fiction that brought meaning to a hero's life through the blurring out of the limits between imagination and historical facts. Biography is characterized as not a mere representation of the hero's life, but a manifestation of his inner qualities through the personal conceptions of the biographer.

emblems in the framework of hagiographic literature. In the form of hagiographic narrative, the early Christian concepts of poverty, humility, and alienation were realized in history through the stories of certain individuals believed to have fulfilled the common expectations of the meaning of Christian discipleship. Through these holy persons the hagiographic narratives expressed what the Christian communities saw as the inner meaning of Christian life.[42] But, as in most kinds of communicative situations, the hagiographer had to stick to what was recognized as truth in the community of readers. In order to be understood, and to fulfill the hagiographic aim of edifying the community of readers, the hagiographer had to proceed from the field of discursive practice, or the horizon of expectations, of the community. Hagiography not only involves the author's creative imagination of holy men but also encompasses the whole process of transference between addresser and the addressee of the hagiographic message. As Averil Cameron concludes in her discussion on why early Christian authors express their ideals in mainly biographical narrative:

> It built its own symbolic universe by exploiting the kind of stories that people liked to hear, and which in their turn provided as mechanism by which society at large and the real lives of individuals might be regulated. The better these stories were constructed, the better they functioned as structure-maintaining narratives and the more their audiences were imposed to accept them as true. [43]

Although based on the same rhetorical elements hagiography was used as vehicle for the maintenance of pre-established ideologies. Thus, proceeding from the inviolability of the system of rhetorical expectations, hagiography represented a persuasive or 'consolatory' form of communication, since it led its readers to accept what was already accepted in the community in a basically emotional way.[44]

---

[42] Cameron, *Christianity and the Rhetoric of Empire*, 115-119. For the relation between hagiography and history, see J. Børtnes, *Visions of Glory: Studies in Early Russian Hagiography* (Oslo 1988), 27, where he suggests that the legends of the saints are 'clearly defined in space and time and by being put forward as true'. Cf. Cox, *Biography in Late Antiquity*, 65.

[43] Cameron, *Christianity and the Rhetoric of Empire*, 93.

[44] Cf. U. Eco, *La struttura assente: introduzione alla ricerca semiologica* (Milano 1971), 89, where this kind of persuasive communication is characterized as '*deposito di forme morte e ridondanti, che è retorica consolatoria,*

In order to produce a specific set of emotional responses, techniques were borrowed from the conventional store of pre-established rhetorical devices and archetypes.

Recognition of hagiography as a mechanism for the creation of monastic culture is one way of eliminating the dangers of the error of perspective that Flusin pointed out to us. It invites the historian to read and interpret hagiographic texts, Chalcedonian as well as anti-Chalcedonian, as the result of textual actions within historically demarcated universes of structured knowledge and memory.[45] Aimed at the preservation of Christian worldviews in the form of popular narrative, hagiography was especially suitable for times of transition and crisis. Since it allowed for multiple manipulations and articulations hagiography was especially profitable for propagandistic purposes, not least in the context of doctrinal controversies during the fifth and sixth centuries. After Chalcedon it became the main form of literary medium in the anti-Chalcedonian movement. The earliest extant anti-Chalcedonian hagiography is a panegyrical account of Dioscorus, originally written by his disciple Theopistus before the patriarchate of Peter Mongus, and preserved in Syriac.[46] Covering the time from the prelude to the Council of Chalcedon to the death of Dioscorus at Gangra in Paphlagonia in 454, the text presents the protagonist as a charismatic opponent of Chalcedonianism, gifted with visionary and thaumaturgic powers. In the course of its history the text has been revised, and later material has been incorporated into its corpus.

At the end of the fifth century, concurrently with the triumph of anti-Chalcedonianism in Egypt, anti-Chalcedonian hagiography moved its center to Palestine. At this point the resistance against Chalcedon was faced with an increasing danger of annihilation. For several reasons the anti-Chalcedonian movement in Palestine was

---

e mira a riconfermare le opinioni del destinatario, fingendo di discutere ma in effetti risolvendosi in mozione degli affetti'.

[45] Cf. the methodological approach of R. Darnton in *The Great Cat Massacre and Other Episodes in French Cultural History* (New York 1984), 4-7, esp. 259-262. For a discussion, see J. E. Toews, 'The Historian in the Labyrinth of Signs: Reconstructing Cultures and Reading Texts in the Practice of Intellectual History', *Semiotica* 83.3 (1991), 351-384.

[46] Theopistus of Alexandria, *Vita Dioscori*, ed. and tr. by F. Nau, *JA*, ser. 10, vol. 1-2 (Paris 1903), 5-108, 241-310.

particularly vulnerable. First, the holy places in Jerusalem made Palestine the stage for considerable international interaction. The never-ceasing flow of pilgrims from the most distant parts of the Empire forced anti-Chalcedonians into contact with Chalcedonians. This made the religious situation in Palestine extremely complicated for the anti-Chalcedonian side. In addition, the holy places, attracting pilgrims from east and west, invested Jerusalem with a symbolic power that rendered the city with a political significance on which the stability of the Byzantine Empire rested. In the fifth century Jerusalem became one of the most important battlefields in the Empire between the Chalcedonian and anti-Chalcedonian factions, were victory was largely determined by the current ecclesiastical policies of the Emperors.[47] One of the most plausible explanations of the marginalization of the anti-Chalcedonian movement in Palestine may thus be traced in the imperial pressures on the ecclesiastic potentates of Jerusalem to keep the city in doctrinal unity with the rest of the Empire.

Secondly, the Chalcedonian faith became firmly rooted in Palestine as a result of the influence of Chalcedonian monasteries such as the Great Lavra or Mar Saba at the Kedron River. Furthermore, there was at the turn of the sixth century an increase in the collaboration between the Chalcedonian monks in Palestine and the ecclesiastical administration in Jerusalem.[48] During the patriarchate of Elias (494-516), this alliance between hierarchy and monasticism was especially prominent when both sides united their forces against the anti-Chalcedonian monasteries. At the time of the deposal of Severus of Antioch in 518 Palestinian resistance against Chalcedon had ended.

---

[47] R. L. Wilken, *The Land Called Holy: Palestine in Christian History and Thought* (New Haven and London 1992), 114. E. D. Hunt, *Holy Land Pilgrimage in the Later Roman Empire AD 312-460* (Oxford 1982), 247-248. In particular relation to the writings of John Rufus, see A. Kofsky, 'Peter the Iberian: Pilgrimage, Monasticism and Ecclesiastical Politics in Byzantine Palestine', *LA* 47 (1997), 209-222.

[48] J. Binns, *Ascetics and Ambassadors of Christ: The Monasteries of Palestine, 314-631* (Oxford 1994), 191-199. S. Rubenson, 'The Egyptian Relations of Early Palestinian Monasticism', in A. O'Mahoney, G. Gunner, and K. Hintlian (eds.), *The Christian Heritage in the Holy Land* (London 1995), 44-46.

Yet, during this very period of crisis anti-Chalcedonian hagiography enjoyed its heyday. Having completed, in the form of a biography, a refutation of Chalcedonian accusations directed against his old fellow-student Severus of Antioch,[49] Zacharias Scholasticus, eventually bishop of Mitylene, wrote a series of lives of the anti-Chalcedonian champions Isaiah of Beth Dalthā, Peter the Iberian (of which only a few lines have been preserved), and Theodore of Antinoë (which is completely lost).[50] From Zacharias has also been preserved two philosophical treaties: the *Antirrhesis*, which is a refutation of the Manichaean heresy, and the *Ammonius*, which is an imitation of the *Theophrastus* by Aeneas of Gaza.[51] The most well-known of Zacharias works, however, is his so-called *Church History*, which has been preserved as books 3-6 in an anonymous Syriac Chronicle written around the year 569, and which is of considerable importance for our knowledge about the period from the Council of Chalcedon to the early reign of Emperor Anastasius.[52]

In a Palestinian monastery, during the same period, the monk and priest John Rufus wrote a biography on Peter the Iberian, an account of the death of Theodosius of Jerusalem, and a collection

---

[49] Zacharias Scholasticus, *V. Severi*, ed. and tr. by M.-A. Kugener, PO 2.1, 5-115.

[50] Zacharias Scholasticus, *Vita Isaiae Monachi*, ed. and tr. by Brooks, CSCO, Script. syri 3.25, 1-16; *Historia de Petro Ibero*, ed. and tr. by Brooks, CSCO, Script. syri 3.25, 17-18 [Fragment].

[51] Zacharias Scholasticus, *Ammonius sive de mundi opificio disputatio*, PG 85, 1012-1144; *Antirrhesis*, PG 85, 1143-1144. Aeneas of Gaza, *Theophrastus siue de immortalitate et corporum resurrectione dialogus*, PG 85, 872-1003.

[52] Zacharias Scholasticus, *HE*, ed. and tr. by Brooks, CSCO, Script. syri, 3.5-6 (Paris 1919-24); eng. tr. by F. J. Hamilton and Brooks, *The Syriac Chronicle Known as that of Zachariah of Mitylene* (London 1899). For a discussion about the identity of the ecclesiastical historian known as Zacharias Rhetor, Bishop of Mitylene, with Zacharias Scholasticus, author of the Life of Severus and the brother of Procopius of Gaza, see E. Honigmann, 'Zacharias of Mitylene', in *Patristic Studies*, Studi e testi 173 (Vatican City 1953), 198-199; Frend, *The Rise of the Monophysite Movement*, 202 n. 5; P. Allen, 'Zacharias Scholasticus and the *Historia Ecclesiasica* of Evagrius Scholasticus', *JTS N.S.* 31.2 (1980), 471-488.

of propagandistic anecdotes known as the *Plerophories*.[53] In the works of John Rufus the element of persuasion, which forms an intrinsic part of hagiographic discourse, is extremely prominent. The reader is confronted with repeated condemnations of the Council of Chalcedon that reveal John as primarily a polemicist. His purpose is not merely to depict the ascetic charisma of holy persons but, above all, to place the reader in the midst of the conflict between the true faith of the holy fathers and the apostasy of the Chalcedonian bishops.

The aim of the present study is to bring forth the characteristic features in the preserved texts of John Rufus in order to explore the motive force behind the opposition against Chalcedon in the Palestinian monastic tradition. By following the lead of hagiographic themes—such as the idea of the holy man, the rhetorical power of miracles and visions, and the representation of heresy—I hope to contribute to our understanding of the manner in which the anti-Chalcedonian population in the Eastern Empire constructed reality.

Aim of Study

This study assumes that the hagiography of John Rufus represents a specific anti-Chalcedonian culture that involves a conception of the world as the arena of a cosmological war between God and the evil powers of the material world, represented by Chalcedonian heretics. It is argued that John Rufus' works uncovers a world vision that is focused on the notion of the absolute initiative of God, whereas the holy men are reduced to merely instruments for God's announcement of his judgement upon Chalcedon. In the cosmological battle between good and evil the orthodox community is characterized as the last stronghold of truth in a world otherwise distorted by global apostasy. The close connection between preserved orthodoxy and the ascetic renunciation from worldly matters will be demonstrated as an inherent part of anti-Chalcedonian mentality that forms the ideological background to the evident sectarian tendencies in John's texts.

In the reconstruction of the world vision of anti-Chalcedonian culture from the hagiographic writings of John Rufus our

---

[53] John Rufus, *V. Petr. Ib.*, ed. and tr. by R. Raabe (Leipzig 1895); *Narr. de ob. Theod.*, ed. and tr. by Brooks, CSCO, Script. syri 3.25, 19-27; *Pleroph.* PO 8.1, 5-208.

investigation proceeds from four main questions: 1) What is the main outline of the historical and geographical context behind John Rufus' texts? 2) What fundamental ideas characterize the hagiography of John Rufus and the culture that he represents? 3) What is the immediate historical situation in which John composed his texts? 4) What argumentative strategies may be revealed in the texts?

The study falls into three sections—first, a few general conclusions about the historical and cultural background to the monastic culture of John Rufus, secondly an inventory of the texts and, finally, an analysis of a selection of hagiographic themes contained in the texts. The first section coincides with Chapter One, has the purpose of providing effective 'building blocks' through which anti-Chalcedonian writers such as John Rufus constructed a literary history of the events that shook the Eastern Empire in the fifth century. The section is divided into five parts, treating in the following order the events in Palestine immediately after the Council of Chalcedon in 451, the monastic milieu at Gaza as the center of anti-Chalcedonianism in Palestine, the idea of Egypt as the bulwark of orthodoxy and the birthplace of monasticism, the ideological tension between ascetic retreat and monastic involvement into the destiny of the church, and the problem of orthodoxy and compromise as expressed in the debate on the *Henotikon* of Emperor Zeno.

The second section, which coincides with Chapter Two, includes an investigation of the sources, beginning with a discussion of the available evidence on the life of John Rufus. The third section, which covers Chapters Three, Four and Five, is devoted entirely to the analysis of a selection of hagiographic themes central for the anti-Chalcedonian polemics of John Rufus. Chapter Three takes as its point of departure the question of the words and actions of holy men in relation to the absolute divine initiative of God. It will be shown that the hagiographic role of holy men is dependent on John Rufus' purpose to point out the ultimate verdict against Chalcedon delivered by God, the holy men themselves having no importance of their own as human beings in the world. The individual ascetic, as a receiver of charismatic virtues, is reduced to the position of a mere mediator of God's claim to complete obedience to his unambiguous declaration of the falsity of Chalcedon. Chapter Four will deal with the frequent stories about visions and miracles in the works of John Rufus. It will be argued that these visions and miracles are important as express confirmations of God's verdict against the Chalcedonian bishops rather than as rhetorical markers of the virtuous qualities of the saintly protagonists. Chapter Five, finally, focuses on the role of the 'enemies' in John's anti-Chalcedonian hagiography. Here the discussion is focused on the relation between heresy and orthodoxy as an important part of the cosmological struggle between the world of the divine realities and the human world of corruption and defilement. This chapter will also address the underlying dogmatic presumptions of John Rufus, placing him in the doctrinal tradition designated by Lebon as 'Severian monophysism'.

Following this format of study, I hope to bring into some light the specific characteristics of anti-Chalcedonian culture that motivated the furious resistance against Chalcedon, thus making a general contribution to the understanding of the early history of the non-Chalcedonian Churches.

1   THE STAGE OF THE RESISTANCE

The Palestinian Mutiny

What occupied the mind of Juvenal, Bishop of Jerusalem, on his way back to Palestine after the closing of the great Council of Chalcedon? Was he satisfied with his achievements at the Council? Was it only on returning to Palestine that he realized that his activities at the council had provoked 'unexpected fury', as suggested by Ernest Honigmann?[1] Of course we cannot know what Juvenal was thinking when he left Chalcedon after the closing session on November 10, 451. But against the background of the expectations of his people that accompanied him to Chalcedon it is not likely that, during his journey home, Juvenal was unaware that his conduct at the Council was to be turbulently questioned by many monks and clergymen in his diocese. The fury that met Juvenal at his return to Palestine could not have been unexpected.

For twenty years Juvenal had been an ardent supporter of the patriarchs of Alexandria in their struggles against the dyophysitic tendencies of the Antiochene Christological tradition. At the Council of Ephesus in 431 he was a staunch ally of Cyril of Alexandria, being the first to declare that anyone who held the views of Nestorius should be anathematized.[2] Eighteen years later, at the second Council of Ephesus in 449, his loyalty to the head of the Alexandrian Church remained as strong as ever. It is difficult to make light of the leading role he played as a supporter of Cyril's successor, Dioscorus. As the first among 113 bishops to vote for the rehabilitation of Eutyches he declared him to be 'most orthodox'.[3] Further, having signed the resolutions regarding the depositions of Flavian and Eusebius of Dorylaeum, he declared the

---

[1] Honigmann, 'Juvenal of Jerusalem', *DOP* 5 (1950), 247.
[2] *ACO* 1.1.2, 31.
[3] *ACO* 2.1.1, 182.

deposition of Ibas of Edessa and took active part in the trial of
Theodoret of Cyrrhus.[4] The reward for these actions was not long
in coming. According to the will of Emperor Theodosius, three
provinces that had been administered by the Patriarch of
Antioch—Phoenicia I and II, and Arabia—were transferred to the
jurisdiction of the bishop of Jerusalem, thus fulfilling what Juvenal
had desired from the very beginning of his episcopacy.[5]

The new political situation that followed on Emperor
Theodosius' death in the summer of 450 does not seem to have
brought about any immediate change in Juvenal's relations with
Dioscorus and the Alexandrines. When, in October 450, Anatolius,
Flavian's successor on the patriarchal throne of Constantinople,
had signed the *Tome* of Leo and sent it out to be subscribed by all
the metropolitan bishops, Juvenal is said to have publicly refused to
sign it. According to John Rufus,

> before his departure for the council, he rejected the so-
> called *Tome* of Leo and ridiculed its blasphemies. And
> he testified before all the clerics and monks of Palestine
> that it was Jewish, worthy of Simon Magus, and that
> anyone who agreed to it deserved to be
> excommunicated.[6]

It may be doubted that this account from the turn of the sixth
century actually states Juvenal's own feelings about Pope Leo and
his *Tome* during the two years that followed the second Council of
Ephesus. Honigmann considers it unlikely that Juvenal did not sign
the *Tome* of Leo at this point, but provides no argument for this
assumption.[7] However, it is reasonable to suggest that, immediately
after the Council of 449, Juvenal's opinions about the *Tome* of Leo
were in concord with those of Dioscorus who, before the opening
session of the Council of Chalcedon, excommunicated Leo as a
dyophysite infected with the teaching of Nestorius.[8] In the eyes of

---

[4] *ACO* 2.1.1, 192; *Akten der Ephesinischen Synode vom Jahre 449*, ed. by J.
Flemming, in *AKWG* 15 (Göttingen 1917), 84, 108.

[5] Honigmann suggests that Juvenal received these three provinces
through a local synod in Constantinople in 450, 'Juvenal of Jerusalem',
238. Cf. *ACO* 2.2.2, 21.

[6] *V. Petr. Ib.*, 52.

[7] Honigmann, 'Juvenal of Jerusalem', 240.

[8] *Sacrorum conciliorum nova et amplissima collectio*, ed. by Mansi, vol. 4,
1009.

Pope Leo himself, Juvenal was simply a Eutychian in need of a severe reproach for having 'harassed innocent catholics' at the Council of 449, which he saw as a *latrocinium*, i.e. a council of robbers. In a letter to Anatolius, dated April 13, 451, he strongly advised him to exclude the names of Dioscorus and Juvenal from the diptychs, so that their names would not be 'mingled indiscriminately with the names of the saints'.[9] The future was in Leo's hands. The new Emperor approved his request for a new council, and decided that it would be held at Nicaea in September 451. The date was eventually postponed to October, and the location was changed to Chalcedon.[10]

Zacharias Scholasticus reports that Juvenal, as soon as he had been summoned to attend the Council of Chalcedon, gathered the monks and people of Palestine and instructed them to withdraw from his communion in case his faith was perverted at the Council.[11] If this report is historically accurate we cannot know, but in any case Juvenal must have realized that it was Leo and Anatolius who were now in control of the situation. Perhaps he even anticipated that they would make efforts to turn the Council into a trial of Dioscorus and the other bishops who, at the Council of 449, had voted for the deposition of Flavian. As regards his own position, Juvenal had probably made up his mind during the days immediately preceding the opening session of the Council.

On October 8, arriving at Chalcedon accompanied by nineteen bishops under his jurisdiction, Juvenal joined over five hundred other bishops in the basilica of St. Euphemia. According to the preserved acts from the council, he and his bishops were obliged to take their seats on the right side of the imperial commissioners, together with Dioscorus and the bishops from Egypt and Illyricum, while the supporters of Leo and Anatolius took their places at the left side.[12] Dioscorus was, however, soon ordered to take his seat in the midst of the assembled bishops, accused by the delegates from Rome of having acted without papal

---

[9] Leo, *Ep. ad Anatolium* (ep. 80), 914-915.

[10] According to anti-Chalcedonian historiography, the change of location was a result of providential intervention, so that Nicaea, the city of the three hundred and eighteen fathers, would not be a meeting-place of rebels. Zacharias Scholasticus, *HE*, 3.1, 148-149.

[11] Zacharias Scholasticus, *HE* 3.3, 156-7.

[12] *ACO* 2.1.1, 65.

authority at the previous council. Immediately, one after the other
of the leaders of the Council of Ephesus—Thalassius of Caesarea
in Cappadocia, Eusebius of Ancyra, Basil of Seleucia, and
Eustathius of Beirut—came forward as Dioscorus' accusers,
assuring the assembly that they had taken no part in the activities at
that council, or that the role they had played was only secondary.
This was a time for many excuses and confessions: 'I let myself be
deceived,' Eustathius of Beirut said, having declared Flavian's
orthodoxy.[13] Even Juvenal averred that he found Flavian's
confession of faith to be in agreement with the words of Cyril of
Alexandria. He then rose from his chair and went over to the left
side, together with the other bishops of Palestine, the bishops of
Illyricum and four of the seventeen bishops who had accompanied
Dioscorus from Egypt.[14] Completely abandoned by his formed
brothers-in-arms, Dioscorus was now left alone to defend his case
before the assembled bishops. In the third session on October 13
the Council finally declared him guilty of breaking ecclesiastical law,
and deprived him of his episcopal office.[15]

As a result of his *volte-face*, Juvenal had managed to escape a
destiny similar to that of Dioscorus. Although he was deprived of
his episcopal dignity during the second and third sessions, he was
readmitted in the fourth session, having given a sworn statement
that the *Tome* of Leo was in accord with the faith established at the
Councils of Nicaea and Constantinople. From the fifth session, on
October 22, he was admitted to the honorable seat next to the
Patriarch of Antioch, and during the same session he was chosen as
a member of the committee assigned to the task of composing the
first draft of the Council's definition of faith.[16] Three days later, in
the sixth session on October 25, a revised form of this document
was brought before the assembled bishops who, in the presence of
the Emperor himself, received it with acclamation and appended
their signatures to it.[17]

---

[13] *ACO* 2.1.1, 112-113.

[14] *ACO* 2.1.1., 115.

[15] *Sacrorum conciliorum nova et amplissima collectio*, ed. Mansi, vol. 4, 1048-
50.

[16] *ACO* 2.1.2, 121, 125.

[17] *ACO* 2.1.2, 130-139. The names of four hundred and fifty-two
bishops who subscribed the document of faith are preserved in the acts,
141-154.

Juvenal was obviously determined to survive the Council of Chalcedon as Bishop of Jerusalem. To secure his position at the Council he voluntarily returned to the Patriarch of Antioch the three provinces that he had received at the second Council of Ephesus.[18] Further, in matters of doctrine Juvenal seems to have been ready to affirm almost any of the resolutions required by the leading members of the Council. However, some inward struggle in Juvenal's mind is indicated during the discussion about the rehabilitation of Ibas of Edessa on October 27. Without any sign that his condemnation of Ibas in 449 was not justified, he approved the rehabilitation of Ibas, with an argument based on nothing more than pity for old men who had converted:

> The Holy Scriptures teaches us to admit the converted; therefore we admit even former heretics. For this reason I also agree with you that pity ['philanthropy'] has been allotted to the venerable bishop Ibas, because he is an old man, with the idea that he shall have the episcopal dignity, since he is [now] orthodox.[19]

It is doubtful that Juvenal could have felt any satisfaction with his accomplishments at the Council. Probably he was relieved that he had been able to cope with the turning tides of doctrinal controversy and that he could return to Palestine still being Bishop of Jerusalem. But the price for his successful adjustment to the new political situation was high. With his freedom of action constrained by the condemnation of the proceedings at the previous council, he had been forced to contradict everything he had believed in 449, supported only by the general opinion that Pope Leo taught the same as Cyril.[20] But it seems likely that, on his departure from Chalcedon, he was aware that the actual accounting for his actions at Chalcedon would be realized to its fullest extent only with his return to Jerusalem. Perhaps he anticipated the threatening clouds already during his stay at Chalcedon, through the furious reaction of a group of Palestinian monks who, led by a certain Theodosius,

---

[18] *ACO* 2.2.2, 20.

[19] *ACO* 2.1.3, 40; tr. by Honigmann, in 'Juvenal of Jerusalem', 246-247.

[20] *ACO* 2.1.1, 81. According to the acts, this was what the bishops exclaimed after the reading of the formula of faith on October 25: 'Leo and Cyril taught alike', *ACO* 2.1.2, 124.

had on their own undertaken the journey to that city in order to observe the proceedings of the Council.[21]

Theodosius and his companions must have left Chalcedon soon after the sixth session of the Council on October 25. It is reasonable to suggest that, before their departure, they had made serious attempts to persuade Juvenal to manifest the same passion for orthodoxy as he had in 449, by defending Dioscorus before the Council and rejecting the *Tome* of Leo. They seem, however, to have left the city in great haste, undoubtedly filled with disappointment and rage. Immediately after their return to Palestine, they informed their compatriots and fellow monks about their bishop's unexpected apostasy. Shaken by these reports, the monks hurried from their monasteries to meet him on his way to Jerusalem, and to correct him for his unorthodox activities at the Council.[22]

The disturbing news about Juvenal's apostasy also reached the monks who lived in a monastery at Maiuma close to Gaza, headed by the archimandrite Irenion.[23] This monastery was the dwelling of a highly respected ascetic, the only son of King Bosmarius, who ruled the kingdom of Iberia in Caucasus. At his birth he was given the name Nabarnugius, but his reputation as a great monastic leader and an ardent champion for orthodoxy was to survive long after he had died under the name of Peter the Iberian.[24] As a king's son from a country that was politically little more than a buffer state between the empires of Rome and Sasanian Iran he became, even as a young boy, a victim of the endless hostilities between the two empires. At the age of twelve, as the kingdom of Iberia was caught in the midst of war between Rome and Persia, he was dispatched to the imperial court in Constantinople as hostage, so that Emperor Theodosius II would be able to prevent Bosmarius from allying himself with the Sasanians. Living for several years as

---

[21] Zacharias Scholasticus, *HE* 3.3; Evagrius Scholasticus *HE* 2.5, ed. by Bidez and Parmentier (London 1898); tr by Festugière, in *Byzantion* 45 (1975), 187-488.

[22] Zacharias Scholasticus, *HE* 3.3.

[23] *Pleroph.* 56.

[24] For the sources to Peter the Iberians life, see Lang, 'Peter the Iberian and his Biographers', *JEH* 2 (1951), 158-168. For Peter's life, there are no evident reasons to doubt the main biographical outline presented in John Rufus' *Life of Peter the Iberian*.

a prisoner at the imperial palace, very well treated by the Emperor but constantly threatened to his life by his servants, he is said never to have ceased to long for the monastic life close to the ascetic fathers in Palestine. After many attempts at escape Nabarnugius finally succeeded in leaving the palace together with his soul mate, the court eunuch Mithridates, and reached Jerusalem, where they entered the monastery of Melania the Younger on the Mount of Olives. Receiving their monastic habits from Melania's foster-son Gerontius, the head of her monastery, the two fugitives assumed the names of Peter and John.[25] Troubled by the daily contact with the world, and by Juvenal's repeated attempts to ordain them as priests, Peter and John eventually settled in Irenion's monastery at Maiuma, from where they frequently visited the cell of the famous Abba Zeno at the village of Kefar Se'arta, fifteen miles from Gaza. Finally Bishop Paul of Maiuma, who was Juvenal's nephew, managed to ordain them, in spite of their unyielding resistance, which was motivated by profound feelings of unworthiness. However, after his ordination, Peter did not exercise his priestly office a single time during the seven years that went by between his ordination and Juvenal's return from Chalcedon.[26]

In the *Plerophories*, John Rufus reports that Peter, when he heard about Juvenal's apostasy and was asked to join the other monks in confronting him, refused to break off his ascetic retreat to consort with courtiers and the people of the world, i.e. Juvenal's imperial escort. But having received a vision in which God rebuked him for seeking peace for himself at a moment when the orthodox faith was at stake, he immediately left his cell and went off with the other monks to meet Juvenal.[27] When the monks arrived at Caesarea the governor stopped them from entering the city because of their large number. Instead they gathered in the Church of the Apostles, close by Caesarea, where they celebrated the Holy Communion while waiting for Juvenal's ship to arrive from Chalcedon. During this celebration of the Eucharist, the priest Maxus later attested, the bread and wine miraculously were transformed into real flesh and blood, an unambiguous demonstration of God's presence among those who ardently

---

[25] *V. Petr. Ib.*, 15-37.
[26] *V. Petr. Ib.*, 47-52.
[27] *Pleroph.* 56.

resisted the doctrinal falsifications produced by the Chalcedonian bishops.[28]

It is likely that Juvenal, as soon as he had arrived at Caesarea, was informed, perhaps by the governor in person, of the immense crowd of monks, clergymen and lay people that had assembled outside the city to correct him for his activities at the Council. While he can hardly have been surprised by the fury caused by his sudden change of policy he may yet have been overwhelmed by the zealous initiative that had made a large number of people march to Caesarea to tell him a few home truths immediately at his landing on Palestinian soil. Presumably, Juvenal soon realized that his control of the diocese was in danger, unless he could persuade the demonstrators that at the Council he had acted in accordance with both canonical law and the orthodox faith. If he failed, there would be no benefit in continuing the journey up to Jerusalem. The sources indicate that he must have left Caesarea hastily, together with his company, in order to meet and confer with the monks and their leaders at the Church of the Apostles, a confrontation vividly described by John Rufus:

> During the discussion between the fathers and the godless Juvenal, the blessed monk Theodosius, whom the believers were to call Patriarch of Jerusalem, openly condemned the apostasy at Chalcedon. For he had been present there the whole time and knew about everything that happened there, and he had exposed the hypocrisy and apostasy of the synod. Juvenal was enraged, and ordered a ducenarius, a man in his escort, to manhandle him, as a disturber of the peace and an adversary to the will of the Emperor. As this was about to be done, the blessed Peter, who was still a monk and had not yet received the episcopate, was filled with burning zeal. Knowing this man since his stay at the court, he threw his stole around his neck and said to him in a prophetic tone of voice: 'You who dare to interfere in a question of faith and to turn everything upside down, did you not do such and such thing that night? I am the least of all the holy men, but if you wish I will speak, and at once fire will come down from the sky that will consume you and those who are in your company!' Trembling with fear the ducenarius

---

[28] *Pleroph.* 10.

recognized him. Throwing himself at his feet he said before everyone: 'Forgive me, lord Nabarnugi, I did not know that your holiness was here'. Thus the ducenarius left the blessed Theodosius in peace. After that he did not dare to say or do anything more against the holy men. He led Juvenal from there and returned to Caesarea.[29]

Juvenal's efforts to defend and explain his conduct at Chalcedon were as vain as the attempts of the monks to make him withdraw his acceptance of the *Tome* of Leo and anathematize the Council. Using Pilate's words 'What I have written I have written,' Juvenal rejected the demands of the monks, who, consequently, refused to accept him as their bishop.[30] Having thus unsuccessfully faced the most influential part of the Palestinian people, i.e. the monks, who revered Dioscorus as the most brilliant champion against Nestorian heresy since Cyril of Alexandria, Juvenal found himself forced to leave Palestine for a life in exile in Constantinople. In his place, the monk Theodosius was appointed as the new head of the Palestinian Church. Several other bishops who had subscribed to the faith of Chalcedon were deposed, and replaced by the followers of Theodosius with monks and clerics from their own ranks.[31] In Maiuma Bishop Paul was deposed and replaced by Peter the Iberian, who from that moment became one of the most prominent champions of the anti-Chalcedonian movement in Palestine.[32]

As soon as the new ecclesiastical order had been established in Palestine, the monks must have realized the importance of maintaining friendly relations with the imperial power. But having asked Pulcheria to put in a good word for them with Emperor Marcian,[33] they were warned not to persist in their rebellion against the Chalcedonian creed and requested to reunite with the orthodox Churches. In exchange, the Emperor would prove his benevolence and reduce the presence of military units in the Palestinian

---

[29] *Pleroph.* 56.

[30] Zacharias Scholasticus, *HE* 3.5.

[31] Zacharias Scholasticus, *HE* 3.3.

[32] Zacharias Scholasticus, *HE* 3.4.

[33] This is indicated through a letter from Emperor Marcian to the monks in Jerusalem. The text is preserved in *ACO* 2.1.3, 125. See Honigmann, 'Juvenal of Jerusalem', 251.

monasteries.[34] The efforts to obtain Marcian's support were
however rendered more difficult by the series of violent incidents
that shook Palestine in the name of anti-Chalcedonian orthodoxy,
in particular the brutal murder of Severianus, Bishop of
Scythopolis.[35] In the eyes of Marcian, the monks were themselves
responsible for these crimes of violence, in spite of their assurances
that these crimes had been caused by strangers and extremist
elements among the people of Jerusalem. Thus, the new leaders of
the Palestinian Church found themselves in the highly precarious
situation of being accused both as Eutychians and instigators of
violent acts, and at the same time completely denied any imperial
support or sympathy. Yet, as a result of the Emperor's cautious
approach to the situation in Palestine, it was not until the summer
of 453 that Juvenal, after twenty months in exile and with the
support of imperial troops, was finally restored as the effective
bishop of Jerusalem.

In February 453, Marcian had decreed the deposition of all the
bishops appointed by Theodosius, while Theodosius himself was
sentenced to death.[36] As the military intervention in Palestine was
about to be carried out during the summer it was ordered that only
Peter the Iberian was to enjoy amnesty.[37] Nevertheless, Peter
preferred to escape, together with Theodosius and several other
anti-Chalcedonian bishops, to Egypt, where he remained for about
twenty years before returning to Palestine, perhaps during the short
reign of Basiliscus.[38]

Turmoil and bloodshed seem to have accompanied Juvenal's
return to Palestine. At Neapolis Juvenal is said to have ordered a
massacre of monks who refused to hold communion with him.
The anti-Chalcedonians perpetuated the memory of this event in a
legendary story about a blind Samaritan who received his sight after
he had smeared his eyes with the blood of these monks, shed by
Juvenal's escort of Roman soldiers and their Samaritan auxiliaries.[39]
However, in another anti-Chalcedonian story that deals with the

---

[34] *ACO* 2.1.3, 127.

[35] *ACO* 2.1.3, 125.

[36] *V. Petr. Ib.*, 57.

[37] According to Zacharias Scholasticus, Peter's life was spared by the
decision of Empress Pulcheria, *HE* 3.5.

[38] *V. Petr. Ib.*, 57; Zacharias Scholasticus, *HE* 3.5.

[39] Zacharias Scholasticus, *HE* 3.5-6; *Pleroph.* 10.

situation in Palestine after Juvenal's return Juvenal is depicted as a penitent and merciful Church leader. Zacharias tells us about the monk Solomon, who emptied a basked filled with dust and ashes over Juvenal's head, saying: 'Shame on you, shame on you, you liar and persecutor!' Moved by his words, Juvenal prevented the Roman guard from intervening, offering him instead a sum of money in exchange for his immediate departure from Palestine. However, the holy man left the country voluntarily, having refused any money from Juvenal's hands.[40]

Thus, the anti-Chalcedonians in Palestine had created their own legends of martyrs, set in the basic narrative of a conflict between charismatic monasticism and ecclesiastical hierarchy. In opposition to the purity of the ascetic virtues nurtured by the monastic supporters of Cyril of Alexandria and his deposed successor Dioscorus, Juvenal became the archetype of any bishop who trusted to the powers of this world rather than to the true philosophy of asceticism. Before Chalcedon, Juvenal was commonly recognized as a patron of the monks, observing the practices of ascetic life in his monastery at Siloe and struggling for the faith at the second Council of Ephesus. After Chalcedon his monastery was left deserted, which by the anti-Chalcedonians was recognized as an obvious sign that Juvenal, because of his treachery to Dioscorus, was another Judas: 'Let his homestead become desolate, and let there be no one to live in it' (Acts 1:20).[41] Instead of being carried in triumph by the monks and the clergy, as he had been after the Council of Ephesus, he was now carried by Roman soldiers and demons.[42] In a culture that saw true faith as essentially dependent upon an ascetic lifestyle, Juvenal was an apostate monk-bishop who had abandoned the ascetic ideals for worldly ambitions. Thus he represented the antithesis of Theodosius the monk, Peter the Iberian, and other holy ascetics who had maintained their renunciation of the world and the purity of their ascetic virtues.

It was not an easy task for Juvenal to convince the Palestinian monks that Chalcedon had proclaimed the same teaching as Cyril. Further, among the minority of Chalcedonians in Palestine the

---

[40] Zacharias Scholasticus, *HE* 3.8.
[41] *Pleroph.* 16.
[42] *Pleroph.* 4.

attitudes towards Juvenal may have been the same as those of Pope Leo, according to whom Juvenal had only himself to blame for the furious rejection of Chalcedon. In the eyes of Leo, Juvenal would never be anything but a converted heretic, struggling with the weeds of heresy he had himself sown because of his previous ignorance of the true faith.[43] Surely the monks and clergy of Palestine had simply been influenced by his own conduct at Ephesus in 449.

It is likely that Juvenal finally gave up his hopes of a general acceptance of Chalcedon in Palestine. Instead, his patriarchal policy seems to have been redirected at improving the conditions for peaceful co-existence between the slowly increasing Chalcedonian population and the still solid majority of anti-Chalcedonians. From John Rufus we learn that Juvenal appealed to the Emperor to let the celebrated monk Romanus, one of the anti-Chalcedonian monastic leaders, return to Palestine from his exile. Juvenal hoped to re-establish peace in his patriarchal see.[44] After Juvenal's death in 458, this policy was inherited by his successors, Anastasius and Martyrius, to such a degree that sixth-century chroniclers and hagiographers are highly ambivalent in their judgements of them. As a result of their close relations with Euthymius the monk both Anastasius and Martyrius were held in high esteem by the Chalcedonian hagiographer Cyril of Scythopolis.[45] Zacharias Scholasticus, in turn, revered Anastasius because of his subscription of the Encyclical of Basiliscus, hence rejecting both Chalcedon and the *Tome* of Leo.[46] Zacharias also seems to have thought highly of Martyrius, not only for his insistence on the *Encyclical* but also for his decree that any teaching, whether promoted in Rimini, in Sardica, in Chalcedon, or in any other place, was to be condemned if contrary to the faith of the three hundred and eighteen holy fathers of Nicaea.[47] Hence, doctrinal unity among the people of Palestine should not be founded on Chalcedon but on the purity of the orthodox tradition from Nicaea, as explicated by the Councils of Constantinople and Ephesus. Evidently the same policy of doctrinal unity guided the

---

[43] Leo, *Ep. ad Juvenalem* (ep. 139), 1103-1104.
[44] *Narr. de ob. Theod.*, 25-26.
[45] See i.a. *V. Euthym*, 51-52, 54-55.
[46] Zacharias Scholasticus, *HE* 5.5.
[47] Zacharias Scholasticus, *HE* 5.6.

Eastern Empire for thirty-six years through Emperor Zeno's *Henotikon*, bringing the confronting factions together on the basis of a formal denial of Chalcedon as a point of controversy.

The sources lead us to the assumption that during the years immediately following Chalcedon the anti-Chalcedonian monks constituted such a powerful political force that they met with no difficulties in ousting Juvenal and taking over the ecclesiastic control over Palestine. After Juvenal's return the patriarchal acceptance of Chalcedon was merely formal, while realist politics was guided by tolerance and indulgence towards the anti-Chalcedonians. But towards the end of the fifth century the attitudes of the Patriarchs of Jerusalem towards the anti-Chalcedonians became tougher. In the early sixth century the anti-Chalcedonian monks in Palestine were for the first time actively opposed by Patriarch Elias, as described by Zacharias Scholasticus in his *Life of Severus*.[48]

This persecution seems to have been simultaneous with a decrease in the anti-Chalcedonian influence in Palestine. Having previously been able to force the patriarchal policy into what Lorenzo Perrone designed as a state of 'minimal Chalcedonianism' in the period from Juvenal's expulsion to the death of Martyrius in 486,[49] the anti-Chalcedonians now faced the turning tides of doctrinal opinion in the Palestinian provinces. One obvious sign of this change of opinion is the emergence of Chalcedonian monasticism in the Judaean wilderness east of Jerusalem associated with the distinguished ascetics Euthymius and Sabas. While anti-Chalcedonianism in Egypt and Syria maintained sufficient strength to force the imperial authorities to redirect their original call for acceptance of the Chalcedonian formula of faith to the conciliatory policy expressed in Emperor Zeno's *Henotikon* in 482, the development in Palestine moved in opposite direction. Why this was so is not evident from the sources, though there are a number of plausible explanations, connected with the religious and symbolic importance of Jerusalem.

The holy places in Jerusalem attracted Christians from all over the Empire and made Palestine particularly cosmopolitan in

---

[48] Zacharias Scholasticus, *V. Severi*, 102-103.

[49] Perrone, *La Chiesa di Palestina e le controversie cristologiche* (Brescia 1980), 138-139.

character. Since the majority of the Emperor's subjects accepted Chalcedon, Palestine became fertile soil for the consolidation of Chalcedonianism among laity as well as monks.[50] Forced to share the holy shrines with crowds of pilgrims in communion with the Chalcedonian patriarchs of the Holy City, many anti-Chalcedonians must have had problems with the rigorous demand to refuse communion with Chalcedonian bishops. It is reasonable to suggest that this situation led to a vast number of conversions among the anti-Chalcedonians to the Chalcedonian side. This is probably also what forms the immediate background to John Rufus' recurrent admonitions to his readers to remain in their cells, in full assurance that they were joined in the communion of the saints by preserving the purity of their faith, rather than to put themselves at risk by sharing communion with Chalcedonian heretics.[51] For strict anti-Chalcedonians like John Rufus the proximity of the Holy Places seems to have been one of the most dangerous obstacles for the strict preservation of the faith. The risk of polluting the faith of their fathers through association with Chalcedonian pilgrims could be averted only by strictly avoiding the Holy Places. One of the most striking expressions of these sentiments is found in the story told by John Rufus of the priest Zosimus, who went to settle at the holy place of Bethel, where Jacob had seen the ladder leading up to heaven. One night he saw Jacob himself sitting on a horse, reproaching him:

> How is it that you, who are orthodox and share the communion with the orthodox, wish to settle here? Do not stray from the faith for my sake but hate the company of the apostates, and you will never lack what is good or tranquility or anything you need.[52]

The scattered remains of anti-Chalcedonianism in Palestine towards the end of the fifth century maintained their position in communities centered mainly along the coast of Palestina Prima, close to cities well known for commercial and intellectual activity, such as Caesarea, Jamnia, Ascalon, and Gaza. Here the anti-Chalcedonian movement managed to retain a vitality that seems to

---

[50] The importance of the holy places is pointed out by Binns as a predominant cause for the consolidation of Chalcedonianism in Palestine, see *Ascetics and Ambassadors of Christ*, 197-199.

[51] For further discussion, see below, chapter 5, 179-184.

[52] *Pleroph.* 30, 79-80

have persisted at least until the reign of Justin I. The ideological solidarity within and between these communities emanated from the monastic settlements in the neighborhood of Gaza and its port Maiuma. The evidence of the influence from these monasteries is limited, resting mainly on the reports of John Rufus, Zacharias Scholasticus, and Severus of Antioch.[53] That these monastic centers, chiefly due to the charismatic leadership of Peter the Iberian, were among the most important strongholds of anti-Chalcedonianism in the East is hard to disprove. Of particular interest is the monastic milieu at Maiuma where John Rufus wrote his hagiographic works.

Anti-Chalcedonianism and the Region of Gaza

Our knowledge of whether monastic settlements existed in the neighborhood of Maiuma and Gaza before the time of Peter the Iberian is limited. But as John Rufus reports, on his arrival in this region Peter found, even before the Council of Chalcedon, a flourishing monastic culture centered around a congregation of 'many holy and cross-bearing monks', led by the archimandrite Irenion.[54] We may surmise that this monastic milieu was merely one fruit of more than a century of extensive migration of monks between Egypt and Palestine. From the apophthegmatic tradition we learn that Abba Silvanus and his disciples left Scetis at the end of the fourth century, eventually making their way to the region of Gaza, where they established a monastery at the village of Gerara. This ascetic group seems to have been of essential importance for the development of monastic life in fifth-century Palestine. Silvanus himself must have died before 412, but a century later he and his disciples, among them Zeno, the prophet of Kefar Seʿarta, were to have a fixed place in the memories of the anti-Chalcedonians.[55]

---

[53] Compared with the chronographic and hagiographic works of Zacharias Scholasticus and John Rufus, the letters of Severus have been surprisingly neglected as sources for anti-Chalcedonian monasticism in Palestine. These letters contain several references to the monastic centers at Maiuma and Eleutheropolis. See Severus of Antioch, *Select Letters*, ed. and tr. by Brooks (Oxford 1902), for example 1.35, 2.42, 9.3.

[54] *V. Petr. Ib.*, 49-51.

[55] For Silvanus, see M. van Parys, 'Abba Silvain et ses disciples', *Irénikon* 61 (1988), 313-30, 451-480. Silvanus is mentioned by John Rufus

At the time of Abba Silvanus' departure from Scetis the monk
Porphyrius left the same place to settle in the Jordan Valley, before
his appointment as Bishop of Gaza at the end of the fourth
century.[56] His biographer Marc the Deacon does not inform us of
the existence of monastic settlements at Gaza and Maiuma in this
period. But as a result of the geographic position it is reasonable to
assume that ascetics, trained in the desert tradition of Egypt,
withdrew to this area as early as the mid-fourth century. Through
Jerome we know that the semi-legendary ascetic Hilarion was born
in the village of Tabatha near Gaza. In the biography we are told
that Hilarion, on his return to Palestine after finishing his studies in
Alexandria, decided to follow the example of the great Antony and
settled as a recluse on the seashore seven miles from Maiuma. The
reputation of the holy man spread quickly, and attracted a number
of visitors to his cell. Soon he was the center of an entire colony of
anchorites.[57] Whether Jerome's account is to be taken as historical
accurate or not, it is quite likely that the position held by the
province of Gaza and Maiuma as a center of Palestinian
monasticism in the fifth century was established already in the
fourth century.[58]

The question about the development of an ascetic culture at
Gaza and Maiuma cannot be isolated from the fact that from
distant antiquity the region served as an important center in trade
and warfare. The city of Gaza, founded by the Philistines, was
situated on the ancient road running along the Palestinian coastline
down to Egypt. It was the final outpost towards Egypt and the first
Palestinian city to receive travelers coming through the Sinai desert.
It was also the western terminus for the caravans from Petra and a
significant commercial center for the desert tribes in the

---

with the epithet 'father of the monks', *Pleroph.* 48. In the *Life of Peter the
Iberian*, Silvanus' disciple Zeno is presented as the spiritual father of Peter,
V. Petr. Ib., 50. Further, two reports of Zeno prophesising against
Chalcedonians are recorded in *Pleroph.* 8, 52.

[56] Marc the Deacon, *Vita Porphyrii*, 4, 11-16, ed. Grégoire and Kugener
(Paris 1930).

[57] Jerome, *Vita Hilarionis*, PL 23, 29-53.

[58] See D. J. Chitty, *The Desert a City* (Crestwood 1995), 13-14; and
Binns, *Ascetics and Ambassadors of Christ*, 155. For the Egyptian connection,
see also Rubenson, 'The Egyptian Relations of Early Palestinian
Monasticism', 35-46.

neighborhood. As a result, Gaza was granted a position of great strategic importance for which it has endured a long and turbulent history. In antiquity the region was repeatedly invaded, and the sovereignty over the city passed almost constantly from one to another of the great rulers of the ancient East. In the Hellenistic age there were several shifts of power during the rivalry of the Ptolemies and Seleucids until, in 96 BC, the city was destroyed by Alexander Jannaeus, and the inhabitants massacred. About forty years later, when the Romans under Pompey had gained control over the area, the city was restored and gradually resettled. For a short period it was incorporated into the kingdom of Herod, only to revert to Roman rule after Herod's death in 4 BC. The following six centuries, until the Arab conquest of 637, were to be the longest period of unbroken peace in the history of Gaza. Mainly as a result of the fact that the city escaped the civil wars, rebellions and invasions that at times struck the Empire and the provinces of the East, Gaza became a prosperous commercial city and a center of higher education in grammar, philosophy and law.[59]

The prosperity of Gaza in the Roman and Byzantine periods depended partly on the importance of Maiuma. Situated at the seashore three miles from Gaza it was the key to the maritime communications and trade of the region. [60] Yet, as the port of Gaza it had no privileges of its own but was incorporated under the public administration in Gaza. The economic effects of this mutual dependency resulted in a latent tension between the two towns. This tension was strongly manifested in the fourth century, when Constantine the Great, impressed by the considerable number of Christian converts in Maiuma, raised the port to the position of an independent *polis*, giving it the name Constantia. The magistrates of Gaza protested, and Constantine's grant was finally withdrawn by Julian. In ecclesiastical affairs, however, the towns of Gaza and Maiuma were in the fourth and fifth centuries split into two

---

[59] A summary on the ancient history of Gaza is given in C. A. M. Glucker, *The City of Gaza in the Roman and Byzantine Periods* (Oxford 1987), 1-5. See also P. M. Meyer, *History of the City of Gaza: from the Earliest Times to the Present Day* (New York 1907); G. Downey, *Gaza in the Early Sixth Century*, (Norman 1963).

[60] Marc the Deacon reports about the presence of many commercial travellers from Egypt in Maiuma and their importance for the Christianisation of the region, *Vita Porphyrii* 58.

separate bishoprics. [61] From Sozomen we know of the existence of a bishop in Maiuma, by the name of Zeno, at the beginning of the fifth century, and that the Bishop of Gaza after the death of this Zeno advocated the idea of incorporating the bishopric of Maiuma under that of Gaza.[62] From John Rufus we know that Juvenalis' nephew Paul held the episcopal throne of Maiuma before the Council of Chalcedon. After Chalcedon Paul was replaced by Peter the Iberian, but it is not known whether the former was restored at Maiuma after the deposal of Peter in 453. However, having returned from his sojourn in Egypt in 477 Peter the Iberian seems to have resumed his duties as bishop among the Palestinian anti-Chalcedonians. It is quite likely that the description of Peter as 'our blessed Abba and bishop' served as a permanent epithet in the veneration of his memory.[63]

The only evidence we have that John Rufus was bishop of Maiuma is the text in the title of the *Plerophories*.[64] But it seems just as plausible to assume that John was never ordained Bishop of Maiuma at all. There is no mention of him or any other bishop of Maiuma in the ecclesiastical records of the sixth century. Instead it is the bishopric of the neighboring city of Anthedon which, in a late ecclesiastic source known as the *Tacticon*, is mentioned as equivalent to that of Maiuma, and so it has been suggested that the two bishoprics in the sixth century were united into one.[65] Still, if this is to be accepted it is remarkable, against the background of the claims made in the preceding century by the people of Gaza, that Maiuma was not incorporated in the bishopric of Gaza. Because of the lack of historical sources the problem is difficult to solve, but one solution would be to connect it with the ecclesiastical policies of the sixth century. The existence of anti-Chalcedonian monasteries at Maiuma at the turn of the sixth

---

[61] *Vita Porphyrii* 43-4. See Sozomen, *HE* 5.7-8, ed. Bidez and G. C. Hansen, GCS 50 (Berlin 1960).

[62] Sozomen, *HE* 5.3. Note that Marc the Deacon does not mention any bishops of Maiuma in *Life of Porphyrius*. The explanation that the omission is due to the rivalry between Gaza and Maiuma is refuted by Glucker, who instead ascribes it to the later editor of the work, 44.

[63] For Peters ordination as bishop of Maiuma and his expulsion, see *V. Petr. Ib*, 52-58.

[64] *Pleroph*. 1.

[65] Glucker, *The City of Gaza* , 25.

century must certainly have influenced the faith of the townspeople of Maiuma. The persecutions during the reign of Justin that seem to have driven a considerable number of anti-Chalcedonian monks into exile were probably the death-blow to these monasteries. But the Christian community of Maiuma must still have been considered anti-Chalcedonian, and to put an end to the controversies in Palestine the ecclesiastic authorities in Jerusalem may have ordered the submission of Maiuma under the (presumably Chalcedonian) bishopric of Anthedon.

One striking feature of the resistance against Chalcedon is the importance of academic intellectuals in the anti-Chalcedonian movement. This is especially evident as regards anti-Chalcedonian monasticism in the Gaza area, which was one of the prominent intellectual centers in the Eastern Empire. In Zacharias Scholasticus' *Life of Isaiah* Aeneas of Gaza, the most significant representatives of the Gazaean Academy, is presented as a devoted admirer of Abba Isaiah.

> Aeneas, a sophist from the city of Gaza—a most Christian and learned man and celebrated for his wisdom—who was one of those who used to visit him, said to me: 'Often when I was in doubt about a paragraph in the expositions of Plato, Aristotle or Plotinus, and could not find the solution in their teachings or interpret them by myself, I asked him, and he enlightened me and revealed to me their mind and what they intended to say. In this way he also refuted their falsehoods and strengthened the truth of the Christian teaching'.[66]

But Aeneas was far from the only intellectual associated with the anti-Chalcedonian movement in Palestine. In fact, there seems to have been close ties between the academic centers all over the Eastern Empire, such as those of Alexandria, Beirut and Gaza, and the monastic centers of the anti-Chalcedonian movement.[67] Here we may consider the group of law students in Beirut who met with Peter the Iberian during his Phoenician journey and eventually became monks under his successors at Maiuma.[68] The most

---

[66] Zacharias Scholasticus, *Vita Isaiae Monachi*, 12.

[67] For the links between anti-Chalcedonians and the schools of Alexandria and Gaza, see i.a. Zacharias Scholasticus, *Vita Severi*, 10-46.

[68] For Peter the Iberian in Beirut, see *V. Petr. Ib.*, 114. See also Severus of Antioch, *Select Letters*, 4. 9, 271.

famous individuals in this group were Severus, the future Patriarch
of Antioch, and the Church historian Zacharias Scholasticus. The
influence of these former law students in the anti-Chalcedonian
circle at Maiuma is evident from the first-hand information
provided in Zacharias' *Life of Severus*. In John Rufus' *Plerophories*
almost a whole section of anecdotes is attributed to them, which
indicates that John maintained close relations with these former
law-students.[69]

Moreover, since higher education was reserved for the wealthy
and influential classes, it seems reasonable to conclude that the
core of the anti-Chalcedonian movement was fairly aristocratic.
This was noticed already by Derwas J. Chitty, who on this basis
ascribed to the aristocratic circle around Peter the Iberian
conservative sentiments that would explain its attachment to the
anti-Chalcedonian cause.[70] This suggestion seems to rest on least
two presuppositions: first, that the proprietary classes were
fundamentally more conservative than other social groups in the
Eastern Empire; and secondly, that anti-Chalcedonianism was the
outcome of reactionary attitudes nursed in the monastic
communities in the East. The main problem with these two
allegations is that they rest on a very general and modern definition
of 'conservatism'. In the world of Late Antiquity, when Christians
ardently resisted every alleged tendency towards doctrinal
invention, the term will provide little help when trying explain what
attracted certain representatives of the well-educated social elite to
commit themselves to the anti-Chalcedonian campaign. Instead, it
would be more fruitful to focus directly on the relationship
between philosophical education and monasticism.

During the second half of the fifth century the turbulence of
Christological controversy in the Eastern academic centers appears
to have been overshadowed by another and much older conflict,
that between Christians and Pagans (*hellenistai*). From the accounts
of academic life in Alexandria and Beirut given by Zacharias

---

[69] In the *Plerophories* there are four anecdotes attributed to these law
students, *Pleroph.* 70-71, 73, 78. Cf. Zacharias Scholasticus, *Vita Severi*, 54-
57.

[70] J. D. Chitty, *The Desert a City*, 74: 'His [i.e. Isaiah] friends were of the
aristocratic and conservative party, most strongly opposed to the
innovations (as they regarded them) of Chalcedon, and intent on
preserving in its purity the old faith and the old life'.

Scholasticus in his *Life of Severus* we learn that Christian students were united in fraternities in which the study of Plato and Aristotle was combined with studying the works of Basil the Great and Gregory of Nazianzus. Closely knitted in their opposition against pagan cults and any dealings with pagan divination and magic rites, they where able, through a synthesis between Greek philosophy and Christian theology, to attract students who had been under the influence of pagan teachers and with them had joined in pagan rites.[71] For Zacharias himself this was explained by the ability of the Christian students to use the arguments of the Classical philosophers as instruments against the magical and mythological character of pagan cults.[72]

Trained in the Greek *paideia* Christian intellectuals were certainly well acquainted with the use of rational arguments. Through the merging of the Greek rationalist tradition with a Christian worldview into a Platonic theology that stressed the spiritual and heavenly essences rather than the corporeal, Christian academics were able to construct philosophically sophisticated arguments against the traditional cults. Analyzing and exposing the theurgic expressions of ancient cults with their magic, oracles and material superstition, they staunchly defended the incompatibility of the spiritual with the corporeal and argued that the divine light could not be attained through veneration of created things. Using rational arguments to reveal the inefficiency of the pagan rites and reject the idea of divine presence in idols or other material things, Christian academics maintained that true knowledge about the divine essence came through transcendence of earthly life by nurturing the spiritual potentiality of man's original nature. In order to be liberated from the irrationality of the material world, man had to gain knowledge about his true self through a rational, philosophic life, transforming himself into his original state of likeness with God. Pagan cults, constantly preoccupied with worldly matters, were recognized as irreconcilable with the philosophic life promoted by Christian teachers at the academic centers in the Eastern Empire. In order to develop his inner

---

[71] Zacharias Scholasticus, *Vita Severi*, 14-44, 58-75. See also F. R. Trombley, *Hellenic Religion and Christianization*, vol. 2 (Leiden 1994), 45-49.

[72] The magic rituals in the temple of Isis in Menouthis near Canopus were dismissed by the Christian intellectual elite in Alexandria with rational arguments, Zacharias Scholasticus, *Vita Severi*, 16-23.

potential of higher knowledge the true philosopher had to
renounce the material world of irrationality and ignorance.[73]

Thus, true intellectual knowledge was defined in terms of
ascetic life and renunciation of corporal matters. This was reflected
notably in Christian academic circles in Alexandria in the fifth
century in which students seem to have ascribed to their
philosophical teachers charismatic gifts traditionally associated with
ascetic holy men. It seems that, in the eyes of his students, an
academic teacher was regarded as an ascetic who had, through hard
work, migrated toward God and become a representation of the
divine. This attitude among the students to their teachers was not
new. In the third century Gregory Thaumaturgus wrote in his
panegyric on Origen:

> For I am proposing to speak about a man who looks
> and seems like a human being but, to those in position
> to observe the finest flower of his disposition, has
> already completed most of the preparation for the
> reascent to the divine world.[74]

Christian intellectuals in the Eastern Empire such as the intellectual
elite in Alexandria known as the *Philoponoi*[75] tenderly maintained the
synthesis between Hellenic philosophy and Christian asceticism
that rests at the center of the intellectual history of Alexandrine
Christianity. Here, we may suggest, the perspective of an
intellectual Platonic worldview the tension between the spiritual
and the material essences was heavily emphasized. In this
intellectual tradition, the notion of the ideal teacher converges with
Platonic-Christian cosmology. Through constant orientation
towards material things man's true nature as a spiritual being has
been forgotten, and must be remembered through the process of
spiritual *paideia*. Knowledge and salvation are thus intimately
connected. To be saved from the irrationality and instability of the
material world, man must have a teacher able to guide him to

---

[73] For an outline of the philosophical and intellectual foundations of
the anti-Chalcedonian movement, particularly that of Platonic
Christianity, see Frend, *The Rise of the Monophysite Movement*, 104-141.

[74] Gregory Thaumaturgus, *Origenem oratio panegyrica* 2.10, ed. and tr. by
P. Guyot, (Freiburg 1996).

[75] Zacharias Scholasticus, *Vita Severi*, 11-13. For a discussion of the
activities of this group, see Trombley, *Hellenic Religion and Christianization*,
10-13, 17-20.

knowledge about his true self and hence about God. Consequently, the perfect philosophical teacher is someone who has transformed himself into an almost spiritual being, having become godlike. The philosophical teacher is a holy man to be imitated in the pedagogical process of transmission of divine knowledge. But the teacher is also as a savior and a mouthpiece of God. He is a citizen and an agent of the divine realms, having rejected his former identity as a material being and liberated himself from the oppressing diversity of the world.[76]

Thus, the qualities of the teacher were those of holy man, and through the personal relationship between teacher and student the divine truth entered history.[77] This was the essential trump card of the Christian intellectuals in their struggles against the pagan elements in the Eastern academic milieus. The ascetic relations between students and teachers in the academic circles in Alexandria also seem to have attracted many Christian intellectuals to relate to the great figures of monastic culture. For example, contacts with the anti-Chalcedonian monastery at Enaton were essential to the *Philoponoi* in Alexandria, as they enlisted forces against the pagan elements in the city.[78]

It is hard to deny that the strength of the anti-Chalcedonian communities in the southwest of Palestine, especially at Gaza and Maiuma, depended on its proximity to Egypt.[79] From the fourth century monks and pilgrims had moved incessantly between Egypt and Palestine. One result of this communication had been the

---

[76] Valantasis, *Spiritual Guides of the Third Century*, 19-25. The idea of the Greek *paideia* as the foundation of Christian knowledge and piety in the early biographies of the Christian saints is examined by Rubenson in 'Philosophy and Simplicity: The Problem of Classical Education in Early Christian biography', *Greek Biography and Panegyric in Late Antiquity*, ed. Hägg and Rousseau (Berkeley, Los Angeles and London 2000), 110-139.

[77] See especially Valantasis, *Spiritual Guides of the Third Century Guide-Disciple Relationship in Christianity, Neoplatonism, Hermetism, and Gnosticism*, Minneapolis 1991, 25: 'The divine realm enters society through a person in a relationship: the student encounters the divine in the person of the teacher'. See also R. Klein, 'Die frühe Kirche und die heidnische Bildung' in Guyot (ed.), Gregory Thaumaturgus, *Origenem oratio panegyrica*, 83-116.

[78] See especially Zacharias Scholasticus, *Vita Severi*, 78. For reports in the *Plerophories* about meetings between Alexandrine students and holy men, see *Pleroph*. 7, 13.

[79] Chitty, *The Desert a City*, 74.

gradual establishment of monastic settlements throughout
Palestine. But perhaps even more significant was the influence on
the Palestinian monasticism of the teaching and spirituality of the
Egyptian ascetics. A historical awareness was nourished that
emphasized the importance of preserving the words and paths of
the holy old men of the Egyptian deserts. A true monk, it was
believed, upheld the heritage of the Egyptian desert saints of Kellia,
Nitria, and Scetis.[80] In Palestine the oral traditions of the lives and
teachings of the desert fathers were gathered, copied, and
translated into the different languages spoken in the cosmopolitan
setting of Palestine.[81] But the notion of continuity involved not
only the preservation of the purity of ascetic life and conduct but
also the maintaining of the faith of the fathers. Asceticism could
never be separated from orthodoxy. It was an essential part of this
desert mentality that the faith of the individual monk was always
connected with the faith of his ascetic father. And the authority of
the ascetic fathers, on their part, depended on their reputation as
witnesses of the one true faith. Orthodoxy, in other words, was one
of the properties of monastic life.

Egypt — The Bulwark of Orthodoxy

Juvenal's affirmation of the Chalcedonian creed wedged the
ecclesiastical hierarchy in Jerusalem from local communities deeply
influenced by a girdle of hermits who nurtured the heritage of
Egyptian monasticism and doctrine. The dependency of the
ecclesiastical hierarchy on the Chalcedonian interpretation of faith,
which lacked support in the local culture, implied a mutual
alienation that would fade only with the emergence of an
alternative Chalcedonian monastic culture. Much of the later
success of this alternative monastic culture, represented mainly in
the works of Cyril of Scythopolis, rested on the promotion of a
world vision that reduced the cultural interdependence of Egyptian
and Palestinian monasticism for the creation of a specifically

---

[80] The words of Abba Isaiah in the title of the sixth book of the
Asceticon may serve as an excellent example of this mentality, *Asceticon* 6.1,
CSCO, Script. Syri 120-123. For the identification of the author of this
work with the above-mentioned Isaiah, see Chitty, 'Abba Isaiah', *JEH* 22
(1971), 61-66.

[81] See Rubenson, 'The Egyptian Relations of Early Palestinian
Monasticism', 44-46.

Palestinian monastic identity.[82] Until then, the cultural dependency of Palestinian monasticism to Egypt, based on the veneration of the great fathers of the Egyptian deserts and the theological heritage of Athanasius, Cyril and Dioscorus, remained as strong as ever.

In the fourteenth anecdote of the *Plerophories* John Rufus recounts a vision perceived by the Egyptian monk Andrew, who saw a number of bishops stirring a blazing fire in a furnace, into which they had thrown a child to be consumed by the flames. When the furnace was opened three days later the child emerged unharmed. The Abba recognized the child as the Savior, and asked him who had thrown him into the fire. The child responded: 'The bishops have crucified me a second time, and decided to deprive me of my glory'. Abba Andrew then noticed at a distance an old man who refused to participate in the wicked acts of the bishops. The Abba asked the child whom the man was and received the answer: 'It is Dioscorus, the Patriarch of the Alexandrines, who alone did not associate with them in their malicious intent'. John then tells that this vision announced the orthodoxy of the bishops of Alexandria who, like Simeon of Cyrene, carried the cross of Christ to the end of their days.[83]

This anecdote is an excellent testimony for the crucial importance of the idea of Egypt as the main 'guardian of orthodoxy' for the anti-Chalcedonian cultural identity. For the anti-Chalcedonians, as indicated in the story of Abba Andrew, Egypt was the paramount symbol of efficient resistance to Nestorian and Chalcedonian heresy. This symbolism was probably established on the general belief that the Chalcedonian bishops, determined to overthrow the decisions of the Council of Ephesus in 431, had martyred the Alexandrine patriarchate for its long unyielding resistanceto Nestorianism. Not only had they disposed Dioscorus, accusing him of uncanonical behavior at the so-called 'Robber

---

[82] Flusin, 'L'hagiographie palestinienne et la réception du concile de Chalcédoine', 44-47: 'Cyrille fait coup double: aux origines de la tradition monastique à laquelle il consacre son œvre se troublent, non pas tel monastère compromis dans les luttes autour de Chalcédoine, mais les saints moines d'Égypte; l'héritage des ascètes égyptiens passe à la Palestine orthodoxe, et ne reste pas dans l'Égypte devenue monophysite après Chalcédoine'.

[83] *Pleroph.* 14.

Council', and neutralized the doctrinal claims of the Alexandrines by accepting Leo's *Tome*, they had also, through their affirmation of the twenty-eighth canon of the Council, subordinated the patriarchate of Alexandria to the primacy of the patriarchal see of Constantinople. Thus, the previous strong influence of the Alexandrine patriarchate in the affairs of the Empire had been permanently broken, to the advantage of the Patriarch of the imperial capital. For the Alexandrines the Christological theology strongly promoted by Dioscorus' predecessor Cyril, against Nestorius' dyophysitic teaching, which was declared orthodox at the Council of Ephesus in 431, had now been destroyed by the plots of Nestorius' disciples. In spite of the express assertion of the Chalcedonian bishops that the doctrinal decree of Chalcedon was in agreement with the faith of Cyril,[84] the majority of the people of Egypt considered it as a disastrous attempt to restore the faith of Nestorius as orthodox. For them the Trinitarian orthodoxy, zealously defended by the Alexandrine Patriarchs Athanasius, Cyril and Dioscorus, had been replaced by an explication of faith that was radically incompatible with the idea of the essential consubstantiality of the Father with the Son. Hence it was thought that the Chalcedonian bishops had sacrificed the orthodox heritage of the Alexandrine patriarchate through a fundamentally blasphemous doctrine.[85]

In 380 this idea of the exceptional position of Alexandrine orthodoxy in the Christian empire had been supported by Emperor Theodosius, rewarding the patriarchal throne of Alexandria for its obstinacy towards the Arian heresy in the times of Athanasius with

---

[84] *ACO* 2.1.2, 81.

[85] The Trinitarian aspect of the Chalcedonian controversy has been highly neglected in previous presentations of the doctrinal history of Early Christianity. But it is very important to notice that Chalcedon, among many anti-Chalcedonians, was considered to have promoted a Trinitarian heresy through its division of Christ into two separate elements in a way that introduced a fourth hypostase in the Trinity, hence a Quaternity, see Timothy Aelurus, *Ep. ad Epictetum* 30*[b]*, ed. and tr. by R. Y. Ebied and L. R. Wickham, 'A Collection of Unpublished Syriac Letters of Timothy Aelurus', *JTS N.S.* 21 (1970), 334. For the Trinitarian aspect of the anti-Chalcedonian resistance in John Rufus, see *Pleroph.* 37. See also Harvey, *Asceticism and Society in Crisis: John of Ephesus and the Lives of the Eastern Saints* (Berkeley, Los Angeles, London 1990), 22.

the honorific 'guardian of orthodoxy', a title shared only with the bishops of Rome.[86] But the recognition of the bishops of Alexandria as the main defenders of the Christian faith may to some extent also be traced to the administrative claims of the Alexandrine patriarchate. The Council of Nicaea had recognized the traditional jurisdiction of the bishop of Alexandria over Egypt, Libya and Pentapolis, i.e. the old province of Egypt before Diocletian's administrative reform of the Egyptian districts in the early fourth century.[87] The authority of the bishop of Alexandria over these provinces was autocratic, which is why most of the Egyptian bishops at Chalcedon refused to sign the doctrinal decree of Chalcedon without the consent of their patriarch, saying that ancient custom forced them to obey him.[88] The jurisdictional autocracy maintained by the bishops of Alexandria seems to have invoked among the Egyptians deep solidarity towards their political and doctrinal claims.[89] One reason for this may be Alexandria's wealth. Beside Rome and Constantinople, Alexandria was the largest city in the Roman Empire, and enjoyed considerable prosperity because of its important port, its industries and its famous university. The patriarchate of Alexandria seems to have reaped the fruits of this wealth since, at the time of the Council of Ephesus in 431, Cyril of Alexandria was able to present the court of Theodosius II with gifts to the value of 1 500 pounds of gold.[90] More important, however, is the close connection between the monastic movement and the patriarchal authority established by Athanasius of Alexandria. By tying the monastic institution to the ecclesiastic hierarchy of the Egyptian Church Athanasius managed to tie the general popularity of asceticism in Egypt not only to his

---

[86] *Codex Theodosianus* 14.1.2, ed. by T. Mommsen and P. M. Meyer (Berlin 1905). See also Frend, *The Rise of the Monophysite Movement*, 15 and 43.

[87] See the sixth canon of the council of Constantinople in *Decrees of the Ecumenical Councils: Volume One: Nicaea I to Lateran V*, ed. and tr. by N. P. Tanner (London and Washington 1990), 8-9; A. H. M. Jones, *The Later Roman Empire 284-602*, (Oxford 1964), vol. 1, 43, and vol. 2, 883-4.

[88] *ACO* 2.1, 309.

[89] Jones, *The Later Roman Empire*, vol. 2, 967.

[90] Jones, *The Later Roman Empire*, vol. 2, 905. For the prosperity of Alexandria, see 714, 759.

own person as the charismatic leader of an essentially ascetic Church but even to his office.

In the fourth century the prominence of the Alexandrine patriarchate was rivaled only by the rising claims of the patriarchal see of Constantinople for primacy in the Eastern Empire. At the Council of Constantinople in 381 the Alexandrine mark of honor as the 'guardian of orthodoxy' in the East was fundamentally contradicted by the canonical promotion of Constantinople to the second rank of honor next to Rome.[91] This was a heavy blow against all the other patriarchal sees that traditionally claimed apostolic origins. This implied a quite new situation of jurisdictional rivalry between the patriarchates of the Roman Empire.[92] At the beginning of the fifth century the most obvious manifestation of the rivalry between Alexandria and Constantinople was the controversy over the legacy of Origen, a conflict that culminated with the expulsion of the Constantinopolitan Patriarch John Chrysostom in 403. In his attempts to control the patriarchal throne in the imperial capital, the Emperor found his case willingly supported by the Alexandrine Patriarch Theophilus. This alliance between the imperial authorities and the Alexandrine patriarchate was maintained to the year before the Council of Chalcedon.

There is reason to regard the Nestorian controversy as a further development of the rivalry between the patriarchates of Alexandria and Constantinople in the times of Theophilus and John Chrysostom. After his death, his nephew Cyril, who for a long time resisted the rehabilitation of John Chrysostom, succeeded Theophilus. Through his engagement in the Nestorian controversy Cyril could continue the policy of Theophilus and extend the claim of the Alexandrine patriarchate for primacy in the Eastern Empire. Unlike his predecessor John Chrysostom, Nestorius was never to be popular among the people of Constantinople, the reason being his express rejection of the popular veneration of the *Theotokos*. This made him an easy target in the dispute with the charismatic and strong-principled Cyril who,

---

[91] Established by the third canon. Text in *Decrees of the Ecumenical Councils*, 32.

[92] Jones, *The Later Roman Empire*, vol. 1, 121-123.

despite the suspicious hostility of the imperial court, made the Council of Ephesus in 431 his own.[93]

The general opinion in the Eastern Empire towards the middle of the fifth century seems to have been that the prestige of the Alexandrine patriarchate had grown out of control. The two councils of Ephesus in 431 and 449 made it clear that no other patriarch, neither of Rome nor of Constantinople, would rule the Alexandrines. But after the death of Emperor Theodosius, and the appointment of Marcian as his successor, forces were released which tried to constrain the canonical and doctrinal claims of the Patriarch of Alexandria. In this way, the Council of Chalcedon marked a new beginning concerning the relations between the patriarchal thrones in the East.

The intention of the imperial authorities to gain control over the patriarchate of Alexandria was most clearly manifested in their support of the Alexandrine priest Proterius, chosen by the Chalcedonian bishops in Egypt to succeed Dioscorus. This was one of the unhappy consequences of Marcian's totalitarian regime, devoted to the universal submission of his subjects under the Chalcedonian faith. Proterius himself, undoubtedly a suitable representative of Marcian's imperial policy, was never to be anything but a stranger in the eyes of the majority of the population in Alexandria and in Egypt. In anti-Chalcedonian history-writing his memory is forever connected with his ambition to make the Egyptians accept the definition of Chalcedon through the persuasive power of armed soldiers.[94] Since Proterius was unable to take control of the situation his pontificate was marked by a long series of popular riots and disturbances. Immediately after Marcian's death in 457 the troubles culminated, as Proterius was deposed by a group of anti-Chalcedonians, consecrating in his place Timothy Aelurus as the new patriarch. With no intentions to yield, Proterius was determined to crush the anti-Chalcedonian rebellion with the support of imperial troops. However, a few weeks later he was murdered by a group of Roman soldiers, who

---

[93] See i.a. the complaint of Nestorius against the autocracy of Cyril at Ephesus in *Liber Heraclidis*, ed. and tr. by Nau, *Le Livre d'Héraclide* (Paris 1910), 117; tr. by G. R. Driver and L. Hodgson, *The Bazaar of Heraclides* (Oxford 1925), 132: 'Cyril presided, Cyril was accuser: Cyril was judge. Cyril was bishop of Rome. Cyril was everything'.

[94] See i.a. *V. Petr. Ib.*, 58-63.

had been demoralized by the endless slaughters in the city of Alexandria.[95]

The case of Proterius is the most striking symptom of Marcian's failure to suppress the patriarchate of Alexandria by force. The deficiencies of Marcian's policy seem to have been immediately realized by his successor, Leo. Although determined to continue promoting the faith established at Chalcedon, he was also determined to establish his own religious policy before restoring the situation in Alexandria. In the first year of his reign he sent out a circular addressed to the metropolitans in the East, calling for the provincial synods to take definite positions about the faith of Chalcedon and the consecration of Timothy Aelurus in Alexandria.[96] The replies to this circular showed that the greater part of the bishops in the Eastern Empire, with the exception of a synod in Pamphylia, accepted that the faith of Chalcedon was in concord with the teachings of Cyril of Alexandria, and that they considered the consecration of Timothy Aelurus to be uncanonical. Encouraged by these results, collected in a so-called *Codex encyclicus*, Emperor Leo decided to take action against Timothy Aelurus.[97]

In the end of 459 an armed force broke into the baptistery in Alexandria where Timothy Aelurus had taken refuge, and arrested him. Timothy was sentenced to exile at Gangra in Paphlagonia, by the Black Sea. He was replaced by Timothy Salofaciolus, an ardent Chalcedonian from the monastery of Canopus who, as a result of the turbulent situation in the province, was forced to adopt a conciliatory attitude towards the anti-Chalcedonian opinion. Dioscorus, who had died in exile in 454, was restored to the diptychs, a political maneuver that proved useless as a way of winning the favor of the Egyptian people. In the hearts of most Egyptians, and to the anti-Chalcedonians in the rest of the Empire, Timothy Aelurus was still the legitimate patriarch, since he maintained the orthodox heritage from Athanasius and Cyril.[98]

The symbolism attached to Egypt and the patriarchs of Alexandria was one of the dominating forces behind the creation of ideological solidarity among the anti-Chalcedonians in the

---

[95] Zacharias Scholasticus, *HE* 4.2-3.

[96] Zacharias Scholasticus, *HE* 4.5-6.

[97] Zacharias Scholasticus, *HE* 4.9.

[98] Zacharias Scholasticus, *HE* 4.11. For a balanced survey on these events, see Frend, *The Rise of the Monophysite Movement*, 160-164.

Eastern provinces.[99] The doctrinal victories of Athanasius and Cyril over the infamous heretics Arius and Nestorius were taken as sufficient evidence that Egypt was the natural home of Trinitarian orthodoxy. The doctrinal views of the Patriarch of Alexandria as true and pure expressions of the faith of the fathers was to many a sufficient guarantee for personal and communal perseverance in orthodoxy. In times of heretical advances Egypt had proved to be the last bulwark of orthodoxy, preserving the true faith in the face of imperial persecutions and eventually bringing it out for ecumenical vindication at the great Councils. Thus, inferiority in relation to imperial Church policy could not be a sufficient argument for rejection of the doctrinal views held by Dioscorus or Timothy Aelurus. To the contrary, Athanasius' struggles against the Arians in the fourth century called for even stronger assurances that Egypt and its patriarchs would fight to the end to preserve orthodoxy.

But Egypt was thought of as something more than a bulwark of orthodoxy. The great variety of ascetic and hagiographic literature preserved from the fourth and fifth centuries shows the symbolic importance of Egypt as the home of Christian monasticism. The Egyptian desert became the predominant metaphor for monasticism and ascetic life. It was the battlefield of the struggle against the attraction of material corruptibility; from there the heavenly realm could be reached through ascetic mortification. From the second half of the fourth century the Egyptian deserts attracted crowds of monks from every part of the Empire. They settled in the monastic centers of Scetis, Kellia and Nitria in order to begin an ascetic life in imitation of legendary desert fathers such as the great Antony. To any monk in the Empire it was essential to embrace the Egyptian desert fathers as true models for a proper ascetic conduct. An emphasis on the precedence of Egyptian Desert monasticism is prevalent in hagiographies written in the midst of the Christological controversy of the fifth and sixth centuries, in the writings of John Rufus as well as in those of Cyril of Scythopolis. To John Rufus and Cyril the heritage of the holy men and women in Egypt was crucial as an

---

[99] This is also pointed out by Frend as one of the most important motives behind the anti-Chalcedonian movement, *The Rise of the Monophysite Movement*, 137.

efficient instrument of monastic propaganda. Both authors recognized the hagiographic importance of linking their saintly protagonists to the heritage of Egyptian monasticism. While John Rufus describes Peter the Iberian as a disciple of the Egyptian monk Abba Zeno, who in turn was a disciple of the famous Scetiote Abba Silvanus, Cyril described Abba Euthymius as the heir of Abba Arsenius of Scetis.[100] Yet there is a radical difference in the way John Rufus and Cyril treats the heritage of Egyptian monasticism. To John Rufus it was essential to preserve orthodoxy by keeping close to the great ascetics of the Egyptian desert. As the holy man Heliodorus, according to John Rufus, told his disciples before Chalcedon:

> Twenty-five years from now there will be an apostasy
> from the faith due to the bishops. When you see the
> beginnings of these troubles you must escape to Egypt,
> because it is there that the remaining orthodox will be
> protected, as well as in Palestine, which they visited.[101]

Cyril of Scythopolis is even more explicit in his approach to establishing an unbroken line between the Golden Age of Eastern monasticism and the Chalcedonian monks in the Judaean desert.[102] As the birthplace of Christian monasticism, and the home of the great pioneers of ascetic life, the Egyptian desert was the main influence in the personal development of Cyril's holy men as ascetic authorities, and as sources for instruction in the customs and rules of Christian asceticism.[103] But through Abba Euthymius, whom Cyril describes as the bridge between Egyptian and Palestinian monasticism, the *locus* of the true ascetic life was transferred to Palestine and the monastic circles preserved his spiritual heritage. To Cyril it is the Council of Chalcedon that forms the turning point of this transition, regarding the preservation of the ascetic charisms as intimately linked to the acceptance of the faith established at this council. As a result of

---

[100] *V. Petr. Ib.*, 47-49; *V. Euthym.*, 34.

[101] *Pleroph.* 31.

[102] This is manifested not least through Cyril's borrowing of passages from other monastic texts, see Flusin, *Miracle et Histoire dans l'œuvre de Cyrille de Scythopolis* (Paris 1983), 41-86.

[103] Cyril of Scythopolis tells us how Euthymius at two occasions admonished his disciples by referring to stories told by Egyptian fathers, *V. Euthym.*, 30, 37.

Dioscorus' and Timothy Aelurus' rejection of the council, Egypt was no longer the home of ascetic authority. Instead, after Chalcedon, correct instruction in the orthodox faith was provided in the Judaean desert by Euthymius and his heirs.[104] Cyril's holy men, then, personify a shift of perspective—from the previous glory of Egypt to the present glory of Palestine—that rests at the heart of his hagiographic approach. This shift of perspective simultaneously involves the precedence of Chalcedonian monasticism in Palestine over anti-Chalcedonian monasticism, and the glory of the new patriarchate of Jerusalem in relation to the ancient patriarchate of Alexandria.[105]

Besides the idea of Egypt as a symbol for orthodoxy and monasticism there is another important ideological feature in the opposition against Chalcedon in the East. It concerns the notion of monks as an active element in the life of the Church, and the tension between the call for subordination of monks under the ecclesiastical hierarchy and the monastic emphasis of freedom and independence from worldly responsibility. This tension, which can be traced back to the period of Athanasius' patriarchate in Egypt, was one of the strongest driving forces behind the monastic resistance against Chalcedon.

Monastic Freedom and the Struggle for Orthodoxy

At the seventh session of the Council of Chalcedon Emperor Marcian announced twenty-seven canons to regulate the life and

---

[104] The idea of such a shift undoubtedly rest in the background of Cyril's account on the arrival of the two Nitrian archimandrites Martyrius and Elias to the lavra of Euthymius, searching peace from anti-Chalcedonian violence after the death of Proterius, *V. Euthym.*, 50-51.

[105] This view on the history of Palestinian monasticism certainly reflected the elevation of Jerusalem to the position of patriarchate at Chalcedon in 451. According to Flusin, Cyril's *Lives* combine hagiographic aims to describe the ascetic charisms of the founding fathers of Chalcedonian monasticism in Palestine with the ambition to defend the position of the new patriarchate in the Empire against the older patriarchates of Alexandria and Antioch. Cyril's use of ascetic and hagiographic sources from both Egypt and Syria for the creation of a Palestinian hagiography that is explicitly connected to the Chalcedonian monasteries of Euthymius and Sabas reflects this ambition, Flusin, *Miracle et histoire*, 86.

organization in the Christian communities.[106] Like any other
canonical regulations established by provincial or ecumenical
councils they reflected urgent problems and concerns in the life of
the early Church. Particularly interesting among the canons which
were established at Chalcedon, and reveal the concerns of the
Church in the fifth century, is the fourth canon, which deals
exclusively with the status of the monks. After a note commanding
the general veneration of monks, the problem is expressed: some
people who call themselves monks bring disorder into the affairs of
the Church and into the civic community. This accusation seems to
be directed mainly against independent monks, the so-called
Gyrovagues or Sarabaites, who were mostly on the move but
occasionally established monasteries for themselves without the
approval of the episcopal authorities. Such activity, criticized
already by John Cassian and later also by Benedict of Nursia,[107] was
now expressly forbidden by the Council. Monks had to remain
within the jurisdiction of the bishops and to live restricted lives in
prayer and *stabilitas loci*.

> It has been decided that no one is to build or found a
> monastery or oratory anywhere against the will of the
> local bishop; and that monks of each city and region
> are to be subject to the bishop, are to foster peace and
> quiet, and attend solely to fasting and prayer, staying set
> apart in their places. They are not to abandon their own
> monasteries and interfere, or take part, in ecclesiastical
> or worldly business, unless they are perhaps assigned to
> do so by the local bishop because of some urgent
> necessity.[108]

The fourth canon of Chalcedon implies a separation of the
Church into two distinct spheres, one institutional and one
spiritual. It prohibits any sort of transgression by the monks of the
borders between these two spheres. The reason behind it was, quite
likely, theological: worldly concerns should not be allowed to
pollute the true philosophical life implied by the spiritual struggles
of the anchorites and coenobites in the deserts. But it seems more
reasonable to suggest that the Chalcedonian bishops primarily

---

[106] *ACO* 2.1.2, 158-163.

[107] John Cassian, *Conlationes* 18, 4-8, SC 64. Benedict of Nursia, *Regula
Monasteriorum* 1, SC 181.

[108] Text and translation in *Decrees of the Ecumenical Councils*, 89-90.

found such a regulation necessary for the repression of the anarchic tendencies in early monasticism. Such anarchic tendencies are easily recognized in the hagiographic accounts by Palladius and the anonymous author of *Historia Monachorum*, where monasticism was presented almost as an alternative culture independent of the institutionalized Church. The immense numbers of people, which were ceaselessly attached to this uncontrollable monastic life, must have been considered even more hazardous to the episcopal authority. At the turn of the fourth century monasticism seems to have grown beyond immediate control in the eyes of the ecclesiastic hierarchy. But despite episcopal attempts to subject them to the supervision of local bishops the monks continued to argue not only their need for spiritual freedom but also their authority to meddle in doctrinal quarrels. The regulation of monastic life settled at Chalcedon can thus be readily explained as motivated essentially by the awareness that the formula of faith established 25 October 451 could be promoted only if the monastic supporters of Dioscorus were subjected to episcopal authority.[109]

The role played by monks in the theological debates in the fourth and fifth centuries, and the Chalcedonian controversy in particular, has long been recognized.[110] The monastic intervention in such disputes was, however, determined by developments going back to the struggle of the fourth-century Egyptian Church against Arianism. In 328 the Alexandrine Patriarch Alexander died, having resisted until the very end Constantine's request that Arius should be received back into the orthodox community of Alexandria. As his successor on the patriarchal throne of Alexandria he had chosen Athanasius, who until his own death half a century later was to continue his predecessor's uncompromising struggle against the Arians. It is all too easy, in the framework of his writings, to estimate the historical significance of Athanasius exclusively in terms of his role as one of the most important architects of post-Nicaean dogma, and of the principles behind the future relations between imperial and ecclesiastical authorities in the Eastern Empire. In order to understand Athanasius' historical importance

---

[109] According to Frend, the fourth canon 'reaffirmed the authority of episcopal government and its vehicle the council', *The Rise of the Monophysite Movement*, 143-144.

[110] See i.a. Roldanus, 'Stützen und Störenfriede', 123-146.

at all, it is essential to recognize the role played by the ascetic movement in Egypt in making him the undisputed leader of the Egyptian Church. Through him a rigid interpretation of the Nicaean faith and the claim for ecclesiastical autonomy combined with the values of the ascetic movement into a political vision. During the turbulent times of the Arian controversy Athanasius built a Church centered around the ascetical and political charisma of the Patriarch. Asceticism and an active life in the service of the Christian community were brought together. It was no longer possible to distinguish the lives of the bishops from the spiritual concerns of early asceticism. The bishop should live like an ascetic in order to receive the charismatic powers of virtue, while the monk, whenever his powers were needed for the spiritual welfare of the Church, should be ready to sacrifice the solitary life in the desert for the life of a bishop.[111]

Particularly important for our knowledge about Athanasius' view on the role of asceticism in the life of the Egyptian Church is his *Life of Antony*, written during his third exile, shortly after Antony's death in 356.[112] As stated in the preface the primary purpose of the *Life* is to picture the hero as an ideal ascetic role model for spiritual discipline.[113] Athanasius fulfils this hagiographic purpose by uniting the ascetic idea of worldly renunciation with a promotion of ascetic intervention in the world. The combination of these two antithetical ideas, which stem from the Athanasian vision of the authority of the ascetic in the Christian community, affects the fundamental narrative structure of the biography. Hence the presentation of the saint's life is clearly subordinated to the ideological preferences of the author. Certainly the chronological account of Antony's early development and ascetic experiences is merely the background that gives meaning to the account of his teaching, miracles, and struggle for the true faith of the Church. But through his chronological presentation of the events the author is also provided with an opportunity to promote his own view of the role of ascetics in the Church. In this way the *Life of Antony* is clearly divided into two parts, each representing a different perspectives of Antony as an ascetic. The first part deals with

---

[111] See D. Brakke, *Athanasius and the Politics of Asceticism*, (Oxford 1995), 11-16.

[112] *V. Ant.*, ed. and tr. by J. M. Bartelink, *Vie d'Antoine*, SC 400.

[113] *V. Ant.* Preface.

Antony's successive departure from the world into the desert, for a life devoted to spiritual exercises. For many years he spent his life in utter solitude, struggling incessantly with demons and other destructive forces, until he finally revealed himself, before the curious crowds of monks gathered around his dwelling, as a perfect human being, initiated into the divine mysteries. At this point he is no longer a mere solitary ascetic but first and foremost a great monastic leader, still a recluse but always ready to bring spiritual support to less experienced monks.[114] The legend of Antony's leaving the deserted fort that had served as his home for twenty years marks an essential turning point in the biography, culminating in Antony's long speech to the monks on proper ascetic conduct.[115] Throughout this section the attention is turned from the individual struggle for peace and self-control in the heart and mind of the ascetic to the active life in the service of the Church. In the second part of the *Life* Antony is transformed from a warrior fighting the enemies of the soul into a warrior of the world, widely renowned as a teacher for the monks, a polemicist against heretics and pagan philosophers, and a spiritual advisor to worldly authorities.[116]

It is, however, not only the fundamental narrative structure of the biography that reflects the Athanasian vision of the position of monasticism in the Egyptian Church. Athanasius' idea of bringing ascetics and ascetic theology into the framework of ecclesiastical policy is also evident from his account of Antony's attitude towards episcopal authority:

> He was tolerant in disposition and humble of soul. Though the sort of man he was, he honored the rule of the Church with extreme care, and he wanted every cleric to be held in higher regard than himself. He felt no shame at bowing the head to the bishops and priests; if even a deacon came to him for assistance, he discussed the things that are beneficial, and gave place to him in prayer, not being embarrassed to put himself in a position to learn.[117]

---

[114] *V. Ant.* 1-15.

[115] *V. Ant.* 14-43.

[116] *V. Ant.* 44-93.

[117] *V. Ant.* 67; tr. by R. C. Gregg, *Athanasius: The Life of Antony and the Letter to Marcellinus*, The Classics of Western Spirituality, (New York, Ramsey and Toronto 1980), 80-81.

In this paragraph Antony appears before us as a humble servant of the hierarchical structures of the Egyptian Church. Here the image of the true ascetic presented by Athanasius is in stark opposition to any view of the monastic movement as an alternative culture in relation to a main stream Egyptian Church mainly governed by administrative and pastoral concerns. Instead, being a true model for untold numbers of people in the cities and the deserts who subject themselves to ascetic practices, Antony remained obedient to the ordained ministry, a mere instrument in the hands of the episcopal authority to keep the Church unified. Through Athanasius' biographical account Antony is thus transformed from the independent teacher of *gnosis*, the author of his seven extant letters, into an illiterate spokesman for the Athanasian Church.[118] He becomes an obedient saint who, when called upon by the bishops to do so, eagerly leaves his mountain for Alexandria in order to reject the Arians in public, proclaiming, in accordance with Athanasian theology, that the Son of God was neither created nor had come into being from non-existence.[119]

Further evidence for Athanasius' promotion of a double-edged vision of the ascetic call, outside the world yet inside the world, is found in his two letters to monks, written sometime during his third exile 356-62.[120] These two letters clearly reveal Athanasius' view on the principles for monastic activity against heresy. The task of the monk is not only to resist the plots of the demons against individual purity of the heart, but also to fight the human demons of heresy. The most striking feature in Athanasius' letters to the monks is his express reduction of the need for theological learning as a tool for monastic denunciation of heretics. Instead, he presents a rather apophatic argument concerning the monastic task of rejecting heretics. Athanasius admits that it is not easy to demonstrate properly the true faith of the Churches, since the nature of God resists any attempt at complete comprehension by means of words. Therefore, it is enough to recognize what does not correspond with an accurate interpretation of the faith. What Athanasius advocates is a confutation of heresy, not by theological expositions but by proclaiming God's verdict upon heresy. Thus

---

[118] Rubenson, *The Letters of St. Antony* (Minneapolis 1995), 143-4.

[119] *V. Ant.* 69.

[120] Athanasius, *Ep. ad monachos (I)*, PG 25, 691-693; and *Ep. ad monachos (II)*, PG 26, 1185-1188.

the bizarre death of Arius would provide a sufficient sign for the just condemnation of the Arians.[121]

This combination in Athanasius' mind of ascetic spirituality and ecclesiastic policy into a coherent political vision, presented in a hagiographic framework in the *Life of Antony*, seems to have met with resistance among many Egyptian monks. The most illuminating evidence for this resistance is provided by the well-known letter to the monk Dracontius, which Athanasius wrote in 354.[122] In this letter Athanasius rebukes Dracontius for rejecting his appointment as Bishop of Hermopolis Parva, and accuses him of being a stumbling block for the Christians in Egypt. Athanasius argues that such rejection of the episcopal office is indefensible since, because of Dracontius' solicitude for his own spiritual welfare the people he was supposed to serve are now left without the leadership they need. The needs of the Church call for sacrifices, and any flight from the responsibility to serve the Christian community—whether such flight is motivated by timidity or by distaste for ecclesiastical administration—is contrary to the order established by God. The Church needs bishops, because without bishops there would be no Christians.[123] Neither should a life in the episcopal office in itself be regarded as contradictory to a true monastic life, since many great monks had become bishops, among them the great Serapion of Thmuis.[124] The episcopal office, therefore, cannot be taken as a pretext for sin, inasmuch as ascetic practices among bishops are not forbidden.

> For we know bishops who fast as well as monks who eat. We know bishops who drink no wine and monks who do. And we know bishops who perform marvels and monks who do not. Many bishops have not even married, while monks have fathered children. [...] For the crown is not given according to position, but according to deeds.[125]

However, Athanasius' condemnation of Dracontius and his 'advisers' for irresponsibly neglecting the needs of the Egyptian

---

[121] Athanasius, *Ep. ad monachos (I)*, 691-693.

[122] Athanasius, *Ep. ad Dracontium*, PG 25, 523-534.

[123] Athanasius, *Ep. ad Dracontium*, 528-529.

[124] Athanasius, *Ep. ad Dracontium*, 529-532.

[125] Athanasius, *Ep. ad Dracontium*, 532-533. Translation by Barnard, 6-7.

Church in a difficult time did not diminish the tension between monastic and episcopal life that many monks felt. The opinion that ordination and ecclesiastical office implied spiritual danger remained an integral part in early monastic teaching. In the Egyptian desert tradition it seems to have been widely accepted that being in the world had a negative effect on the relationship with God, since being among men constantly exposed the individual to the temptation of falling into pride and vainglory. Athanasius realized that such an attitude motivated what he considered a kind of withdrawal that was essentially nothing but an escape from the moral responsibility for the unity of the Church.[126] Instead of putting their own personal need for spiritual freedom before the needs of the Christian community, monks should submit themselves to the rule of the Church and the superiority of the bishops, just as the great Antony had done.

Athanasius linked the monks to the episcopate by making them part of his vision of a unified Church. But his idea of the Egyptian Church as a heavenly *politeia*, centered around the Patriarch of Alexandria and his bishops, also implied efforts to translate the ascetic spirituality of monks and virgins into an established program for the entire Christian population. As Athanasius defined the role of monks within the framework of episcopal hierarchy, he also developed a new model of episcopal authority in terms of ascetic leadership. This model of episcopal authority was closely linked to his understanding of the aims and means of asceticism. To Athanasius, the idea of ascetic withdrawal formed an important element in his view of the Christian life as a departure from the earth for a journey to heaven. However, ascetic withdrawal was not seen, as it traditionally was in the Egyptian desert tradition, as a quest for freedom from worldly affairs and social relations, but rather in terms of a practical and social concern for the truth of faith within the Christian community. As expressed in the second *Festal Letter*, withdrawal makes each Christian a friend of God in the same way as Abraham was made a friend of God when, having withdrawn from the lands of darkness to the light of the heavenly Jerusalem, he spoke with God face to face.[127] In order to receive eternal joy in a heavenly fellowship with God Christians

---

[126] See Brakke, *Athanasius and the Politics of Asceticism*, 106-107.
[127] See Brakke, *Athanasius and the Politics of Asceticism*, 157-161.

must withdraw from the darkness of those who lack faith. Ascetic withdrawal is thus profoundly associated with the virtue of turning away from heretics. According to Athanasius, asceticism is nothing but practiced orthodoxy, conceived as a struggle for the purity of the soul. Since ascetic fathers, because of the spiritual authority they achieved after years of ascetic practices, offered less experienced monks instruction on ascetic progress, they were expected to use their authority to defend the entire Church, viewed as an ascetic society, against heresy. Experienced monks could not simply refuse facing such an obligation, implied by their spiritual authority, just as Antony did not reject his obligation to serve as a spiritual teacher for the Christian population. What in the early Egyptian monastic tradition was a basic conflict between spiritual purity and activity in the world was by Athanasius regarded as a harmonious unity between ascetic struggle and struggle for orthodoxy. The common skepticism among monks towards ordination and episcopal ministry he rejected simply as a symptom of spiritual egocentricity that disregarded the Church as a coherent unity of believers.[128]

Athanasius' significance for the early history of Christian monasticism rests on the fact that he drew up the normative principles for monastic activity in the Egyptian Church. But in the times of Athanasius' successors the policy to put monasticism under the control of the ecclesiastical hierarchy proved to be a source of considerable turbulence as regards the relations between monks and the patriarchal authorities. This latent tension was clearly manifested after the appointment, in 385, of Athanasius' disciple Theophilus to the patriarchal throne of Alexandria. Throughout his career Theophilus made efforts, in the same way as his great mentor did, to place charismatic monks under his authority by investing them with clerical offices. Just as in Athanasius' case the motive was to strengthen the internal unity of the Alexandrian patriarchate. But towards the end of the fourth century the historical conditions that had determined Athanasius' ambitions had dramatically changed. As a result of the Council of Constantinople the Arian movement in Egypt was eventually dissolved, and on the initiative of the Emperor the remaining pagan cults were more or less successfully suppressed. Thus the

---

[128] See Athanasius, *Ep. ad Dracontium*, 525.

efforts to keep the Church united were no longer motivated primarily by the danger of heresy, but by the necessity to defend the jurisdictional position of the Patriarch of Alexandria. In order to claim effectively their leading role in the affairs of the Eastern Church, the successors of Athanasius had to guard their own position as heads of the Egyptian Church. For the realization of this ambition the monks were regarded as a source of support as well as a menace. As long as they acknowledged their subordinate position in the Church hierarchy, the monks served as useful political instruments in the hands of the Patriarch. But when the monks found their own spiritual freedom threatened by the political ambitions of the Patriarch, conflict was inevitable.[129] Further, at the time when Athanasius was composing his *Life of Antony*, monasticism was still a movement that attracted only a limited number of the Egyptian people. At the end of the fourth century, however, some ten thousand monks lived in the Egyptian deserts.[130] In the days of Theophilus the Athanasian vision of an ascetic Church had thus been realized in a far too literal manner to be easily regulated by the episcopal authority. The political implications of this intense development of Egyptian monasticism were made particularly clear in the Origenist controversy at the turn of the fifth century, culminating in Theophilus' expulsion of several hundred ascetics from Egypt in A.D. 400.[131]

One of the most notorious expressions of Theophilus' pretensions as a head of the Egyptian Church was his extensive activity as a builder. Theophilus' engagement in building projects provoked severe criticism from many ascetics, among them Palladius, who accused him of being obsessed by stones in the same manner as the old Pharaohs had been, and Isodore of Pelusium who called him a 'stone-loving worshipper of money'.[132]

---

[129] For a further discussion, see J. Goehring, 'Monastic Diversity and Ideological Boundaries in Fourth-Century Christian Egypt', *JECS* 5 (1997), 61-84.

[130] At the end of the fourth century, according to Palladius, there were about five thousand monks in Nitria, *HL* 7, ed. and tr. by C. Butler, Text and Studies 6, (Cambridge 1892).

[131] E. A. Clark, *The Origenist Controversy: The Cultural Construction of an Early Christian Debate* (Princeton 1992), 37.

[132] Palladius, *Dialogus de vita Iohanni Chrysostomi* 6, ed. and tr. by M. Malingrey, SC 341 (Paris 1988); Isodore of Pelusium, *Ep.* 152, PG 78, 285.

The power and wealth of the Alexandrine patriarchate, expressed in Theophilus' building activity, evidently caused a great deal of skepticism among the desert monks. In the pharaonic ambitions of the Patriarch they recognized the symptoms of spiritual corruption caused by the worldliness of the episcopal office. To many ascetics the case of Theophilus became a conclusive argument for refusing episcopal ordination. From Palladius and Socrates Scholasticus we learn that Abba Ammonius cut of his left ear, hoping that this act of self-mutilation would disqualify him from being ordained by Theophilus, and that for the same reason Evagrius of Pontus cut out his tongue.[133] Also the four distinguished monks from Nitria known as the Tall Brothers refused ordination, until Theophilus eventually forced them into the clerical office by his authority. Two of them were assigned to Alexandria, in the immediate proximity of Theophilus:

> They, constrained by necessity, performed the duties thus imposed on them successfully; nevertheless they were dissatisfied because they were unable to follow philosophical pursuits and ascetic exercises. And as in process of time, they thought they were being spiritually injured, observing the bishop to be devoted to gain, and greedily intent on the acquisition of wealth.[134]

According to the account given by Socrates they eventually, as a result of Theophilus' greedy conduct, refused to continue their office, and tried to convince him to let them leave the city. As the Patriarch realized that their wish was motivated by a profound dislike of his conduct he became furious, and began to accuse them of being corrupted by the teachings of Origen.[135] Socrates' allegation that it was Theophilus' obsession with money that ultimately motivated his involvement in the Origenist controversy can be substantiated by the account given by Sozomen of the conflict between Theophilus and his closest advisor, the monk Isodore of Pelusium. According to a story related by Sozomen, the

---

[133] Socrates, *HE* 4.23, ed. and tr. by G. C. Hansen, GCS N.F. 1 (Berlin 1994); Palladius, *HL* 11.

[134] Socrates, *HE* 6.7; tr. by A. C. Zenos, *Church History from A.D. 305-439*, in A Select Library of the Nicene and Post-Nicene Fathers of the Christian Church, ser. 2, vol. 11 (Grand Rapids 1983), 143.

[135] Socrates, *HE* 6.7.

hostility of Theophilus against Isodore was based on a disagreement about a legacy received by Isodore to be distributed to the poor. When Theophilus claimed money to finance his building projects Isodore refused to yield before the Patriarch, declaring that to restore the bodies of the suffering, the true temples of God, was better than to build walls. As a result Isodore was excommunicated by Theophilus, and returned to the desert to join the Tall Brothers.[136]

Theophilus' need for money to finance his building projects seems to be a recurrent theme in the polemical accounts of his enemies. Indeed, the image of Theophilus provided by these sources is in stark contrast to that of the ascetic and charismatic leadership of Athanasius. To many monks Theophilus failed to embrace the Athanasian vision of a Church guided by ascetic bishops, to the extent that it also damaged his position as a teacher of the true faith of the Church. This is particularly clear from the remarkable hagiographic account of Abba Aphou of Pemdje, a monk who was sent by the Lord to rebuke Theophilus for having, in his Paschal Letter of 399, made an incorrect exposition of the Christian faith.[137] The story about Abba Aphou's encounter with Theophilus, dealing with the question of in what way man should be regarded as the image of God, is presented in terms of the marked contrast between a simple desert monk and the powerful Patriarch of Alexandria. We are told that Aphou went to Alexandria dressed in a worn-out cloak, and patiently waited for three days outside the gate of the patriarchal palace until Theophilus finally received him. Moved by the monk's humble appearance the Patriarch let himself be enlightened on the true meaning of faith.[138] Finally, profoundly impressed by Aphou's exposition of the faith, he fell down on the ground, saying:

> Those who live in solitude and peace shall truly be teachers. For our thoughts have confused us, so that

---

[136] Sozomen, *HE* 8.12, ed. and tr. by J. Bidez and G. C. Hansen, GCS 50 (Berlin 1960).

[137] *Vita Aphou*, ed. E. Drioton, *La discussion d'un moine anthropomorphite audien avec le patriarche Théophile d'Alexandrie en l'année 399*, ROC 10 (= 20) (1915-1917), 92-110, 113-128.

[138] *Vita Aphou*, 95-100, 113

we in this way have erred utterly because of our foolishness.[139]

As the story proceeds, Aphou explains to Theophilus,

Your powerful position cannot raise you over foolishness so that you can master your own will. [...] But truly you have shown that you have converted entirely from pride to the purity and simplicity of humbleness.[140]

For the author of the *Life of Aphou*, ascetic practices create an authority through which it is possible to teach and rebuke even the patriarchs, since asceticism opens the mind for divine inspiration. Clerical offices do not necessarily protect orthodoxy, since the temptations associated with such offices may give the Devil opportunities for plots to promote heresy. Consequently, Theophilus must give attention to the words of the inspired men of the desert in order to serve the Christian community properly, instead of leading it into the abyss of heresy.

To conclude, to Athanasius asceticism was crucial in his vision of the formation of the Egyptian Church. The ascetic notions of renunciation and imitation were integrated into a political program resting on episcopal organization and a strict interpretation of Nicaean theology. Asceticism was no longer a concern exclusively for virgins and anachoretic monks, but for the whole Church, as a single body of believers. Ascetic withdrawal was essential for the perfection of all Christians, but was not to be taken as a pretext for solitary isolation from the Christian community. Fundamentally, ascetic withdrawal implied a responsibility to partake in the struggles of the Athanasian party and to keep the Christian community from being polluted by Arian, Meletian or pagan impiety. Thus the idea of withdrawal should motivate the whole Church to unite behind Athanasius' anti-Arian struggle, ordinary Christians together with the ascetic elite in the deserts. To fulfill this vision Athanasius needed the charismatic leadership of experienced ascetics such as Ammoun or Serapion of Thmuis, and tried to draw them under his authority by making them bishops. The monk Dracontius refused to receive this ordination, since he feared the consequences of the loss of ascetic independence. To Athanasius such a refusal was nothing but an irresponsible kind of

---

[139] *Vita Aphou*, 114.
[140] *Vita Aphou*, 115

withdrawal that jeopardized the spiritual well fare of the Christian community. Ascetics were expected to obey the Patriarch and to follow him in his struggles against heresy. It is this conviction that forms the main ideological background to the *Life of Antony*.

The *Life of Antony* provided a long-lasting model for the anti-heretic activity among monks that was based on the necessity of obedience towards the ecclesiastic hierarchy. But at the same time it did not solve the question that arose among many Egyptian monks at the turn of the fifth century of how to act before prelates who distorted the truth because of their excessive concern for worldly matters. Instead, this question was solved by the anonymous author of the *Life of Aphou*, advocating the idea that the clerical office could not by itself protect the purity of faith. Only if such offices were associated with an ascetic conduct of life, the Holy Spirit would enlighten the soul on the true meaning of faith. Knowledge about the divine realities presupposed ascetic independence of worldly matters. Many ascetics were ordained bishops, but as bishops they constantly had to watch their own will so as not to fall into temptations associated to administrative concerns. So much better then to withdraw to the desert and return to the world only as a warrior of faith whenever the believers were threatened by the plots of the heretics. Consequently, when Theophilus asked Abba Aphou to stay by him in Alexandria Aphou's simple answer was: 'I cannot'. The spiritual independence of worldly matters could not be compromised. It was this concern for independence that, according to Zacharias Scholasticus, made the great Abba Isaiah to leave Egypt and settle in Palestine, where he eventually became one of the great legends of the anti-Chalcedonian resistance.[141] In the end many monks preferred independence of the ecclesiastic hierarchy in order to preserve their ascetic freedom. At the same time they were, like Antony, constantly prepared both to support and to correct their bishops, whenever the purity of faith was endangered.

Behind this way of thinking with its duality between the spiritual aim of monastic practices and material responsibilities as a main cause of heresy we meet with a Platonic emphasis on the cosmological division between the spiritual and the material world. As he was himself a hypostatic unity of soul and body a monk

---

[141] Zacharias Scholasticus, *Vita Isaiae Monachi*, 4.

should not take pleasure in ecclesiastic authority, even if forced to hold such authority. A monk should *take* part in the responsibilities of ecclesiastic offices, but under no circumstances submit to the material condition of *being* part of such responsibilities. Monastic life is about the *theoria* of the soul, not the *theoria* of corruptible matter that would entail the risk of putting oneself straight in the hands of the demons. For the anti-Chalcedonians such attraction to the world of perceptible things was the essential point of failure as regards the bishops at Chalcedon. Evidently, these bishops had chosen to safeguard the material pleasures of their ecclesiastic power by depriving the Son the honor of being wholly God, and by reducing his very essence to a part of this corruptible world.[142] Instead of devoting themselves, in accordance with their responsibilities as spiritual leaders of the Christian community, to the struggle against the blasphemous teaching of Nestorius as revived in Leo's *Tome*,[143] they had desacralized the Son into a material idol and turned him into an image of their own corruptibility. In such a state of ecumenical apostasy, who could find any remains of orthodoxy and true responsibility for the Christian community except among the monks of Egypt and Palestine, who were still devoted citizens of the divine realm.

To adhere to the teaching of Chalcedon was, in the eyes of the anti-Chalcedonians, to confess Christ as divided between the two fundamentally incompatible and conflicting realms of spirit and matter, thus denying the Trinitarian dogma of the Son as true God. Such a theology of compromise, promoting the veneration of Christ in two self-subsistent parts, one essentially divine and the other essentially material, not only reduced the divinity of the Son but also implied a menacing compromise with Nestorian heresy. To compromise with heretics, veiling their heterodoxy by misusing the theological language of orthodox doctors such as Cyril of Alexandria, was in itself an act of heresy that deserved condemnation. It was this view of the danger of compromising orthodoxy that underlay the internal crisis that shook the anti-Chalcedonian circles at the end of the fifth century, following the imperial formula of doctrinal unification known as the *Henotikon*.

---

[142] Cf. *Pleroph.* 14.
[143] Cf. *Pleroph.* 40.

Compromising Orthodoxy

During the second half of the fifth century factions arose in the
anti-Chalcedonian movement who considered the Patriarchs of
Alexandria to have failed quite seriously in the pursuit of orthodox
purity. A major reason for this division within the anti-
Chalcedonian movement was the question of whether or not to
compromise, a debate centered on Emperor Zeno's formula of
unity of 482, known as the *Henotikon*. The internal anti-
Chalcedonian debate on the *Henotikon* which persisted from its
establishment in 482 until long after its withdrawal in 518 is
attested as a present reality in a letter by Severus of Antioch,
written sometime between 520-534. In this letter Severus
complains about the circulation of prophecies and visions intended
to persuade ordinary people not to maintain communion with the
churches in Egypt. From Severus we learn that the reason behind
this refusal to receive communion from the Egyptian bishops was
the communion established with the Chalcedonian bishops by the
Alexandrine Patriarch Peter Mongus in 482 on the basis of
Emperor Zeno's *Henotikon*. In his letter, Severus makes it clear that
he does not think highly of the promulgators of such visionary
stories, and he is clear in his conviction that dreams and prophecies
are too often, for lack of rational arguments, used to pollute the
truth for personal gain. Clearly annoyed with those prophecies he
regards them as a phenomenon characteristic of communities
suffering from suppression and persecutions, while there is no such
talk about prophecies and visions in times of orthodox
hegemony.[144] Instead, he accuses those who relate such visions
and prophesies of an unjust judgement of the orthodoxy of the
Egyptians, who, since the anti-Chalcedonian Council of Tyre in
514, had rejected any communion with the Chalcedonians.

The promotion of the *Henotikon*, which for thirty-six years
represented the official faith of the Eastern Empire, caused
considerable debate among the anti-Chalcedonians. According to
the *Henotikon*, the faith to be confirmed was that of Nicaea, as it
had been confirmed in Constantinople and in Ephesus and by Cyril
in his twelve propositions against Nestorius. Christ, truly God and
truly man, was to be confessed as of the same nature with the
Father in the Godhead and of the same nature with us in the

---

[144] Severus of Antioch, *Select Letters*, 5.11.

manhood, not as two sons but as one. Any other conviction would be condemned together with Nestorius and Eutyches and their adherents, whether expressed in Chalcedon or elsewhere.[145] However, nowhere in the document was there an express rejection of the Council of Chalcedon, something that for many anti-Chalcedonians obstructed the possibilities of a complete restoration of orthodoxy. Severus, in turn, clearly expressed his opinion that the *Henotikon* had to be accepted, since from the very beginning it had been supported by the great legends of the anti-Chalcedonian movement.

> Who cannot but be disgusted with men […] who have fallen so far into conflict with God as they presume to condemn the edict under which—as those men say in so many words—the followers of Julian the priest, whose soul is at rest, preserved communion with Peter [Mongus], who became bishop of the city of the Alexandrines after Timothy [Aelurus], unto this day, and went into the church with him. Do they not know that they are condemning men whom, as they think, they ascribe as their fathers? For how is it that, the right confession being contained in the edict, they sought to have that which is wanting added, that is a rejection of the Council of Chalcedon, and when this was not added withdrew from communion? If the edict deserved condemnation, they should never have assented to this in the first place. But instead they should have demanded that it also ought to be repudiated, like one of the repudiated doctrines.[146]

The history behind the *Henotikon* goes back at least to 474, when Emperor Leo died and was succeeded by Zeno the Isaurian. The anti-Chalcedonians in Egypt seized the opportunity and sent a petition to the imperial capital to persuade the newly appointed Emperor to restore Timothy to the patriarchal throne of Alexandria. But when the petitioners arrived in Constantinople in early 475 they found the situation in the imperial capital dramatically changed. A revolution had expelled Zeno from the city, and the imperial throne was now occupied by the Germanic warlord Basiliscus. The new Emperor received the Egyptians and

---

[145] For the text, see Zacharias Scholasticus, *HE* 5.8. Also in Evagrius Scholasticus, *HE* 3.14.

[146] Severus of Antioch, *Select Letters*, 5.11.

gave his full support to the anti-Chalcedonian cause. Timothy
Aelurus was recalled from exile and re-established as Patriarch of
Alexandria. Also Peter the Fuller, the anti-Chalcedonian Patriarch
of Antioch who had been deposed by Leo in 471, was permitted to
return to his see.[147]

For the first time the anti-Chalcedonians found their cause
supported by imperial authorities. Basiliscus' political agenda was
obviously determined by his ambition to unite the Eastern
Churches in the condemnation of Leo's *Tome*. In the spring of 475
an imperial encyclical letter was written in which the *Tome* of Leo
and the Council of Chalcedon were expressly rejected as contrary
to the Nicaean creed.[148] Timothy Aelurus and Peter the Fuller,
together with Patriarch Anastasius of Jerusalem, Paul of Ephesus,
and a considerable number of the Eastern bishops, signed this
document, known simply as the *Encyclical*.[149] Only Acacius, the
Patriarch of Constantinople, refused to sign the encyclical letter,
undoubtedly because of his ambition to preserve the privileges
granted   at   Chalcedon   to   the   patriarchal   throne   of
Constantinople.[150]

However, the days of Basiliscus' reign were running short.
Reports reached him that Zeno prepared his return to the imperial
throne, and riots were stirred up against Basiliscus in the capital,
which was predominantly Chalcedonian. A new edict was written,
rejecting the *Encyclical* but also the heresies of Nestorius and
Eutyches. This *anti-Encyclical* fell far short of providing Basiliscus
with the political strength he needed at Zeno's return to
Constantinople. In August 476 Zeno entered the capital and re-
established himself on the imperial throne. Every single one of
Basiliscus' decrees was officially nullified, the two encyclicals as
well as the restoration of the patriarchal positions of Peter the
Fuller and Timothy Aelurus. The latter, however, was released
from banishment only by his death in 477.[151]

---

[147] Zacharias Scholasticus, *HE* 5.1.

[148] Zacharias Scholasticus, *HE* 5.2.

[149] Zacharias Scholasticus, *HE* 5.3.

[150] See Frend, *The Rise of the Monophysite Movement*, 170-173.

[151] Zacharias Scholasticus, *HE* 5.5. Frend, *The Rise of the Monophysite
Movement*, 173-174. John Rufus places the withdrawal of the *Encyclical* and
the promulgation of the *anti-Encyclical* immediately in connection with

Timothy Aelurus was succeeded by his archdeacon, Peter Mongus.[152] It was soon made known from the imperial capital that the ordination had been effected contrary to the will of Emperor Zeno, who instead ordered the restoration of Timothy Salofaciolus. Peter Mongus was forced to leave the patriarchal throne of Alexandria in great tumult.[153] Anti-Chalcedonian feelings were strong, and Acacius soon saw the fatal consequences of an open breach between the Eastern Churches. In order to defend his position as the head of the Eastern Churches he finally followed the example of Martyrius, the Patriarch of Jerusalem, and decided to accept Chalcedon, but only as an instrument by which Nestorius and Eutyches were condemned.[154] When Timothy Salofaciolus died in 482, Acacius would accept Peter Mongus as Patriarch of Alexandria on the condition that Peter signed a new imperial edict of unity, the *Henotikon*, written by Acacius.[155]

Peter Mongus signed the *Henotikon*, and Acacius immediately recognized his patriarchal dignity. Communion between Constantinople and Alexandria was secured. Also Martyrius in Jerusalem accepted the *Henotikon*, while Calendion in Antioch did not. Calendion regarded the edict as a furtive refutation of Chalcedon, and in 484 he allied himself with the rebels of the Isaurian general Illus in a civil war against Zeno. As a result of his treason Calendion was deposed from the patriarchal see of Antioch, and Peter the Fuller was reinstalled, immediately accepting the *Henotikon*. Through his diplomatic skills Acacius had,

---

Zenos restauration and the banishment of Peter the Fuller, see *Pleroph.* 22, and *V. Petr. Ib.*, 80.

[152] For Peter Mongus, see C. Haas, 'Patriarch and People: Peter Mongus of Alexandria and episcopal Leadership in the Late Fifth Century', *JECS* 1.3 (1993), 297-316.

[153] Disturbances also characterized the situation in Antioch, where Stephanus, the Chalcedonian successor of Peter the Fuller, is said to have been murdered by anti-Chalcedonian priests in 479 and his body thrown in the Orontes. See below, chap. 2, sec 1.

[154] Zacharias Scholasticus, *HE* 5.5-6. The text of Martyrius' encyclical letter from 479 is found in Zacharias Scholasticus, *HE* 5.6.

[155] Zacharias Scholasticus, *HE* 5.7.

at least officially, managed to achieve concord between
Chalcedonians and anti-Chalcedonians in the East.[156]

In Rome, Pope Simplicius was enraged by Acacius'
acknowledgement of Peter Mongus as the legitimate patriarch of
Alexandria. A schism developed between Rome and
Constantinople that would last until the reign of Emperor Justin.
But even in the East the *Henotikon* met with opposition, particularly
from a group of anti-Chalcedonians in Egypt who were disturbed
by the absence of an express condemnation of Chalcedon and
Leo's *Tome*. At the request of this group Peter Mongus pronounced
his official condemnation of the *Tome* and the Council, and thus
managed partly to avoid a schism within the Egyptian Church.
However, certain groups of Egyptian monks were far from
impressed by the condemnation Peter had pronounced against
Chalcedon, since he remained in communion with those patriarchs
who had not openly condemned the *Tome* and the Council. As a
result these monks refused communion with Peter Mongus, and
were therefore designated as the *akephaloi*, i.e. the headless, those
who rejected the ecclesiastic leadership of the Patriarch of
Alexandria and his bishops.[157]

The following years were marked by a sudden shift of power
on almost every important stage of authority in the Eastern
Empire. Peter the Fuller died in 488, Acacius in 489, Peter Mongus
in 490 and Emperor Zeno in 491. In Constantinople the former
soldier and civil servant Anastasius entered upon the imperial
throne.[158] Like his predecessor Zeno, Anastasius wished to protect
the doctrinal unity of the Eastern Empire. In the first years of his
reign he was also determined to put an end to the breach between
Constantinople and Rome in terms of accepting Chalcedon.
Negotiations were conducted between the popes of Rome and the
East, but were interrupted by the Persian war (502-5), which

---

[156] Zacharias Scholasticus, *HE* 5.9. See Frend, *The Rise of the Monophysite Movement*, 179-181.

[157] See Zacharias Scholasticus, *HE* 5.9.

[158] For Emperor Anastasius, see P. Charanis, *Church and State in the Later Roman Empire: The Religious Policy of Anastasius the First, 491-518* (Thessaloniki 1974).

necessitated political support from the Eastern provinces.[159] The policy of Anastasius was now mainly directed towards the religious quarrels within the Eastern Empire. In 508 he received Severus, the future Patriarch of Antioch, who had been sent from his monastery at Maiuma at Gaza to complain about the measures taken by Elias, the Patriarch of Jerusalem, against the anti-Chalcedonians in Palestine.[160]

In the following years Severus managed to convince Anastasius that supporting the anti-Chalcedonian cause was the only way to attain unity in the East. The Emperor soon appointed him his imperial *magister*, and in order to assure the people and magistrates in the imperial capital of the purity of his faith he wrote a number of refutations directed against Eutychians, Apollinarians, Nestorians, and Origenists. However, the main threat against the unity of the Eastern Churches did not derive from those quarters. Instead, the greatest problem with Eastern ecclesiastical policies for the time was to decide whether the *Henotikon* should be taken as the official doctrine or as a first step towards a final condemnation of Chalcedon. Flavian, the Patriarch of Antioch, was a supporter of the former policy, while Philoxenus of Mabbug wanted a total rejection of Chalcedon. Severus was summoned by the Emperor to arbitrate between the two factions, and a formula of satisfaction, the so-called *Typos*,[161] was written. This *Typos* implied not only the acceptance of the *Henotikon* but also an express rejection of Leo's *Tome* and the formula 'in two natures'.

Meanwhile the Trisagion controversy concerning Peter the Fuller's addition to the doxology—'one of the Trinity has been crucified'— broke out between Severus and the Patriarch Macedonius of Jerusalem. The outcome of the dispute meant victory for Severus, and Macedonius was deposed in 511. For a year the new doxology was recognized as official in the East until

---

[159] For a discussion about the early reign of Anastasius and the negations between Rome and Constantinople until the Persian war, see Frend, *The Rise of the Monophysite Movement*, 190-201.

[160] See Zacharias Scholasticus, *Vita Severi*, 100-105.

[161] Part of the text is preserved in an Armenian translation and is edited by C. Moeller, 'Le Type de l'empereur Anastase I', *SP* 3 (=TU 78) (Berlin 1961), 240-247.

Anastasius was forced to recall it, following severe riots in the capital in 512.[162]

The next step for Severus and Anastasius was to replace the *Henotikon* with the *Typos* as the official doctrine of the Eastern Empire. A synod was summoned at Sidon in 511, but the result was a great disappointment for Severus. A vast majority of the bishops summoned, among them also the Egyptians, decided to stick to the *Henotikon*, and rejected the thought of breaking communion with the Chalcedonians.[163] In Antioch, however, the spirit of revolt was fomented by Philoxenus' agitation, and Flavian was deposed by a council at Laodicea in 512.[164] In November the same year Severus replaced him, and at that moment all patriarchal sees in the East, except that of Jerusalem, were controlled by anti-Chalcedonians. The schism caused at the synod of Sidon by the disagreement between the supporters of Severus and Philoxenus on the one hand, and the Egyptian bishops on the other, still had to be healed. In 514 Anastasius summoned a new synod to Tyre, where the *Henotikon* was accepted by all the patriarchs of the Eastern Empire as a rejection of Chalcedon and the teaching of the dyophysite faith, without any mention of the *Typos*. Communion was restored between Severus and the Patriarch of Alexandria, and would last until Severus' death. But the days were counted for the *Henotikon* as the fundamental document of faith. In 518 Emperor Anastasius died, having governed the Eastern Empire for twenty-seven years with a policy inclined towards a moderate non-Chalcedonian solution. His successor Justin immediately initiated a Chalcedonian restoration in the Empire, leading to the expulsion of Severus from Antioch and the withdrawal of the *Henotikon*. Severus escaped to Egypt where, until his death in 538, he carried out his duties as a distinguished leader of the anti-Chalcedonians in the Roman East. But although the *Henotikon* had been replaced, following a violent campaign for Chalcedonianism, the controversy on the *Henotikon* within the anti-Chalcedonian movement was still not over.

---

[162] For the *Trisagion* controversy, see Pseudo-Zacharias, *HE* 7.7-9, ed. and tr. by Brooks, CSCO, Script. syri 3.5-6. For the riots in Constantinople in November 512, see Evagrius Scholasticus, *HE* 3.44.

[163] Pseudo-Zacharias, *HE* 7.10. For Severus of Antioch's opinion on the synod of Sidon, see *Select Letters*, 4, 2.

[164] Evagrius Scholasticus, *HE* 3.32.

There is no direct mention of the *Henotikon* in the works of John Rufus. But in a lengthy autobiographical anecdote in his *Plerophories* that deals with the attempt of John's former friends, Peter and Solomon, to make him return to the service of Peter the Fuller in Antioch, there is an important clue to a general conclusion about John's opinions about the *Henotikon*. In this story we learn that, after his restoration in 484, Peter the Fuller sent Peter and Solomon to deliver a synodical letter to Martyrius, the Chalcedonian Patriarch of Jerusalem. In Palestine the two couriers found John in Peter the Iberian's monastery at Maiuma, and tried to persuade him to accompany them back to Syria. But John refused, while Peter and Solomon were struck with a dangerous fever. When John visited them in their distress, Peter confessed that he had been deceived by his desire for the episcopate and had therefore strayed from the true faith.[165]

This story provides the most manifest illustration in the *Plerophories* of the idea that compromise is tantamount to heresy. The purpose of the story is simply to demonstrate that the communion that Peter the Fuller and Martyrius had established on the basis of their mutual acceptance of the *Henotikon* had made them both adherents of the council of the renegades. In other words, signing the *Henotikon* was quite simply the same as signing the *Tome* of Leo. Communion with those who had approved the *Henotikon* thus had to be rejected, since the *Henotikon* implied the danger of being tainted by the impurity of heresy. This seems to be the main theme in John's works. John was concerned about the situation in which he and his friends lived, a time when the Eastern Empire had been united following the *Henotikon*, a compromise worked out in order to bring the Chalcedonians in line with the anti-Chalcedonians without any express condemnation of Chalcedon. This was a time when the faithful had to react, and the precise manner in which John Rufus reacted will be elucidated in the following chapters.

---

[165] *Pleroph.* 22.

2 THE TEXTS

The Author

In the chronicle of John Malalas, written in the 560's, we are given a short report of the assassination of Stephanus, Patriarch of Antioch, on the ninth of March, 479. Leading a procession outside the city walls of Antioch to celebrate the commemoration of the forty martyrs of Sebaste, the Patriarch was suddenly surrounded by his own retinue of priests and pierced with reed pens all over his body until he was dead. His body was then thrown into the river Orontes. Furious at this fanatical outrage, Emperor Zeno appointed as the successor of the murdered Patriarch the harsh Chalcedonian Calendion, who immediately sent the priests responsible for the cold-blooded murder into exile.[1]

About the same time, we learn from another source that a man came down from Antioch to Palestine to join his old fellow student Theodore as a disciple of the great anti-Chalcedonian protagonist Peter the Iberian. Describing himself in third person as 'the most worthless of men,' he informs us that he had served as a priest in Antioch under Peter the Fuller but escaped when Calendion had taken hold of the patriarchal throne in Antioch. The account of his admission into the monastic circle of Peter the Iberian is characterized by an extreme self-effacement, expressed through metaphors borrowed from Luke 15:

> He [i.e. Peter the Iberian] was seized with sympathy and love towards this useless person, and received him and made him his companion in his cell. He did everything and cared for his salvation like a compassionate father, liberating him from the bonds of

---

[1] John Malalas, *Chron.* 15, ed. by L. Dindorf (Bonn 1831), 381. A similar account is provided in Pseudo-Dionysius of Tel-Maḥrē, *Chronicon*, 229-30, ed. and tr. by J.-B. Chabot, CSCO, Script. syri 3.5; in Evagrius Scholasticus, *HE* 3.10, 109; and also in Michael the Syrian, *Chron.* 9.6 ed. Chabot, 1899, 254.

death and from evil habits. He led him on the true way
of penance and like a good shepherd brought this lost
sheep before the Lord, carrying him on his shoulders in
joy and inviting all his beloved friends and neighbors to
rejoice, since he had found him.[2]

The man behind these penitential words of unworthiness is known
to us by the name John of Beth Ruphinā, or John Rufus, priest at
the monastery of Peter the Iberian at Maiuma and most likely the
spiritual leader of the anti-Chalcedonians in Palestine after the
death of Peter 489. The sources of our knowledge about his life are
scant and—except for a short biographical report in the *Life of
Severus* by Zacharias Scholasticus—limited to few autobiographical
notes in his works, the *Life of Peter the Iberian* and the *Plerophories*. Yet
it is possible to sketch at least a preliminary portrait of him.

From the information delivered in the title of the *Plerophories*
we learn that his name was John Rufus of Antioch, that he was a
disciple of Peter the Iberian, and that he was a priest and later
Bishop of Maiuma at Gaza. The problem of the historical
authenticity of John's episcopate of Maiuma was treated in the
previous chapter. From the lack of information about any bishop
of Maiuma at the turn of the sixth century it would be plausible to
suggest that John never was Bishop of Maiuma. Yet we know that
Peter the Iberian, although expelled from his bishopric of Maiuma
in 453, in the eyes of the anti-Chalcedonians in Palestine continued
to be the true bishop and spiritual leader of the Palestinian flock.[3]
It is thus not unlikely that the anti-Chalcedonians in Palestine
consecrated John as the successor of Peter the Iberian, so as to
maintain their claim to be independent of the Chalcedonian
patriarchs of Jerusalem.

From the *Plerophories* we learn that John was born in the
province of Arabia, and that he was a monk before being ordained
priest in Antioch by Peter the Fuller 'in the time of the *Encyclical*,'
i.e. about 475. During the exile of Peter the Fuller he left for
Palestine, where he subordinated himself to the spiritual authority
of Peter the Iberian and Abba Isaiah.[4] Phrases such as 'our Abba
related to us', which several times in the *Plerophories* introduce
stories told by Peter the Iberian, suggest that John was one of his

---

[2] *V. Petr. Ib.*, 81.

[3] *V. Petr. Ib.*, 77.

[4] *Pleroph.* 22. See also 88, 89.

chief disciples. Otherwise the information provided in the *Plerophories* is meager but, on the whole, consistent with what is revealed in the anonymous *Life of Peter the Iberian*. Here we learn that the author, together with his friend Theodore of Ascalon, who later became one of Peter the Iberian's successors, had been a law student in Beirut before his ordination to the priesthood by Peter the Fuller in the days of Basiliscus. Later, when Calendion became Patriarch of Antioch, John took refuge in Palestine under the spiritual leadership of Peter the Iberian.[5] After Peter's death his monastery at Maiuma was expanded, under the leadership of Theodore of Ascalon, and the altar in the new-built monastery church was entrusted to the author of the *Life*.[6] This clearly corresponds with the information given by Zacharias Scholasticus in his *Life of Severus*, that Theodore of Ascalon was entrusted with the leadership of the monastery of Peter the Iberian after Peter's death, and that the altar was reserved for John, 'surnamed Rufus'.[7] Zacharias then tells us that this John—or Lazarus, as he also seems to have been called, because of the grave expression of his face and the physical asceticism he had subjected himself to—belonged to the clergy of Antioch during the time of Peter the Fuller and before he embraced the monastic life in Palestine under Peter the Iberian.[8] Our sources, thus, give a fragmentary but at the same time surprisingly uniform picture of John Rufus. Yet it was not until 1912 that the identity between the author of the *Plerophories*, the author of the *Life of Peter the Iberian*, and the monk-priest mentioned by Zacharias Scholasticus as John Rufus, was finally established.[9]

Our sources are, however, remarkably silent on the circumstances that forced John Rufus to leave Antioch for Palestine. Turning once more to John Malalas' report on the death of Stephanus, and knowing that John Rufus served as a priest in Antioch until Calendion's patriarchate, we are immediately confronted with the intriguing question whether John was present at the very moment of Stephanus' violent death. Did he actually have a share of the responsibility for the assassination of Stephanus, and is it possible to explain the utter self-effacement

---

[5] *V. Petr. Ib.*, 79, 81.

[6] *V. Petr. Ib.*, 143-145.

[7] Zacharias Scholasticus, *V. Severi*, 86.

[8] Zacharias Scholasticus, *V. Severi*, 86-87.

[9] Schwartz, 'Johannes Rufus', 9.

and humility reflected by the text quoted above as the words of a sincerely penitent murderer? Nevertheless, intriguing as these questions might be, it is preferable to put them aside, because of the lack of evidence in our sources. Without completely rejecting the historicity of John Malalas' report, it must be observed that the earliest report on the assassination of Stephanus seems to be that of John, while Zacharias Scholasticus, though closer in time to the events reported, says nothing at all about this incident. The course of events in the patriarchal see of Antioch during Peter the Fuller's second exile is, on the whole, historically obscure, and has for long been the object of controversy.[10] Taking a sober view of these matters it should be sufficient to assume that John, when Calendion took control of the patriarchal see of Antioch, found it impossible to continue his ecclesiastical service under a man he would later describe as a 'rapacious wolf that did not spare even his own flock',[11] and therefore left the city, probably in 482.[12] Furthermore, John's words, when he describes himself as a lost sheep and a prodigal son, should be considered against the background of his role as a hagiographer, using his alleged lack of worthiness as a rhetorical ornament for an appropriate account of Peter the Iberian's life.

There are, in all, three works extant by John Rufus, each contributing in its own way to our understanding of the literary and rhetorical expressions of the anti-Chalcedonian movement.[13] First, there is the important *Life of Peter the Iberian*, to which we owe much of our knowledge about the first generation of opposition to Chalcedon. Secondly, there is the much less extensive *Commemoration of the Death of Theodosius*, written as an appendix to

---

[10] See Stein, *Histoire du Bas-Empire*, vol. 1 (Paris 1949), 20-21, esp. 21, n. 1. Honigmann, *Évêques et évêchés monophysites d'Asie antérieure au VIe siècle* (Louvain 1951), 4 with n. 4.

[11] *V. Petr. Ib*, 81.

[12] Here I accept Honigmann's suggestion that Calendion, although consecrated bishop by Acacius in 479, did not take office until 482, *Évêques et évêchés monophysites d'Asie*, 4. Whether Calendion then succeeded John Codonatus or the second Stephanus (Stephanus III) mentioned by Zacharias Scholasticus, *HE* 4.12, cannot be determined here.

[13] For a notice on the authorship of John Rufus, see Flusin, 'L'hagiographie palestinienne et la réception du concile de Chalcédoine', 34-44.

the *Life of Peter the Iberian*. This text deals with the martyrdom of the rebellious monk Theodosius who after Chalcedon and Juvenal's exile was made bishop of Jerusalem. But the most fascinating of the writings of John Rufus is his third work, the *Plerophories*. It was written during the Patriarchate of Severus of Antioch 512-518, and consists of a somewhat bizarre collection of eighty-nine anecdotes about prophesies, visions and other signs received by holy men against the blasphemous teaching of the two natures of Christ. But with its constant emphasis on the holy man's position as the principal witness of truth, it follows the general monastic and hagiographic patterns of anti-Chalcedonian literature.

Texts and Versions

The Life of Peter the Iberian

In 1895 Richard Raabe published an edition of two anonymous Syriac manuscripts, dated 741 and 1197 respectively, describing the life of one of the most prominent figures of the anti-Chalcedonian movement, Peter the Iberian:[14]

[A] Berlin syr. 321, fol. 68-103, Sachau, n. 26, p. 96
[B] British Library, add. 12.174, fol. 48-78, Wright, vol. 3, n. 960, p. 1124

On the whole the two manuscripts show considerable agreement, though there are numerous linguistic and grammatical differences. Unfortunately the Greek original behind these manuscripts seems to have been lost at a fairly early stage, but in the *Church History* of Evagrius Scholasticus the existence of a Greek original is reported without reference to the author.[15] Apparently the anonymity of the *Life of Peter the Iberian* was preserved from the very beginning, probably in accordance with the author's intention. The *Life* gives the impression of having been written fairly soon after Peter the Iberian's death in 491.[16] In 1912 E. Schwartz solved the question

---

[14] *Petrus der Iberer. Ein Charakterbild zur Kirchen- und Sittengeschichte des fünften Jahrhunderts*, ed. and tr. by R. Raabe (Leipzig 1895).

[15] Evagrius Scholasticus, *HE* 2.8: 'Peter the Iberian, [bishop] of the small town of Maiuma, as the author of the Life of Peter reports on this subject'. For Evagrius, see G. F. Chesnut, *The First Christian Histories: Eusebius, Socrates, Sozomen, Theodoret and Evagrius*, TH 46 (Paris 1977).

[16] Particularly striking is the contemporary character of the description of Peter's death. John Rufus, *V. Petr. Ib.*, 137–146. I accept Schwartz's

about the authorship of the *Life*, suggesting on the basis of the autobiographical notices in the text that the author of the *Life* could hardly be anyone but John Rufus.

The author emphasizes in the foreword his ambition to recount as carefully and detailed as possible the course of Peter the Iberian's life. In the foreword John Rufus expresses his intention to depict a bishop and a monastic leader who, even after his death, serves as a true model for his disciples.[17] The purpose of the *Life* is to admonish the surviving disciples to seek the good and joyfully strive for a pious death in imitation of their great leader. In the *Life* an ascetic doctrine is presented that focuses on the career of the great protagonist, but with constant emphasis on true monastic and orthodox conduct as a fruit of God's grace.[18]

The structure is strictly chronological but at the same time geographical, primarily as a result of the strong emphasis on Peter's frequent travels. The narrative structure of the *Life* can be divided into five distinct sections that correspond to the different stages of the personal development of a holy man in the framework of Eastern hagiographic tradition. The first section deals with the saint's pious upbringing and his gradual reaching of spiritual maturity. Besides the presentation of the ascetic piety of Peter's family, this stage includes his decision on a radical dissociation from the material world in order to submit himself completely to the ascetic way of life. The ambition of completeness of detail indicated in the foreword is realized in the pages immediately following the foreword, where considerable attention is given to Peter's parentage. Behind this attention on Peter's family we may, presumably, trace John Rufus' intention to stress that one of the most honorable of the non-Chalcedonian leaders was in fact a prince of the blood who had renounced the heritage of his father's kingdom to become a monk, and to be a champion for the purity

---

suggestion in 'Publizistische Sammlungen zum acacianischen Schisma', in *ABAW* 10.4 (München 1934), 111, n. 2, where he corrects his previous statement that Peter died in 489, presented in 'Johannes Rufus, ein monophysitischer Schriftsteller', 17-26. Schwartz's later statement is supported by M. Van Esbroeck, 'Esbroeck, 'Peter the Iberian and Dionysius the Areopagite: Honigmann's thesis revisited', *OCP* 59 (1993), 224.

[17] *V. Petr. Ib.*, 3.
[18] *V. Petr. Ib.*, 3-4.

of faith.[19] But the most manifest features of this section are the Christian belief, pious virtues and ascetic conduct of Peter's ancestors. John provides, for instance, the following description of Peter's maternal grandfather, Bakurius:

> Three times a week the faithful Bakurius, dedicated to fasting, praying and almsgiving, swept the church of the city. Since he was possessed by extreme love for the poor, he did not find it below his dignity to prepare various kinds of meals in his palace. He then carried the food in baskets to the poorhouse that he himself had built, and fed with his own hands those who lived there.[20]

The ascetic virtues of the king Bakurius and his love for the poor were shared by Peter's mother Bakurdukia, who lived as an ascetic in the Iberian villages and built houses for the poor and the sick. Born into such a pious family Peter was raised from the beginning to perform virtuous acts, carry the cross of Christ and keep the orthodox faith.[21]

When he was brought to Constantinople as a hostage at the court of Emperor Theodosius II he found that everyone who resided in the imperial palace lived as if they were in a monastery, fasting, praying and performing all kinds of ascetic practices. Under the influence of the pious Empress Eudocia his own personal zeal for the ascetic life increased day by day until he, still merely a young boy, was entirely filled with virtue and grace. The courtiers and the Senate venerated him for his ascetic zeal and spiritual insight, and many people gathered around him to observe his ascetic practices. One day, when he spoke to some ascetic-minded courtiers about matters of use for salvation, he saw Christ appear among them in the guise of a monk.[22] From the moment of this vision he was determined to leave the palace to become a monk, and after a few attempts at he finally managed to leave Constantinople, together with his companion John the Eunuch.[23] John Rufus' report on

---

[19] For a treatment of the historical value of the hagiographic presentation of Peter's ancestry, see Flusin, 'Naissance d'une Ville sainte: autour de la Vie de Pierre l'Ibère', in *Annuaire de l'Ecole Pratique des Hautes Etudes, Section des Sciences Religieuses* 100 (1991-92), 365-368.

[20] *V. Petr. Ib.*, 7.

[21] *V. Petr. Ib.*, 12-13.

[22] *V. Petr. Ib.*, 19.

[23] *V. Petr. Ib.*, 20-23.

Peter and John's escape is put into the framework of a conflict
between the powers of the material world and the supernatural
realm of holiness. While worldly forces, described as 'demons and
men', were trying to prevent their escape, holy martyrs came
forward as their helpers and protectors, so that, miraculously, they
could pass unnoticed through the city gate. Protected by God and
the holy martyrs, whose relics they carried in a golden casket, they
traveled on foot through Asia Minor until they finally reached
Jerusalem.

The account of Peter's arrival in Jerusalem introduces the
second section of the *Life*, which focuses on Peter's early monastic
career and his discipleship under Abba Zeno, the disciple of
Silvanus. After the initial reports about Peter's ascetic mind and
ambitions as a young prince, the story proceeds with a presentation
of Peter's early monastic career. Having been welcomed by Melania
the younger and her husband Pinianus in their monastery on the
Mount of Olives, they received their monastic habits from
Melania's foster-son Gerontius. Subsequently they spent all their
royal wealth on establishing a guesthouse for pilgrims at the eastern
gate of Jerusalem, inspired by the celebrated Abba Passarion's love
for strangers and for the poor.[24] Close to the Tower of David they
also built a monastery, which at the time of the composition of the
Life was still known as the Monastery of the Iberians. They devoted
their time to charitable works for the poor and for pilgrims until
Abba Zeno advised them to live in the monastery under the
guidance of an ascetic authority, a life that for them was the more
profitable since they were still young.[25] Peter was nevertheless soon
reminded of the world that he had forsaken, when Empress
Eudocia arrived to Jerusalem to visit the holy places and the
monastery of Melania. With some hesitation he obliged her wish to
meet with him, fearing that it would be a temptation. Some years
later she again insisted on seeing him, and with a troubled mind he
hastened to Abba Zeno for instruction. Advised to save himself
and flee Peter immediately left Jerusalem and settled in the
monastic community of Irenion, between Gaza and Maiuma. Soon
Peter was forced into the priestly office by Bishop Paul of Maiuma,

---

[24] *V. Petr. Ib.*, 27-35.
[25] *V. Petr. Ib.*, 44-47.

Juvenal's nephew, but for seven years refused to perform any
service at the altar.[26]

With the report of the Council of Chalcedon the narrative
proceeds into a third stage that deals with the responsibility of the
true monk to leave his ascetic retreat for the sake of the purity of
the orthodox faith. This section covers almost twenty-five years of
Peter's life, i.e. from his ordination as bishop of Maiuma to his
return to Palestine from voluntary exile in Egypt. When
Theodosius was established on the patriarchal throne in Jerusalem,
as an immediate response to Juvenal's acceptance of the decisions
at Chalcedon, Peter was consecrated bishop of Maiuma, despite
protesting his unworthiness. For six months he held his episcopal
office at the church of Maiuma, until Juvenal returned to Jerusalem
and the bishops appointed by Theodosius were deposed.[27]
Following Theodosius' advice the anti-Chalcedonian bishops of
Palestine chose to go into exile as a result of his conviction that

> saving the lives of those who preached the truth would
> be more pleasing to God than that the orthodox
> people, if they died or were killed, were deprived of
> those who brought them edification and support.[28]

Thus Peter departed to Egypt to comfort and support the
orthodox people of Alexandria during the Chalcedonian
patriarchate of Proterius. Hiding from the authorities and
celebrating the divine service in secret, he strengthened the faith
and zeal of the believers during the slaughter ordered by Proterius
on the orthodox townsfolk. After a sojourn in Oxyrhynchus in
Thebais, where he had fled when he could no longer hide from
Proterius, he returned to Alexandria at the time of Emperor
Marcian's death and participated in the consecration of Timothy
Aelurus as the rightful successor of Dioscorus.[29] When Timothy
Aelurus was banished by Emperor Leo and sent in exile to Gangra,
Peter remained in Egypt to give edification and support to the
orthodox people there.

> When he saw the faithful brothers troubled and
> abandoned in the house of the dead, deprived of those
> who could edify and support them as they were in the

---

[26] *V. Petr. Ib.*, 48-51.

[27] *V. Petr. Ib.*, 51-56.

[28] *V. Petr. Ib.*, 57-58.

[29] *V. Petr. Ib.*, 58-65.

risk of stumbling in the true faith, Peter – this devoted servant of God in the likeness of the great Moses – was filled with divine zeal. To his death he made himself observe and consider the following well-known words of the Apostle: 'Who is weak, and I am not weak? Who is made to stumble, and I burn not?' Giving up the peace he loved as inappropriate for the moment, he remained in the city of the Alexandrines and the monasteries nearby. He visited many other towns and villages of Egypt and traveled everywhere in secret, edifying and supporting the orthodox flock, becoming, like a second Paul the Apostle, 'all things to all men'. His conduct and manners in words and deeds was an exemplary demonstration of the teaching about the pious life and divine zeal. As to he wonders and great signs performed there through God's grace, the powers he had received, and the numerous deeds of healing and miracles, our weakness does not allow us to describe them in full detail.[30]

Urged to visit his own Palestinian flock, which had for so long been deprived of spiritual guidance, Peter finally decided to return to Palestine, where he settled in the village of Palaea near Ascalon.[31]

The return of Peter the Iberian to Palestine marks the beginning of the fourth section of the biography, which deals with his role as an authority on asceticism and orthodoxy. In this stage Peter resumes his obligations as bishop and becomes the ascetic master of a circle of disciples. Peter no longer appears merely as a supporter of the believers, in the absence of true teachers, he is in fact an authority in his own right, as a father to the monks and a legitimate bishop to the faithful. His role as an ecclesiastical leader is emphasized by the reports on his frequent travels in Palestine, Arabia and Phoenicia, i.e. the provinces of Juvenal's patriarchal jurisdiction after the second Council of Ephesus. In this way John Rufus confronts his readers with the image of a non-Chalcedonian patriarch who provides the people under his jurisdiction with edification and strict expositions of the orthodox faith.

---

[30] *V. Petr. Ib.*, 71.
[31] *V. Petr. Ib.*, 77.

Immediately on his return to Palestine Peter gathered a group of disciples around him, thus creating a monastic community around him.

> Many people came from all places to see him. Some he strengthened, others he enlightened and brought into the orthodox Church. Some he persuaded to forsake the material world, making them strive for perfection, distribute their possessions among the poor and carry the cross of Christ to follow him alone. To him came the blessed Procopius, in every respect an honorable man who was in truth the epitome of a man of God, and Cyril, this lamb of Christ. Both of them he brought from the world and carried to the place of the angels. There was also Theodore Scholasticus, who would eventually inherit his evangelic conduct, his zeal and the leadership of his monastery, together with Abba John, a most venerable old man, beloved, worthy, and adorned with all the virtues of monasticismespecially that of humility. Many others came to him, not only men but also women. He made them the soldiers of Christ. As he admonished them to carry the gentle yoke of Christ, he prepared for the Lord an exalted and zealous people that prospered on good deeds.[32]

Peter mostly led the life of a vagabond, without recognizing any specific place as his permanent residence. After his stay in Ascalon he left Palestine and spent almost a year in the province of Arabia.[33] He then settled for three years in the village of Magdal Tutha near Gaza, where Dionysius, a scholastic from Gaza, had built him a monastery.[34] During that time he maintained close relations with Isaiah of Beth Dalthā, the great Egyptian ascetic whose *Life* was written by Zacharias Scholasticus.[35] But when Cosmas, Emperor Zeno's chamberlain, invited him to the imperial

---

[32] *V. Petr. Ib.*, 78. Abba John, known as the Canopite, is referred to in Zacharias Scholasticus, *Vita Severi*, 86.

[33] *V. Petr. Ib.*, 83-98.

[34] *V. Petr. Ib*, 100-101; For Dionysius of Gaza, see also Zacharias Scholasticus, *Vita Isaiae Monachi*, 8-9.

[35] Zacharias Scholasticus, when describing the friendship between Peter and Isaiah, writes: 'They never ceased to think of each other and to be by each other in the Spirit', *Vita Isaiae Monachi*, 12. For Isaiah in the works of John Rufus, see *Pleroph.* 12, 22, 48, 65, 73, and *V. Petr. Ib.*, 101-103, 124-126. See also Zacharias Scholasticus, *Vita Severi*, 83.

capital he escaped to Phoenicia and provided spiritual support to
the anti-Chalcedonians there. On this Phoenician journey Peter
met with a group of law students in Beirut who finally decided to
become monks in Palestine.[36] A number of these students, known
from Zacharias Scholasticus' *Life of Severus*, eventually left Beirut to
become monks in Peter's monastery.[37]

With John Rufus' description of Peter's return to Palestine the
biography enters the fifth and final stage, which deals with the
death of the holy man. In a village close to Jamnia, Peter and his
monks were at their supper when they received the news of the
death of Isaiah of Beth Dalthā. John Rufus provides the following
report on this event:

> When we had finished the meal and were about to rise
> one of the brothers, named Zacharias, said to him:
> 'Honorable father, the orthodox have been struck by a
> great sorrow, since Abba Isaiah has departed'. But he
> replied, untroubled and calm, as if this was not
> unknown to him but as if he had been told what he
> already knew: 'What is strange about the death of
> Isaiah? Are not all the patriarchs and prophets and all
> the saints also dead? Why is it peculiar that also Isaiah
> has now gone the same way, in a manner that makes us
> astonished? After these words he stood up and went to
> the cell where he used to stay, and wept bitterly in his
> seclusion. The only thing we heard him say was: 'Now
> it is my turn'.[38]

Four months later Peter the Iberian died, having a last time
admonished his disciples to remain firm in the orthodox faith until
death, and to condemn the Council of Chalcedon and the *Tome* of
Leo.[39] His earthly remains were taken to his former monastery at
Maiuma and buried—between the remains of his old companion
John the Eunuch and an Egyptian ascetic named Abraham of
Athribis—with the honors due to a legitimate bishop of that city.
On the first anniversary of his death his remains were finally
moved to the newly built monastery, dedicated to Peter and headed

---

[36] For Peter the Iberian in Beirut, see John Rufus, *V. Petr. Ib.*, 114. See
also Severus of Antioch, *Select Letters* 4.9.

[37] Zacharias Scholasticus, *Vita Severi*, 51-57.

[38] *V. Petr. Ib.*, 124-125.

[39] *V. Petr. Ib*, 134-135.

by Theodore of Ascalon in the same area, and placed under the altar in the chapel where John Rufus performed his priestly duties.

Deeply rooted in the early Christian hagiographic tradition, John Rufus presents an interpretation of reality that includes almost every aspect of the mythology of Christian asceticism in Late Antiquity. Combining the rhetorical features of the Hellenistic biographical-anecdotal tradition with the Christian emphasis on biblical images and metaphors, he shows himself clearly dependent on the whole continuum of Christian hagiographies written in the fourth and fifth centuries. The style of the *Life* is realistic. Obviously determined to put the story about Peter the Iberian into a historical framework, the author provides us with numerous important references to the historical, political, and social setting of the Eastern Empire in the fifth century. The reader is given a detailed and vivid description of Peter's world and the people around him, although the historical and social context is carefully set within a strictly hagiographic presentation. Written in a highly rhetorical style, and dressed in the pious ornaments of Christian ascetic literature, the text markedly displays the literary ideals of antiquity. There is also an obvious tendency to unrestrained exuberance, manifested in the author's preference for lengthy digressions. Frequently given to exhaustive descriptions in a somewhat nonsensical jargon, he exploits the stereotypes of contemporary monastic literature in numerous comments on the holiness and orthodoxy of the protagonist.

Throughout the *Life* the highly sophisticated style is liberally sprinkled with biblical quotations and allusions to biblical characters. By presenting him as a new Paul, Noah or Moses, Peter the Iberian not only represents himself but also the holy persons of the Scriptures, thus becoming in his own person an interpretation of the Biblical narratives. In this way the present is connected with the past into a relationship focused on God's plan for the salvation of man. The realism of the *Life* involves a highly mythological conception of a world characterized by the conflict between good and evil. The saintly protagonist stands in the center of a world constantly involved in a struggle between the powers of the material world and the heavenly realms. To the advocates of the orthodox faith are allotted the common attributes of blessedness and holiness in the panegyric style, while the enemies of faith are given imaginative portrayals, complete with attributes fetched from the darker side of nature. In this way, Proterius is described as an apostate dragon and a merciless and bloodthirsty wolf that rejoices as he is told about the death of the blessed Dioscorus.[40]

The harsh polemical tone used against the enemies of the non-Chalcedonian faith is clearly the most important feature in John Rufus' *Life of Peter the Iberian*. At the same time, the *Life* should not be regarded merely as a controversial pamphlet. As a monastic text, it represents much of the development of the genres and sub-genres of late antique hagiographic discourse, with its constant focus on the ascetic ideals and spirituality in early Eastern monasticism and the idea of the struggle for faith as an essential concern of monastic life.

The Commemoration of the Death of Theodosius

In the *Life of Peter the Iberian* John relates an incident that took place during Peter's visit in the town of Oxyrhynchus in Thebais. According to John, the Patriarch, Proterius, had sent a letter to be read out in the churches of Egypt, demanding, under threat of excommunication, general acceptance of the Chalcedonian faith. Disturbed by its contents, Peter carried the document to a public place and fastened it to the base of a statue of an emperor. Suddenly, in a vision, he saw Theodosius, the rebellious bishop of Jerusalem who had only recently died in prison in Constantinople. Strengthened by the words of the martyred bishop, Peter immediately tore the document to pieces. As he describes this event, John tells us, that 'if God wants it, we will later give a full report about the way in which he [i.e. Theodosius] died'.[41]

In the introduction to John Rufus' *Commemoration of the Death of Theodosius*, we read:

> As I remember, I promised earlier to relate the manner
> in which the blessed Theodosius, bishop of Jerusalem,
> confessor and martyr, died. It is now necessary to
> fulfill this commitment in a few [words].[42]

The text was edited in 1907 by E. W. Brooks from two Syriac manuscripts preserved in the same codices as those of the *Life of Peter the Iberian*.

---

[40] *V. Petr. Ib*, 62-63.

[41] *V. Petr. Ib*, 62.

[42] *Narr. de ob. Theod.*, 21.

[A] British Library, add. 12.174, fol. 141-142, Wright, vol. 3, n. 960, p. 1126.

[C] Berlin syr 321, fol. 103-104, Sachau, vol. 1, n. 26, p. 96.[43]

In spite of the lack of attribution in the text John's authorship of it cannot be disputed, since it is difficult to consider this brief text as anything but an appendix to the *Life of Peter the Iberian*.[44] This assumption is also supported by the striking similarity between a passage in this text with an anecdote in the *Plerophories*. In the *Commemoration of the Death of Theodosius* the passage runs as follows:

> When he [Theodosius] lived out his days the blessed Peter, our Abba, was in Alexandria. During that very night he saw him in a vision, carried by a multitude of angels and dressed in a white stole, in the same way that the archbishops of Jerusalem used to be dressed when baptizing. In this way he was lifted up to heaven.[45]

In the *Plerophories*, the wording is almost identical, but adapted to the form of a brief anecdote:

> Our Abba said: When I was in Egypt, at the time when the blessed Theodosius, Archbishop of Jerusalem lived out his days in Constantinople as a witness for the truth, I saw him during that very night being lifted up to heavens. He was dressed in a white stole in the same way that the bishops of Jerusalem used to be dressed when they baptized, shiny and bright, until he entered heaven.[46]

Despite the fact that the *Commemoration of the Death of Theodosius* is an appendix to the *Life of Peter the Iberian*, there is reason to treat it as an autonomous work, since its contents diverge from the account of Peter's life.

The short text begins with Theodosius' exile in Egypt, when he had been expelled from Jerusalem after Juvenal's return. At that time Abba Romanus, the celebrated archimandrite of the monastery at Tekoa, was arrested and imprisoned in Antioch together with Timothy, archimandrite of the monastery of

---

[43] In the Berlin codex, the text follows immediately on the *V. Petr. Ib.*. Sachau does not treat it as a separate text from that of the Life.

[44] See Schwartz, 'Johannes Rufus', 11.

[45] *Narr. de ob. Theod.*, 24.

[46] *Pleroph.* 54.

Hypatius close to Jerusalem. While in Egypt Theodosius was eventually reached by the disturbing news that, during their imprisonment in Antioch, these distinguished monks were quarrelling about doctrinal matters. It was said that Timothy was accused of being a Eutychian, and that he avoided the expression 'consubstantial'. Fearing that this conflict would cause public offence Theodosius decided to travel to Antioch in secret, to bring the two monks at one with each other. But John Rufus also informs us that, according to some reports, his journey to Syria may have been motivated by a wish to visit Simeon the Stylite, celebrated for his immaculate conduct and dissociation from heretics such as Theodoret of Cyrrhus. At the city gate of Antioch Theodosius was, however, immediately arrested and brought in great humiliation to Constantinople. The Emperor, who could not persuade him to accept the Chalcedonian definition of faith, eventually sent him to the Chalcedonian monastery of Dios. Imprisoned in a small cell full of lime Theodosius soon died, beset by hunger, cold and starvation. John Rufus reports that immediately after Theodosius' death the dyophysites tried to seize his bodily remains in order to bury them in their own churches, thereby able to spread the rumor that at the end of his life Theodosius had accepted the Chalcedonian doctrine. To prevent these plans the faithful immediately brought his relics to a non-Chalcedonian monastery on Cyprus, where they were buried.[47]

Subsequently, John Rufus turns his attention to the destiny of the monk Romanus. Forced to live as a prisoner in Antioch he remained firm in his faith and converted many from their state of unfaithfulness, despite the Chalcedonian majority of that city, which was described as 'the mother of the impious Paul of Samosata and Nestorius'. At that time Palestine was plagued with drought and starvation. Protests were raised against Juvenal, since many regarded this affliction as a manifestation of God's wrath at the exile of the blessed Romanus. In fear of a popular uprising Juvenal reluctantly arranged for the return of Romanus and all the other anti-Chalcedonian leaders. On his return to Palestine Romanus settled close to the city of Eleutheropolis where, with the support of Empress Eudocia, he founded a monastery. There he lived out his days, and was buried under the altar in the monastery

---

[47] *Narr. de ob. Theod.*, 21-25.

church, where he was given his last resting-place in a miraculously created cave in the rock.[48]

The immediate purpose of the *Commemoration of the Death of Theodosius* is to present, in the form of a short narrative, the importance of remaining steadfast in the orthodox faith until death. It is a story of martyrdom that requires the faithful to be prepared to participate fully in the sufferings of Theodosius and Romanus. In this text John Rufus reveals an ambition to draw a line of spiritual continuity between the holy Christian martyrs of ancient times and the contemporary orthodox minority, concerned at their inferior numbers in comparison with the vast majority of Chalcedonians in the Eastern Empire. The text is characterized by the concept of the anti-Chalcedonian struggle as a monastic struggle, fought by experienced and charismatic monks armed with the virtues of ascetic life. Here John demonstrates in full clarity the monastic conception of ascetic life as inseparable from the struggle for the true faith, a constant theme in all his extant works.

The Plerophories

The collection of anti-Chalcedonian anecdotes preserved under John Rufus' name, known as the *Plerophories*, was edited by F: Nau in 1911.[49] The text has been transmitted to us in a great number of manuscripts and fragments. Yet the whole text is preserved only in two Syriac manuscripts kept in the British Library:

[A] British Library, add. 14.650, fol. 90-134, Wright, vol. 3, n. 949, p. 1104.
[B] British Library, add. 14.631, fol. 17-44, Wright, vol. 3, n. 933, p. 1080.

The oldest manuscript (A), written about 875 in a monastery near Dulikh (today Dolik, Turkey), fortunately also happens to be the most fully preserved. The other manuscript (B) dates back to the tenth or eleventh century, but much of it has been mutilated during

---

[48] *Narr. de ob. Theod.*, 26-27.

[49] *Jean Rufus, évêque de Maïouma, Plérophories. Témoignages et révélations contre le concile de Chalcédoine*, ed. Nau, PO 8.1 (Paris 1911). The most comprehensive study on the *Plerophories* is Perrone, 'Dissenso dottrinale e propaganda visionaria: Le Pleroforie di Giovanni di Maiuma', *Augustinianum* 29 (1989), 451-495. See also Witakowski, 'Syrian Monophysite Propaganda in the Fifth to Seventh Centuries', *Aspects of Late Antiquity and Early Byzantium*, 1993, 57-66.

the centuries and leaves are missing, several at the end and one at the beginning.[50] The differences between the two manuscripts are negligible, and almost exclusively to be found in style and details, such as the choice of words and the spelling of place-names and personal names. In the margins of the oldest manuscript there are, moreover, additions that often recur in the text of the later manuscript, which suggests that the later manuscript is a copy that includes in the text the marginal notes made by a reader of the older manuscript.[51]

However, Nau also made use of two other important witnesses of the text. The first is the *Chronicle* of Pseudo-Dionysius of Tel-Maḥrē, in which 13 chapters of the *Plerophories* have been incorporated.[52] This chronicle, which is extant in a manuscript written in the ninth century,[53] was presumably written by an anonymous non-Chalcedonian monk in 775.[54] Apart from introductory notes and additions, the text follows the manuscripts of the British Museum almost literally. The far-reaching agreement, broken only by orthographic and a few grammatical differences, and by the chronicler's need to adjust the text to the historiographical genre, seems to confirm that add. 14650 is a fairly faithful copy of an older but lost manuscript, used also by the anonymous writer of the *Chronicle* of Pseudo-Dionysius. The second witness is the *Chronicle* of Michael the Syrian, completed in Syriac in 1195. Of this chronicle only one Syriac manuscript is preserved, written in 1598.[55] Michael the Syrian, who based his chronicle almost entirely on other sources, devoted the eleventh chapter of the eighth book to 72 chapters of the *Plerophories*, the

---

[50] As a result, Wright fails to identify add. 14.631 as the *Plerophories* in spite of an accurate identification with add. 14.650.

[51] See Nau, 'Introduction', PO 8.1, 5.

[52] Pseudo-Dionysiys of Tel-Maḥrē, *Chronicon*, ed. Chabot, *Incerti auctoris chronicon anonymum pseudo-Dionysianum vulgo dictum*, CSCO, Script. syri, 3.1 (Paris 1927), 209-223.

[53] S. E and J. S. Assemani, *Bibliothecae apostolicae Vaticanae codicum manuscriptorum catalogus*, vol. 3.1 (Rome 1759), 328.

[54] For the dating, see Witakowski, *The Syriac Chronicle of Pseudo-Dionysius of Tel-Maḥrē* (Uppsala 1987), 90.

[55] A transcript of the text was made by Chabot in 1899 and published as the fourth volume of his critical edition of the text, Michael the Syrian, *Chronicon*, vol. 4, 203–215.

order of the chapters following that of the two British Museum manuscripts. However, the text provided by the chronicler consists merely of summarized versions of the anecdotes, grammatically adjusted to the demands of the chronicler. The text has been modified to such an extent that little more can be said than that the text used by Michael the Syrian represented at least the shared tradition of the London manuscripts and Pseudo-Dionysius of Tel-Maḥrē.

There is yet another manuscript, written in 1826, which gives a paraphrased version of chapters 28, 29, and 30 of the *Plerophories*.[56] At times it follows add. 14650 literally, but there are also considerable differences. Nevertheless the dependency of this text upon the tradition behind the British Museum manuscripts and Pseudo-Dionysius is evident from the agreement between these texts as regards word order and choice of words.

In Coptic, only four fragments or collections of fragments have been identified as excerpts of the *Plerophories* of John Rufus:

1. A Bohairic fragment of two folios from the monastery of St. Macarius containing the opening lines of the 26th chapter of the Syriac collection. The folios, kept in the Coptic Museum of Cairo, are nos. 6 to 12 of a lost codex and are all that is left of a work that may have been a collection of anecdotes about Timothy Aelurus. The preserved text is, with the exception of the few lines of the *Plerophories*, identical with two sections from John Rufus' *Life of Peter the Iberian* dealing with Timothy's patriarchate until his deposal and exile in 460. The fragment is dated to the eighth century, and was edited in 1926 by H. Evelyn White.[57]

2. A Sahidic fragment on two folios containing the end of the 26th chapter and the opening of the 27th. This severely mutilated fragment, which dates back to the seventh century, was edited by Crum in 1913, and during the publication bought by the private Library of Pierpont Morgan in New York. A third passage in the second folio, which mentions the name of one Emperor

---

[56] Recorded by Sachau under catalogue number Berlin Syr. 175 (n. 329), *Die Handschriften-Verzeichnisse der Königlichen Bibliothek zu Berlin*, vol. 32: *Verzeichnis der syrischen Handschriften*, (Berlin 1899), vol. 2, 556; edited by Nau in PO 8.1 as chapters 90-93 of the *Plerophories*. The manuscript is unquestionably non-Chalcedonian and not, as Nau supposed, Nestorian.

[57] Evelyn White, *New Coptic Texts from the Monastery of St. Macarius*, 1926, 164-167 (no. 31).

Theodosius, cannot be identified with any anecdote in the Syriac collection.[58]

3. A group of seven fragments, probably from the seventh century, kept in the Michigan University Library. Most of them are small and thus difficult to identify, but the largest consists of the end of the 51st chapter of the Syriac version and the opening of the 87th, the latter numbered as 72. Further more, two fragments are analogue to the twelfth chapter in the Syriac collection. Orlandi, who edited the fragments in 1979, suggests that the scribe copied only a minor part of a Coptic collection similar to the Syriac version.[59]

4. A fragment consisting of two folios, dated to the ninth century and kept in the National Library of Vienna. The text was edited in 1974 by T. Orlandi and consists of chapters 59, 64, 70, and 71 of the Syriac version. In the fragment they are numbered 62–65, which, according to the editor, suggests that the text is part of a Coptic collection of the *Plerophories* of about the same extent as the Syriac version.[60] The Vienna folios are unquestionably most valuable, since they provide the largest continuous and least mutilated excerpt of the Coptic version of the *Plerophories*.[61]

The Vienna folios is unquestionable the most valuable fragment, since it provides the largest continuous and least mutilated excerpt of the Coptic version of the *Plerophories*. However, a comparison between this Coptic fragment and correspondent passages of the Syriac version shows the Coptic text more compressed than the Syriac. On the principle of *brevior lectio probabilior* this would mean that the Coptic text hardly could be a translation of the Syriac version, a conclusion also supported by Orlandi.[62] Also regarding the second fragment, edited by W. E.

---

[58] Crum, *Theological Texts from Coptic papyri*, (Oxford 1912), 62-64 (no. 13).

[59] *Coptic Texts in the University of Michigan Collection*, ed. by W. H. Worrell (London 1942), 16; T. Orlandi, 'Un frammento delle Pleroforie in Copto', in *StRiOC* 2 (Rome 1979), 3-12. Kept under catalogue number Inv. 4945.

[60] Orlandi, *Koptische Papyri theologischen Inhalts* (Vienna 1974), 110-117 (no. 8). Kept under catalogue number K 2502a-b.

[61] Orlandi, *Koptische Papyri*, 114-115.

[62] Orlandi, *Koptische Papyri*, 112: 'Il copto non è traduzione dal testo siriaco che noi abbiamo, ma con ogni probabilità da un testo greco che sta all'origine'.

Crum, it has been suggested that the text behind the Coptic is simply the Greek original. However, Orlandi has objected to too confident a conclusion on the origin of the text.[63] That the text of the fragment from the monastery of St. Macarius is based on Greek versions of the *Plerophories* and the *Life of Peter the Iberian*, as was suggested by the editor of this text, remains undisputed. But it should be noted that this conclusion is based on insufficient arguments and rests mainly on the assumption that the *Plerophories* was originally written in Greek.[64]

Though the dispersion of the Coptic fragments makes it difficult to isolate conclusive evidence about the Coptic version, it is interesting that a Coptic version of the *Plerophories* was mentioned, in an ostracon dating from the sixth or seventh century, as *The Plerophoria of Abba Peter the Iberian*.[65] An explanation which, although supported by Evelyn White, can easily be refuted has been put forward by Crum, who attributes to John Rufus the role of having compiled and translated into Syriac a Greek collection allegedly written by Peter himself.[66] But the note in the ostracon makes it evident that a collection of the *Plerophories* once existed in Coptic. With the support of the fragments we are surely in the position to say that there were actually several collections in Coptic, these being either translations from the original language or, as in the case of the Michigan fragments, simply secondary compilations from some earlier Coptic collection. What is left unresolved is the problem of what original language is concealed behind the collections.

There is no decisive information in the *Plerophories* about the date of the work. However, a casual reference in the text to the removal of the name of Basil of Seleucia from the diptychs at the installation of Severus as Patriarch of Antioch makes it possible to

---

[63] Crum, *Theological Texts*, 62: 'That this Coptic text is not a translation of the latter [*i.e.* the Syriac translation] is clear from divergences in detail which even its dilapidated condition allows us to recognize'. For the objection against Crum, see Orlandi, 'Un frammento delle Pleroforie in Copto', 5: 'Il testo conservato e' comunque esattamente uguale a quello siriaco'.

[64] Evelyn White, *New Coptic Texts*, 164 n.

[65] See Crum, *Theological Texts*, 62; also Orlandi, 112.

[66] Crum, *Theological Texts*, 62; and Evelyn White, *New Coptic Texts*, 164 n.

establish late 512 as the *terminus post quem* for the composition of the work.[67] The presentation of this event in a clearly present tense would, moreover, seem to indicate that the work was written in the early years of Severus' pontificate. Narrowing the date to this period—the most triumphant years of anti-Chalcedonian history— finds support in another anecdote in the *Plerophories*, which mentions 'the current strength' of the orthodox faith.[68] In the light of this expression it is hardly probable that the collection was written after the expulsion of Severus in 518 and during the persecutions against the anti-Chalcedonians that lasted until 530.[69] It is thus quite reasonable to conclude that the *Plerophories* were written during Severus' tenure of the patriarchal throne of Antioch in the last years of the reign of the aged Emperor Anastasius. This was the high noon of anti-Chalcedonianism, when the communion between the majority of the sees in the East was based on the express condemnation of Chalcedon and the *Tome* of Leo.[70]

As a collection of short hagiographic sketches, gathered together with scant consideration for the internal continuity of content and chronology, the *Plerophories* follows a genre deeply rooted in the Byzantine Middle Eastern monasticism.[71] In the background of this monastic genre we find a tradition of anecdote writing represented by classical Greek writers such as Plutarch, and

---

[67] *Pleroph.* 23.

[68] *Pleroph.* 24.

[69] The proportions of these persecutions is difficult to determine, but the measures taken by the imperial authorities against the anti-Chalcedonians during Justin's reign seem to have affected all levels of the ecclesiastical hierarchy; laymen as well as monks and bishops. See Zacharias Scholasticus, *HE* 8.5. The matter is discussed in Frend, *The Rise of the Monophysite Movement*, 247-248.

[70] Nau himself is cautious when dating the text: 'Il a écrit le présent ouvrage pendant que Sévère ètait patriarche d'Antioch (512-518)', 7. For Honigmann, who meant that it was probably the source of one *Life of Dioscorus of Alexandria*, the *Plerophories* were written after 518, 'Juvenal of Jerusalem', 265.

[71] It would here be appropriate to observe that scholars regularly have been uncertain about how to categorize the *Plerophories*. In general, they have avoided to place the work within the genre of hagiographical collection and considered merely as a dogmatic polemic record of theological and ecclesiastical events in the fifth century, i.e. belonging to the genre of historiography.

later also by Lucian.[72] However, the development of this literary form into a hagiographic genre cannot be separated from that of the aphoristic tradition in early monasticism. The anonymous writer of the *Historia Monachorum* at the end of the fourth century seems to have pioneered the informal genre of monastic anecdotes, incorporating the characteristic features of monastic biography and of the apophthegmatic tradition. It was further developed around 420 in the *Historia Lausiaca* by Palladius and the *Historia Religiosa* by Theodoret of Cyrrhus. During the following centuries, and in particular in Syrian monasticism, the popularity of such anthologies of monastic anecdotes continued to increase.[73]

As a collection of originally independent *logia*, the literary and rhetorical orientation of the work is not to be traced in the sequence of stories only, from the first story to the last. Rather, since each story contains its own logic of persuasion, the *Plerophories* is organized as an arbitrary chain of persuasive stories internally connected only by the overall concern to show that, through his divine judgement, God has unambiguously condemned the Council of Chalcedon as a revival of Nestorianism.

The conviction that Chalcedon had implied a revival of Nestorianism is noticeable in the very first anecdote, which describes the demoniacal spasms which suddenly afflicted Nestorius when, in a sermon in Constantinople, he had dared to deny the Blessed Mother her position as the Theotokos.[74] This story clearly sets the tone for the collection, and is followed by a group of stories of visions seen by the monk Pelagius that reveal, in an almost logical sequence, God's condemnation of Emperor Marcian, Empress Pulcheria and Bishop Juvenal of Jerusalem.[75] The stories that follow seem, however, almost randomly organized, since they differ in length, rhetorical structure and immediate

---

[72] Plutarch, *Vitae*, ed. B. Perrin, *Plutarch's Lives*, LCL (London and Cambridge [Mass.] 1914-1926).

[73] For example, John of Ephesus, *Lives of the Eastern Saints*, ed. and tr. by Brooks, PO 17-19, 1923-1925; John Moschus, *Spititual Meadow*, ed. and tr. by R. de Journel, *Jean Moschus: Le pré spirituel*, SC 12 (Paris 1946). Thomas av Marga, *Historia monastica*, ed. and tr. by E. A. Wallis Budge, *The Book of Governors. The Historia Monastica of Thomas Bishop of Marga* (London 1893).

[74] *Pleroph.* 1.

[75] *Pleroph.* 2-4.

concerns. A few chunks of stories seem to be more clearly associated than others with common themes or protagonists, but the rest of the stories in the *Plerophories* is a rather unsystematic mixture, each story adding its own argument against Chalcedon and its advocates. The collection rounds off with two anecdotes in which John gives an eye-witness account of a man who had settled in front of the imperial residency in Antioch and who, in obedience to a divine command, lived for many years in utter humility and total silence. In the last story, dealing with the violent confrontation between this holy man and the apostate bishop Nonnus of Quennesrin, the narrative turns into a fire-and-brimstone sermon against Chalcedon reminiscent of Old Testament prophetic wrath against the apostate people of Israel.[76]

In the center of each anecdote contained in the *Plerophories* is God's condemnation of Chalcedon, or rather the different ways through which God communicates this judgement to mankind. Through a variety of signs, visions and miracles God provides the last remnants of his orthodox people with full assurance (*plerophoria*) of the anathema laid upon Chalcedon and its adherents. This divine communication is achieved above all through the mediation of distinguished and holy monks, knowledge of God's will which they have received due to their purity of mind and perseverance of the orthodox faith. Holy men, such as Peter the Iberian, Abba Isaiah, Abba Pelagius or Abba Romanus, appear constantly as trustworthy spokesmen of the Lord, and ambassadors of the heavenly Jerusalem, in a world distorted by the irrational wickedness of heresy. Since the text is fundamentally monastic it is the holy monks who are trustworthy mouthpieces for the announcement of God's judgement to the world, although John Rufus does not exclude the common man as a witness to God's truth. But throughout the collection it is the holy men, his dearest friends among mortals, who dominate the stage and are brought out as a particularly effective instrument in the narrative process of persuasion. The precise elaboration of John Rufus persuasive argumentation as founded on the reliable authority of the holy men will be the focus of the next chapter.

---

[76] *Pleroph.* 88.

3   THE IMAGES OF AUTHORITY

Setting out to explore the mental world of the anti-Chalcedonian movement as conveyed in the hagiographic writings of John Rufus, it might be useful to start with a consideration of the protagonists in these texts. Who, then, are the characters that we encounter in John's writings and whose words and deeds form the heart of his narratives? In order to answer this question we might first consider the opening lines of the *Life of Peter the Iberian*, where the author presents the immediate purpose of his undertaking to depict the life of his beloved master:

> Concerning our leaders Paul, the apostle of God, gives us a command, saying: 'Remember your leaders, those who spoke the word of God to you; consider the outcome of their way of life, and imitate their faith'. Since we now will fulfill this pious duty, which is pleasing to God, and observe the command of the apostle, it is required that we will do so with exactness. Truly it is a great benefit for the disciples in their labor for salvation as they pursue the good and joyfully strive to be like those who through their virtuous conduct were leaders divine spirit. Yet we have made it our task not only to remember a leader, but also a good shepherd, a loving father, a pious bishop, a confessor of the true religion and a perpetual witness for faith, equally cherished by speakers and hearers, so that we properly and with all joy may fulfill the speaking and hearing about him, putting trust in his holy prayers that deliver from sinfulness, not according to merit but by good will.[1]

Here John Rufus makes it clear that the duty to remember the holy fathers is intimately connected with imitation, and as essential for salvation. From this perspective, to strive for salvation is basically to live according to a model of perfection transmitted from the

---

[1] *V. Petr. Ib.*, 3-4.

past by the process of collective remembrance. Thus, in his preface
to the *Life of Peter the Iberian*, John Rufus, in the words of Jerome,
reveals his intention to write a 'history of chastity for the chaste',[2]
aimed at remembrance of a godly man as a model for anyone who
seeks to attain virtue.

The connection between proper ascetic life and imitation of
distinguished men or women recognized as true image of ascetic
perfection is certainly one of the most important features of
hagiographic literature. This connection finds a particularly striking
expression in the preface of the most famous and widespread
hagiographic text ever produced in Eastern monasticism, that is,
the *Life of Antony*.

> You have entered on a fine contest with the monks in
> Egypt, intending as you do to measure up to or even to
> surpass them in your discipline of virtue. [...] Since you
> have asked me about the career of the blessed Antony,
> hoping to learn how he began the discipline, who he
> was before this, and what sort of death he experienced,
> and if the things said concerning him are true—so that
> you also might lead yourselves in imitation of him—I
> received your directive with ready good will. For simply
> to remember Antony is a great profit and assistance for
> me also. I know that even in hearing, along with
> marveling at the man, you will want also to emulate his
> purpose, for Antony's way of life provides monks with
> a sufficient picture for ascetic practice.[3]

Athanasius presents Antony primarily as a model to be imitated by
monks determined to join the Egyptian monks in their spiritual
combat for perfection. When Antony leads his disciples to ascetic
progress through his own self-sufficient perfection he serves as a
didactic device. Thus the educational function of early hagiography
is strongly manifest in the *Life of Antony*. From the study of several
late antique hagiographies it is evident that hagiography was more
than simply stories about the ascetic progress of holy men and
saints.[4] Rather, it seems that one of the main purposes of

---

[2] Jerome, *Vita Malchi*, PL 23, 54-60.

[3] *V. Ant.* 1; tr. by Gregg, *The Life of Antony*, 29.

[4] The connection between hagiographic presentation, edification and
ascetic instruction is evident in, for instance, Palladius, *HL*, prologue. See
also the Cyril of Scythopolis' prologue to *V. Euthym.*, '...restoring to
memory things worthy to be remembered and providing a fine model for

hagiographic literature was to present models for imitation, so that the community of readers might come as close to God as the protagonists had. In fact, it seems that the holy men, whether historical or not, gained their power and prestige for the local communities of believers primarily when oral and written tradition had transformed them into models for proper ascetic conduct.

However, the function of being a model of true ascetic life to imitate is far from the only image of the holy man in late antique hagiography. In the quotation above from the *Life of Peter the Iberian* we perceive the image of the holy man as an intercessor whose posthumous prayers before God deliver men from sin. Later on in the *Life* John Rufus provides an expressive representation of the protagonist as a new Noah, who by his holy prayers rescues those who are about to drown in the waves of sinfulness, lifting them up to safety on his Ark of virtue.[5] This image of the holy man as an intercessor, nurturing the virtues of his beloved disciples with holy prayers, appears frequently in early hagiographic literature. We find it, for instance, in the following anecdote from the *Historia Monachorum* about Abba Apollo:

> One of the monks asked the father abruptly to pray for
> him that he might be granted some grace or other.
> When the father had prayed for him, the grace of
> humility and gentleness was granted to him, so that all
> were amazed at him and the extraordinary degree of
> gentleness which he had attained.[6]

The role of the holy man in protecting spiritually weak disciples with his prayers is an inherent part of the hagiographic making of ascetic authority. Through this role the rather impersonal image of the holy man as an ideal or a model to imitate is balanced with an image that emphasizes his personal care for those striving to be like him. The holy man is not merely a model, standing on a pedestal like the image of a pagan demigod, but a character that constantly participates in the ascetic struggles of his disciples with paternal

---

those who read such a painstaking endeavor as this'; tr. by R. M. Rice, *Cyril of Scythopolis: The Life of the Monks of Palestine*, CS 114 (Kalamazoo 1991), 2.

[5] *V. Petr. Ib.*, 13.

[6] *HM* 8.42, ed. and tr. by A.-J. Festugière, *Historia monachorum in Aegypto*, Sub. Hag. 53 (Bruxelles 1971); tr. by N. Russel, *The Lives of the Desert Fathers* (Kalamazoo 1981), 76.

attention. As the disciple proceeds on the narrow path of ascetic progress he is never left completely alone. He is always followed by the prayers of his saintly master, who pleads for him before God and actively defends him from all the evils of the world, whether still alive on earth or as a citizen of the heavenly realms.[7]

The life of the holy man as a didactic pattern for ascetic life is given further variations when we look at the prophetic aspect of his earthly activities. This aspect, which includes predictions of the future and insight in the divine realities, is certainly one of the most frequently reported charisms of holy men, related in order to emphasis their authority and spiritual powers entrusted to them by God.[8] But accounts about holy men and their prophetic gifts are more than just miraculous stories; sometimes they also clarify the close connection between the activities of the holy man and truth. Through his account about Antony's visionary experience of the future rebellion of the Arians, Athanasius not only represents his hero as a character gifted with the charism of clairvoyance, but primarily as a witness for the orthodox faith.[9] The terrible things seen by Antony function as an immediate call for adherence to the orthodox faith and watchfulness against the plots of the heretics.

The image of the holy man as a prophetic witness to the truth is constantly found in John Rufus' *Plerophories*. While the images of the holy man as a model to imitate and a intercessor praying for his disciples rests at the very heart of the hagiographic representation in the *Life of Peter the Iberian*, those images are clearly put aside in the *Plerophories*, in favor of a focused attention on the holy man as a prophetic witness of truth. Here, the holy men appear to us not primarily as ascetic masters worthy of imitation but rather like prophets from the Old Testament, proclaiming divine messages of judgement and admonition. As in the case of the Old Testament prophets it is not the holy men themselves who are the core of the stories in the *Plerophories* but their messages, delivered directly from God through all manner of manifestations. Though the holy men

---

[7] Serapion of Thmuis, *Letter to the Disciples of Antony*, ed. and tr. by R. Draguet, 'Un lettre de Sérapion de Thmuis aux disciples d'Antoine (A.D. 356) en version syriaque et arménienne', *Le Muséon* 64 (1951), 4-17.

[8] See B. Ward, "Signs and Wonders': Miracles in the Desert Tradition', *SP* 18 (Oxford, New York 1982), 539-542; Flusin, *Miracle et histoire*, 155-217. Binns, *Ascetics and Ambassadors of Christ*, 218-244.

[9] *V. Ant.* 82, 91.

appear as the main characters in most of the anecdotes in the collection, they are essentially subordinated to the real protagonist of the stories—God. The holy men themselves are reduced to messengers, whose virtuous and ascetic conduct calls for trust in the veracity of their testimonies.

As a fourth image of the holy man as he appears in the hagiography of John Rufus we may bring to attention yet another representation of holiness, one which has no immediate connection with the role of the holy man as a didactic pattern but is instead closely related to his prophetic function. This fourth image, which deals with the holy man and his ascetic labors as a sign for something else, finds expression throughout the range of late antique hagiography but is particularly prevalent in the context of Syrian asceticism. We find it, for instance, in Theodoret of Cyrrhus' account of Simeon the Stylite, whose rigorous and eccentric asceticism resists outward imitation but attracts many admirers as he expresses what can be described as a prophetic behavior.[10] In the stories about Simeon we encounter the image of the holy man as an eye-opener, whose ascetical practices are grating in the eye of the beholder and call for undivided attention to the essential message behind these practices. For Theodoret, Simeon is above all a representation of true philosophy rather than an ascetic model to imitate. Through sometimes shocking exercises of asceticism, undertaken in obedience to God's command rather than by personal initiative, Simeon presents an interpretation of his outward behavior that reveals the true path to the virtuous life.

This image of the holy man as a sign is remarkably absent in the works of John Rufus. One exception is the eyewitness account in the *Plerophories* that deals with a man in Antioch who one day, probably during Peter the Fuller's second tenure of the patriarchal throne in 475-77, settled down in front of the imperial residency. Dressed in simple—not to say vile—clothes he lived, John tells us, for many years in a tent during summer and winter, in cold and nakedness, constantly weeping and praying. When John finally asked him why he had chosen this location for his retreat instead of the wilderness, far from the glamour of city life, the holy man

---

[10] Theodoret of Cyrrhus, *Historia Religiosa* 26, ed. and tr. by P. Canivet and A. Leroy-Molinghen, SC 257 (Paris 1979). See Harvey, *Asceticism and the Society in Crisis*, 15-16.

responded by simply pointing to the sky with his right hand, as if to say: 'God has commanded me'.[11] In this account the holy man is presented mainly as a sign pointing at the willingness to submit oneself to God's instructions. The eccentric form of asceticism performed by him does not call for immediate imitation of his outward ascetic conduct. Instead, it is the virtues symbolized in his behavior that are the focus of the story.

Hagiographic representations of holy men – either as didactic patterns of ascetic conduct or as prophetic witnesses for the divine truth – played a considerable role in the Christological controversies of the fifth and sixth centuries.[12] It is important to notice that the significance of holy men in these theological conflicts rested far more on the conceptions of their contemporaries and disciples than on their actual historical actions. We should not deny that many of those acknowledged as saints in later hagiographic reports were even in their lifetime venerated as spiritual authorities, because of their rigorous renunciation of all temporal matters. But as we, in our search for the late antique holy man, are heavily dependent on the aims and intentions of the hagiographers we must realize that history has forever concealed the true characters behind the persons commonly recognized as holy men.[13] Contact with these illusive figures can established only through their disciples and admirers, who were far closer to their own time and world than we are but are susceptible to blame for having, through the pious and creative imagination of hagiographic discourse, transformed the holy men into a mythical characters. In the course of their mission to preserve for posterity the activities, words, and examples of the holy men, they emphasized or censored, and even added certain elements, to their earthly lives, to make them fit the standards of cultural expectations. Thus they became 'good patrons', humble in their service of guiding his disciples into the true monastic life, and uncompromising in his defense of the faith of the fathers. As a mythical character, easily exploited as an effective instrument of persuasive communication, the holy man became a symbol of the common value system of the

---

[11] *Pleroph.* 88.

[12] Cf. Brown, *Authority and the Sacred: Aspects of the Christianisation of the Roman World* (Cambridge 1995), 72-73.

[13] Brown, *Authority and the Sacred*, 63.

ascetic community.[14] Consequently, when the hagiographers invited their readers to imitate the ascetic progress of the holy protagonists, and to follow them as true models for monastic life, they also invited them to preserve the identity and conformity of the community.[15]

Starting from these assumptions about the holy man as an idea of perfection and a didactic model of pre-established behavioral patterns of a certain ascetic community we will now explore the ways in which the holy man was used in the anti-Chalcedonian hagiography of John Rufus. John Rufus was a monk, and his readers were primarily to be found in the monastic communities settled in the southwest of Palestine, recognizing as their leaders the disciples of Peter the Iberian at Maiuma close to Gaza. John's world was a monastic world containing a wide range of ideals linked to distinguished persons, whose patterns of life and utter devotion to God served as symbols for the bountiful fruits of ascetic virtue and closeness to God. It was a world in which holy men were the main source for the preservation of communal identity and faith. In his texts John Rufus reveals a society of archetypes, based on the veneration of holy men and women who after years of ascetic training were believed to have achieved total impassivity towards the material and corruptible world, as well as spiritual insight, and supernatural qualities. Over and over again ascetic fathers such as Peter the Iberian, Abba Isaiah, or Abba Zeno, appear before us as instruments of grace through which the divine truth is mediated into the temporal realm. The constant references to holy men become the principal means by which John raises his works to the prominence of divine legitimization.

In the following pages we will put forward some aspects of the idea of the holy man and ascetic authority as revealed in John Rufus' works. The first aspect treats the ways in which holy men are legitimized as proper models for ascetical conduct and orthodox faith. It will be argued that the holy man's position as a witness of truth could not be taken for granted unless warranted by his ascetic qualifications. Spiritual authority was something that was earned after a successful and often spectacular career of self-

---

[14] Brown, 'The Rise and Function of the Holy Man in Late Antiquity', 86-87, 93-94.

[15] See Rousseau, *Ascetics, Authority and the Church*, 68-76.

mortification. In short, the basic criterion of veracity was an authentic ascetic lifestyle. To this concept of the holy man's authority as closely connected with ascetic progress also belonged a common recognition of his natural place in the ascetic lineage that went back to the great pioneers of Egyptian monasticism. In John Rufus' hagiography the past is given an essential importance, since it is through the historical continuity of ascetic discipleship that ascetic authority is made.

For the second aspect our attention will be directed to the important role of ascetic renunciation in John Rufus' presentation of his holy men as witnesses of truth and earthly mediators of the divine command and judgement. Truth seems to be present only in the divinely inspired activities of persons who attain purity of conduct and faith by completely dissociating themselves from the material culture and living as absolute strangers to the world. The idea of renouncing the world of institutions and civilization as a particular virtue of ascetic leadership places the jurisdiction of ecclesiastical institutions in opposition to the direct command of God, which is reflected in the words and deeds of holy men.

The third aspect is how the consequences of this are elucidated in the treatment of the relation between personal ascetic authority and the institutionalized authority of the ecclesiastic offices. It is evident that John Rufus' concept of authority is centered on personal and concrete imitation, rather than on doctrinal expositions of faith as presented by the bishops and patriarchs of the Church. The doctrinal position of John Rufus, it will be made clear, rests on the personal authority of virtuous and charismatic holy men rather than on the institutionalized authority of ecclesiastic office.

The Power of the Past

In hagiographic presentations organized as biographical accounts of a holy man's life from birth to death, the focus rests on the personal development of the saint to ever increasing degrees of ascetic perfection, their aim being to incite the readers to progressive emulation of his ascetic labors. Thus the narration of the saint's progressive struggle for perfection is an essential part of the hagiographic purpose to create an ascetic ideal to be imitated. In short, it was the hagiographic narrative in itself that elevated the historically obscure individuals behind the pious legends into ascetic stars.[16] Athanasius' *Life of Antony* provides us with a particularly illuminating example of how hagiographic texts delineate ascetic ideals. In one of the most crucial passages in this text we learn how the protagonist was finally forced out from the fort where he had lived for twenty years, after his friends had wrenched off the door by force.

> Antony came forth as though from some shrine, having been led into divine mysteries and inspired by God. This was the first time he appeared from the fortress for those who came out to him. And when they beheld him, they were amazed to see that his body had maintained its formed condition, neither fat from lack of exercise, nor emanicated from fasting and combat with demons, but was just as they had known him prior to his withdrawal. The state of his soul was one of purity, for it was not constricted by grief, nor relaxed by pleasure, nor affected by either laughter or dejection. Moreover, when he was the crowd, he was not annoyed any more than he was elated at being embraced by so many people. He maintained utter equilibrium, like one guided by reason and steadfast in that which accords with nature. Through him the Lord healed many of those present who suffered from bodily ailments; others he purged of demons, and to Antony he gave grace in speech. Thus he consoled many who mourned, and others hostile to each other he reconciled in friendship, urging everyone to prefer nothing in the world above the love of Christ. And when he spoke and urged them to keep in mind the future goods and the affection in which we are held by God, *who did not spare his own Son, but gave him up for us all,* he persuaded many to take up the solitary life. And so, from then on, there were monasteries in the mountains and the desert was made a city by monks, who left their own people and registered themselves for the citizenship in the heavens.[17]

The circle of friends and admirers gathered outside Antony's dwelling place to see the great man, and perhaps receive a word of wisdom from his mouth, finally saw him come forth 'as from a

---

[16] Brown, 'The Saint as Exemplar in Late Antiquity', *Representations* 1.2 1983, 1.

[17] *V. Ant.* 14; tr. by Gregg, *The Life of Antony*, 42.

shrine', marked by his ascetic practices but with an almost angelic appearance. Reluctantly, but still prepared to fulfill the duty of the experienced monk to provide instruction for those eager to attain perfection, Antony submitted to his new role as an ascetic authority.

What is revealed in this passage is an image of the ascetic authority as a person who is, through successful warfare against evil powers, completely transformed into a state of original and natural holiness. As a human being Antony was still the same, yet he was filled with the Spirit of God and rewarded with knowledge of the divine mysteries. No demons could beset him anymore, since he had reached a state of utter indifference towards material vanity. He had been initiated in the mysteries, and his mission was now to provide his disciples with instruction about the ascetic progress towards spiritual perfection.

In Athanasius' presentation of the ideal of ascetic authority we find one of the most characteristic features in the hagiographic representations of the great Egyptian ascetics of the fourth century, namely the ideal of the holy man as essentially self-made, or at least taught by God alone (*theodidaktos*).[18] The holy men of the fourth century appear before us as individuals without a history. Their status as ascetic authorities was not immediately dependent on their conforming to a previous tradition of ascetic teaching. In fact, among the hagiographers of the fourth century there was an evident tendency to attribute to the Desert Saints the role of being pioneers of the true monastic life, clearly demonstrated in Jerome's preface to the *Life of Paul the First Hermit*:

> It has been a subject of widespread and frequent discussion what monk was the first to give a signal example of the hermit life. For some going back too far have found a beginning in those holy men Elia and John, of whom the former seems to have been more than a monk and the latter to have begun to prophesy before his birth. Others, and their opinion is that commonly received, maintain that Antony was the originator of this mode of life, which view is partly true. Partly I say, for the fact is not so much that he preceded the rest as that they all derived from him the necessary stimulus. But it is asserted even at the present

---

[18] Cf. *V. Ant.* 66.

day by Amathas and Macarius, two of Antony's
disciples, the former of whom laid his master in the
grave, that a certain Paul of Thebes was the leader in
the movement, though not the first to bear the name,
and this opinion has my approval also.[19]

This image of the ideal ascetic as a pioneer of monastic life
corresponds to the idea found in Athanasius' reports of Antony—
that the truth rests constantly with the holy man himself as a seed
of natural holiness that has to be protected against the instability of
the material world. The most important instrument for the
protection and nurturing of his natural holiness is simplicity and
single-mindedness, which in Antony's debates with heretics and
pagan philosophers becomes itself an argument for truth.[20] This
single-minded stability is linked both to the holy man's natural
holiness and his allegiance to the Church. Truth has its place in the
orthodox Christian community, but at the same time truth is
emphasized as something natural, perceived through natural virtues
rather than philosophical arguments.[21]

However, in hagiographic representations from the fifth
century we find the opposite tendency of playing down the holy
man's natural holiness to emphasize the truth as received from a
glorious tradition of ascetic life. To John truth is closely connected
with the notion of discipleship to old and venerable ascetics in the
past, as is stated by the following words that introduce one of the
stories in the *Plerophories*:

The following reports may not convince all, and for
some they may even appear as incomprehensible, but
when I report then it is because pure, old and in faith
worthy men and holy monks have told them.[22]

This short passage seems to summaries much of the Eastern
monastic notion on the close relationship between ascetic authority
and the monastic progress of virtue. Authority could not be
separated from the achievement of perfect virtue as a result of
renunciation, prayers and contemplation. The recognition of the

---

[19] Jerome, *Vita Pauli* 1, PL 23, 17, tr. by W. H. Fremantle, *The Principal Works of St. Jerome*, A Select Library of the Nicene and Post-Nicene Fathers of the Christian Church, ser. 2, vol. 12 (Grand Rapids 1983), 299.

[20] *V. Ant.* 72-80.

[21] *V. Ant.* 20; Rubenson, *The Letters of St. Antony*, 135.

[22] *Pleroph.* 10.

holiness of the protagonists grants genuine assurance that their
words are to be taken as authentic signs of God's verdict against
heresy. But, more importantly, these words reveal an idea of truth
as communicated through a historical chain of spiritual authority.
In order to maintain the purity of the orthodox truth everybody
must enter into this continuity of truth as a humble disciple, ready
to be instructed by those who through their ascetic progress have
received the gift of distinguishing the teachers of truth from the
teachers of falsehood. As Epiphanius, who lived in a monastery
near the Palestinian village of Aphta, plainly declared when the
priest of the village was trying, by torturing him, to make him enter
into communion with the Chalcedonian bishops: 'It is not possible
for me to reject the faith I have received from the holy fathers'.[23]

Truth is received from the personal authority of spiritually and
ecclesiastically distinguished men. Any claim for truth is impossible
in separation from the historical continuity of transmitted faith. As
John Rufus instructs his readers to respond to accusations from
Chalcedonians:

> It is not through our own [personal] authority and
> judgement that we anathematize, but it is from the
> apostolic canon and the decrees of the holy fathers that
> we regard you as transgressors and condemned.[24]

Words of truth uttered by an ascetic master were commonly
acknowledged as signs of his spiritual power. But as such verbal
icons they did not derive from the ascetic master himself but were
transmitted, in the past and in the present, from master to disciple.
This idea of transmitted truth finds its clearest expression in the
collection of ascetic teaching attributed to the monk Isaiah, a
collection most probably derived from the anti-Chalcedonian
circles at Gaza and Maiuma in the fifth century.

> Brothers, everything that I heard and saw in company
> with the old I have transmitted to you without having
> added or removed anything, so that we may be worthy
> to share their inheritance as we walk in their path.[25]

---

[23] *Pleroph.* 48.

[24] *Pleroph.* 59.

[25] Abba Isaiah, *Asceticon* 6.1. For the attribution of the *Asceticon* to
Isaiah, the monk at Beth Dalthā and the friend of Peter the Iberian, see
Chitty, 'Abba Isaiah', *JTS* 22 (1971), 47-72. Cf. Zacharias Scholasticus,
Vita Isaiae Monachi, 3. For a survey of the debate, see L. Regnault, 'Isaïe de

From these words it is evident that every aspect of the ascetic life is profoundly connected with transmitted knowledge. The personal authority of an ascetic master is acknowledged only in relation to tradition and his maintaining a true discipleship under the holy fathers of the past. Fundamentally, it is that discipleship that made the spoken word of a holy man an indisputable evidence of truth. Due to the preservation of true discipleship God himself spoke through the holy man, revealing the true meaning of orthodox faith and anathematizing the Chalcedonian bishops who had rejected the Holy Trinity by imposing the teaching of Nestorius as an accurate explanation of faith.

The idea of truth as something transmitted lends a supreme prominence to the past. In the ascetic communities in Palestine in the fourth and fifth century the constant call for preserving the wisdom of the past was closely associated with the idea of Egypt as the cradle of monasticism as well as of Trinitarian orthodoxy.[26] Particularly in the polemical anecdotes contained in the *Plerophories* we find a close link between the literary expressions of John's anti-Chalcedonian hagiography and the Egyptian tradition of asceticism. The impact of Egyptian ascetic theory and practices on Palestinian monasticism cannot be denied, and seems to have operated independently of the conflicting dogmatic traditions in the area.[27]

The clear-cut features of the spirituality of Egyptian monasticism in the hagiography of John Rufus do not distinguish him rhetorically from his pro-Chalcedonian colleagues in the sixth century. We have seen that the ideals of the Egyptian tradition are emphasized by both Cyril of Scythopolis and John Rufus. It is evident that the ascetic heritage of the Egyptian deserts was a shared source for the ideological consolidation of two fundamentally conflicting doctrinal traditions within Palestinian monasticism. This is particularly obvious when we consider the concept of ascetic authority within each tradition, since the traditions emphasize aspects of the shared Egyptian heritage in a

---

Scété ou de Gaza? Notes critiques en marge d'une introcuction au problème isaïen', *RAM* 46 (1970), 33-44.

[26] The idea of the prominence of Egypt in the cultural vision of Palestinian anti-Chalcedonanism has already been discussed in the first chapter.

[27] See Cyril of Scythopolis, *V. Euthym.*, 34

way that creates a point of radical difference between the two
traditions in Palestinian monasticism.

The Road of Renunciation

During the last days of his earthly life Peter the Iberian gathered all
monks in his monastery around his deathbed in order to tell them a
few final words of admonitions. He exhorted them to maintain the
orthodox faith fixed and unchanged unto death and to reject all
kinds of heresy, especially the council of Chalcedon and the
ungodly *Tome* of Leo:

> in the same way as I have many times have brought
> witness, before you and all people, when I said: If you
> ever see me, being according to your own words and in
> your eyes a saint, changing my mind and saying to you
> that there is no harm in the council of Chalcedon, you
> will separate yourselves from the Father, the Son and
> the Holy Spirit if you not separate from my face and
> escape from me as from an unbeliever and a person
> that has part in the traitor Judas. Next to faith you must
> care for the holiness of soul and what is profitable for
> the body and preserve firm accuracy, without which no
> one will see the Lord. Preserve the love towards each
> other and unity in a way that, following the Scriptures,
> comes from the heart and emanates from good
> consciousness and non-hypocrite faith. Preserve
> yourselves also from thoughtless speech when
> conversing with outsiders, but also with each other,
> since boundless frankness enlightens and produces
> every passion. Always consider and read the blessed
> bishop Basil's book on the ascetic life, the *Ascetic Rules,*
> and direct your conduct and manners in accordance
> with his rules and prescriptions. For in the same way
> that the by God inspired Scriptures presents an image
> of the Holy Spirit, so has also this book been produced
> through divine grace and the Holy Spirit in order to
> lead to accuracy, correction and redemption for the
> monastic life everywhere.[28]

In the center of this final address of Peter the Iberian we find the
close connection between preserved orthodoxy and the ascetic life.
Orthodoxy and asceticism is a part of the same life in complete

---

[28] *V. Petr. Ib.*, 134-135.

obedience under God and that through which intimacy with Christ is founded. The connection between orthodoxy and ascetic life is one of the most essential features in the works of John Rufus. This close relation between orthodoxy and ascetic life finds its most concrete expression in John's notion of renouncing the visible world by various forms of exile based on a twofold view of the world—as an idea of material dependency as well as the home of heresy. As we read in one anecdote in the *Plerophories*:

> Brother Anastasius, a monk from Edessa who had been a scholastic, had a similar dream. When he still lived in Beirut and belonged to the apostates he saw a holy and truly honorable old man who said to him: 'If you want to be saved, take a horse and keep in close company with the bishop Peter the Iberian. Then you will receive the true light and be saved'. Thus he left everything and went to find the Abba, who then lived at Aphthonia by Abba Gregory. He told him his vision as he had done to many that he had met in Antioch and on his journey. The vision announced that he was to renounce the world and that he was ordered to leave and escape the world completely, and he was convinced and received instruction about the orthodox faith by Peter. Having anathematized the council of Chalcedon he lived close to him as a monk and renounced the world.[29]

Central to ascetical life in early asceticism is the renunciation of all worldly matters. To renounce the world is to create an absolute independence of everything that puts the monk into the risk of being tied to corruptible and temporal matters. Renunciation is nothing but a quest for the freedom to serve God with undivided love. It is a quest for freedom from possessions, bodily satisfaction, and people.[30] In the end monastic freedom implies the freedom to love and serve God with all one's heart. Without this fundamental freedom there is no path for a monk to reach a perfect relationship with God. In John Rufus' hagiography, as in early monastic literature as a whole, renouncing the world is the starting-point for individual perfection. In John's texts we constantly hear about

---

[29] *Pleroph.* 71.

[30] For evidence in the apophthegmatic literature of early Egyptian asceticism, see, *AP*, ed. PG 65, Macarius 18, Theodore of Pherme 1, Tithoës 3, Antony 33, Arsenius 13; Abba Isaiah, *Asceticon* 15.59-61, 67.

people leaving the world, in the strict geographical sense, to become monks and disciples of celebrated ascetic masters.[31] At times, however, the ideal of renunciation is even more radically expressed, through the ascetic feature of voluntary exile. In two cases in the *Plerophories* the exile as an ideal appears in the honorary epithet of 'wanderer'.[32] In one of these cases, in an anecdote dealing with Abba Zeno of Kefar Se'arta, the disciple of the legendary Egyptian monk Silvanus, the relationship between exile and maintaining the orthodox faith is clearly stated.

> Abba Stephanus, who was a monk and finally became a deacon in Jerusalem, wanted to go off to foreign countries to serve God and participate in the perfection of exile. Thus he went to Zeno to consult him. Zeno foretold him following, before the Council of Chalcedon: 'Go and stay in peace, since a persecution and a rebellion of heretics will shake the churches as regards the orthodox faith. If you love the orthodox faith, keep wandering'. And this was what he did. He went off to foreign countries and died in this state because of the Council of Chalcedon.[33]

Here the willingness to submit oneself to voluntary exile is expressed in terms of particular excellence. The flight is undertaken by free will, not as the result of actual persecution. It is a question of a continuous flight from the turbulence and disturbance of a world that has fallen into the hands of heretics. To move from one place to another becomes a form of ascetical labor, through which the monk gains the strength to maintain the virtue of impassivity and avoids mixing with people who might endanger his true faith and conduct. But the Eastern monastic concept of exile can sometimes be even more radically expressed. In the *Plerophories* John Rufus relates the ascetic career of the holy man Heliodorus, who retired from the world of men to live an anachoretic life in the forests and mountains of Taurus in Cilicia. Living with wild animals

---

[31] For instance, John Rufus relates that Peter renounced the court of Constantinople to become a monk in Palestine, where he submitted himself to the spiritual authority of Melania the younger and Gerontius, *V. Petr. Ib.*, 19-32. Later we are told that he renounced city life in Jerusalem to live as a monk at Maiuma, in contact with Abba Zeno of Kefar Se'arta, 49-50. See also *Pleroph.* 52, 70-71, 80, 87.

[32] *Pleroph.* 8, 20 (*metkarkānā*), and 30, 72 (*aksnāyā*).

[33] *Pleroph.* 8.

he fed on wild plants and shoots from trees, until at last he had altogether forgotten the world of men. One day, however, he was discovered by a group of huntsmen who believed that they had come across some kind of strange animal. The holy man was caught, but being revealed as a human being he left these wild areas and settled in a monastery, where eventually he became head of the monks.[34] The depiction of Heliodorus as a man living in harmony with wild animals, sustaining himself only on what is provided by nature itself, serves as an evident demonstration of his ascetic sincerity and humility, indicating the true meaning of monastic independence and freedom. Almost the same life story recurs later in the *Plerophories*, where John tells us about a deacon from Antioch named Basil, who was inspired by the young Peter the Iberian, still living at the court of Theodosius, to commit himself to a monastic life:

> Our blessed Abba said about him that he renounced the world, carried the cross of Christ, and kept to it. For thirty-five years he lived alone in the desert at Thebais, until he finally heard a voice coming down from the sky, saying: 'Basil, go to the world of men and fight for the sake of the faith, because a denial of God's only-begotten son has there been set up by the bishops and the kings'. When he had arrived in the lands of the province of Lycia, he found on the coast a den, a secluded place. Here he lived for twelve years and submitted himself to the same ascetic training as Abba Heliodorus, whom I have mentioned previously. But one day a ship landed, and he was discovered by the seamen, who were downhearted in their distress. Having been discovered in this way, he became well known all over the country. And he was requested by the people in this region to depart for the populated regions of Lycia. There he founded two monasteries for holy monks, one for men and another one for women.[35]

The notion of exile is once more connected with the demand of maintain and struggle for the orthodox faith in times of apostasy from the true faith of the fathers. Stories like these, emphasizing the natural wilderness and purity through the removal of all contact

---

[34] *Pleroph.* 31.
[35] *Pleroph.* 35.

and memory of civilization, verge on the extreme but are frequently found in early monastic hagiography. We find them in the *Life of Antony* as an essential part of Antony's spiritual struggles, making the wild desert the garden of paradise as he lives in harmony even with the beasts. Only by separating himself from the material world, and by nurturing and preserving his inner stability and unaffectedness through his retreats into the wilderness, will he be ready to confront the civilized world, appearing as an ascetic master in whom God is always present.[36]

In the *Life of Antony* we find that Athanasius depicts his holy man as fulfilling two different kinds of ascetic missions. The place where Antony is transformed into an ascetic authority is the isolated wilderness of the desert. As he has perfected himself through his spiritual struggles with demons he is ready to appear to his admirers as from a shrine, in order to guide the establishment of a new civilization in the desert, making it a city. But Antony's role as a cultivator of the desert is in the *Life* combined with another aspect of authority, that of a helmsman of the orthodox faith. As a perfected ascetic Antony possesses the truth within himself, recognizing his ecclesiastical mission to defend it candidly against falsity and invention. Whenever truth is at stake Antony breaks off his retreat in the desert to confront the heretics.

Both these sides of the mission of the ascetic authority are traceable in the hagiography of John Rufus and Cyril of Scythopolis. But at they same time they seem to differ in their emphasis on each of these two aspects. In the works of Cyril of Scythopolis the protagonists certainly appear as gladiators of orthodoxy, in fierce opposition to anti-Chalcedonian and Origenist heretics. But in addition to the successful attempts of Cyril's holy men to win over schismatic monks to the communion with the Chalcedonian patriarchs of Jerusalem, they are also eagerly engaged in making the desert of Palestine a suitable home for orthodoxy. This is the background of Cyril's frequent description of his holy men as cultivators and colonizers of the Judaean deserts. For instance when, according to Cyril, the Patriarch Elias sends a letter to Emperor Anastasius asking him to receive Sabas in the imperial capital, he describes Sabas as 'the colonizer and guardian of our

---

[36] *V. Ant.* 49-53.

desert and luminary over all Palestine'.[37] By his descriptions of how
Euthymius and Sabas make cells out of caves,[38] tame wild beasts
into harmless sheep, or drive away Saracens and robbers, Cyril
manifests his view of the young patriarchate of Jerusalem as being
in a state of wilderness. The uncivilized condition of the land of
Palestine is turned into a grand metaphor for the wilderness of
anti-Chalcedonian and Origenist heresy which holy men are
destined to tame. The struggle for Chalcedonian orthodoxy, hence,
is for Cyril a struggle against nature. The divine task of the holy
fathers of the deserts is to tame the beasts of heresy and to bring
order to the land of Palestine. Cyril's emphasis on law and order as
a condition for the proper profession of faith is incongruous with
John Rufus' hagiographic depictions of ascetics living in the midst
of nature. Stories that emphasize the natural wilderness and purity
through the removal of all contact with and memory of civilization
are a frequent theme in early monastic hagiography. But with the
Lives of Cyril, the theme of the holy man is sorted out from the
storage of hagiographic commonplaces and replaced by a strong
emphasis on the necessity of discipline and order for the spiritual
conditions in the Eastern monasteries.

While Cyril emphasizes the role of taming the wilderness as a
main theme in his depiction of the protagonists, it is obvious that
John Rufus stresses the aspect of the holy men as representatives
of true faith. As ascetic authorities they have but a single mission,
which is to mediate God's verdict against Chalcedonian heretics.
For example, in the *Plerophories* we read the story of how Romanus,
the archimandrite of Tekoa, was finally assured of the heresy of
Chalcedon. John tells us that Romanus, as soon as the
transgression at Chalcedon and the apostasy of Juvenal had
become known all over the East, was urged by his monks not to
accept the Council but to leave the monastery and stand up for the
faith. To convince him that the Council was to be anathematized
and that he should withdraw from the communion of Juvenal, he
received confirmation from those who had accompanied Juvenal
on his way to Chalcedon and who had heard the bishop say, before
the Council, that those who accepted the *Tome* of Leo should be

---

[37] *V. Sab.*, 141.

[38] See *V. Euthym.*, 15-25, 38-39, 61-65; *V. Sab*, 90-107, 110-126, 138-
139, 167-169.

circumcised in the same way as Jews. Still uncertain on what to do, Romanus went into the Judaean desert to receive from God a final affirmation of the heresy of the Chalcedonian bishops. After ten days and ten nights he heard a voice from heaven, say: 'Go and keep to the faith of the three hundred and eighteen, in accordance with your baptism, and you will be saved'. Romanus returned to his monastery and related this auditory revelation. But the holy monks doubted the vision—did not even those who were gathered at Chalcedon claim to have affirmed the faith of the three hundred and eighteen fathers, i.e. the Council of Nicaea? Romanus left his monastery for a second time in order to find the truth in the desert. Some days later God spoke again, instructing him to follow the faith received from Peter of Alexandria, Gregory Thaumaturgus, Julian of Rome, Athanasius of Alexandria, Basil of Caesarea, Gregory of Nazianzus, John Chrysostom, and Cyril of Alexandria. Having returned to the monastery the monks remarked that, in order to deceive the simple-minded, even the renegades claimed to rest their faith on the great doctors of the church. Romanus went into the desert a third time, and submitted himself to a severe asceticism of solitude, prayer, and lamentation. Finally he saw a great letter descend from heaven, in which it was written: 'Those who were at Chalcedon are renegades. They have transgressed the faith. Woe betide them, and may they be in anathema'. This was the clear and unambiguous confirmation from God that the holy monks at Tekoa had waited for. At once Romanus anathematized Juvenal and supported the monk Theodosius as Patriarch of Jerusalem instead of him.[39]

The most interesting feature in this story is the role that John Rufus ascribes to the holy man. It strikes us that, in spite of his position of an ascetic authority, Romanus appears very uncertain in his attitude towards the Council of Chalcedon. While his monks strongly urge him to condemn the Council, he is himself utterly in doubt on how to act. He is fully assured only when, after some time, he receives clear instruction directly from heaven. This story presents an image of the holy man that is quite characteristic of the hagiography of John Rufus, as formed mainly in the *Plerophories*, i.e. an evident reduction of the importance of the holy man as a bearer of truth, and an emphasis on the absolute initiative of God. Thus

---

[39] *Pleroph.* 25. Cf. 21.

the story about Romanus is not to be read as a confirmation of the
holiness and orthodoxy of the holy man, but rather as evidence
that God has made his verdict known. The holy man becomes
merely a messenger of this verdict, delivered by the actual
protagonist in John Rufus' works, i.e. God himself. This is an
evident point of divergence from many other hagiographic
presentations composed within the cultural framework of Eastern
monasticism, for instance the *Life of Antony*, the *Historia Lausiaca*,
the *Historia Religiosa*, and the Chalcedonian hagiography of Cyril of
Scythopolis.

A further notion that constitutes a foundation of John's
images of ascetic renunciation is the close relationship between the
holy man and God. Sometimes the authority of the holy man is
legitimized by showing his closeness to God. Peter the Iberian is
once described as 'a man of God',[40] and another holy man, living in
a monastery in the neighborhood of Jerusalem, is mentioned as
'one of those great old ascetics who were close to God'.[41] Essential
is also the relationship between a holy person and Christ. One of
John's informants is described as a servant of Christ,[42] and the
blessed Eliana, the wife of the prefect and governor Damianus, is
said to have loved Christ beyond everything.[43] Moreover, a few
times we come across individuals who are described as godfearing.
John tells about a blessed woman near Ascalon, named Miqa, who
was nearly hundred years old and had lived all her life as an ascetic,
'in complete purity and fear of God',[44] and later on he gives an
account of a vision experienced by 'a man who feared God'.[45] The
fear of God was a salient feature in the spirituality of the Desert
Fathers, a necessary quality for the attainment of virtues. In a
saying in the *Apophthegmata Patrum* it is even recognized as the most
important principle, next to prayer and charity.[46] It is a principle of
humility and a shield against the attacks of the passions.[47] However,

---

[40] *Pleroph.* 19.

[41] *Pleroph.* 17 See also 74, where Themision of Alexandria is mentioned
as 'a friend of God'.

[42] *Pleroph.* 24

[43] *Pleroph.* 36.

[44] *Pleroph.* 43.

[45] *Pleroph.* 60.

[46] *AP* Poemen 160.

[47] See *i.a.* Abba Isaiah, *Asceticon* 15.118.

it must be noted that in the works of John Rufus fear of God is associated not with the commitments of ascetic labor, but with keeping the faith of the orthodox fathers. To fear God seems to John to imply the necessity of standing up for the true faith. But, at the same time, we must remember that for John there is no contrast between orthodoxy and the ascetic pattern of life. The monk's relationship with God or Christ involves both principles. The 'mystery of the fear of God, which is to be entrusted only to people acknowledged as worthy and reliable, includes the orthodox faith as well as the teaching of the ascetic fathers.[48]

Charisma and Institution

In John Rufus' hagiography the power of a holy man rested on the public recognition of his authority and influence. Monastic authority was not created by itself, it was the fruit of the fruit of the experiences and expectations of the holy men's ascetic labors within the community.

In the works of John Rufus there is no emphasis on any specific monastic pattern of life. Rather than depicting organized forms of ascetic conduct he intends to bring forth the holy man as a model for imitation. Important is the holy man's personal virtues, received through his humble discipleship under the ascetic masters. It is the virtues of the holy man that constitute the main evidence for his holiness and natural stability. Through his virtues the holy man appears as a witness for God's presence on earth. This is illustrated in a passage in the *Life of Peter the Iberian* where John Rufus displays the virtues of the protagonists, exalting his master to a level of unreachable perfection:

> Each of his virtues and gifts, which by the grace of God were manifested in various times, ways and deeds: in asceticism and monasticism as well as, in the words of the Apostle, in afflictions, hardships, calamities, persecutions, labors, fasting, watchings, struggles, beatings, and wrestlings, not only against sin and not against flesh and blood but against the rulers and authorities, against the powers of darkness and the spiritual forces of evil, through great endurance, in powerful signs, wonders, and healings, and by the powers of the Holy Spirit through the arms of

---

[48] *Pleroph.* 89.

righteousness, to the right and the left, in honor and shame, in blasphemies and praise. As he was both unknown and known, he knew only his God when he heard that he was known. In the flesh he was like a dead man, but in the spirit always alive and passionate. He was like a poor man, but made many men rich when he gave proper nourishment in soul and body to each and every one. He was as one who has nothing, and yet he possessed everything, not only in the world but also treasures that are in heaven. For the treasures he possessed always remained hidden in his heart, mind and virtues.[49]

In this passage standard phrases drawn from the hagiographic tradition of late antiquity are candidly mingled with epithets derived from the Pauline letters into excessive praise of the great protagonist. In the focus is, however, the view of the completed progress of ascetic life as the basis for ascetic authority. As a result of his ascetic virtues, Peter received every single one of the charismatic gifts associated with Christian leadership. He had fought well against his own flesh, as well as against all the dark powers of the universe, and is now to be imitated for the attainment of the good, of virtue and of the proper faith.

Enumeration of ascetical virtues, as in the quotation above, has a natural place within hagiographic discourse. In fact, they serve a distinctive and calculated purpose of rhetorical legitimization of a holy man's words and deeds. Especially in John Rufus' *Plerophories* such remarks about the ascetic characteristics of the orthodox protagonists play an essential rhetorical role for the legitimization of the anecdotes contained in the collection. Often found in the openings of the stories these remarks on the holy men's virtuous lives have no immediate significance for the actual contents of the stories. Still they serve as sufficient proof of the authority of the holy men, or of the informant. For instance:

> This Abba told us another story, about the blessed Pelagius of Edessa, who was steadfast in *a perfected life*.[50]

and

> The blessed John, priest of Alexandria, who was named Beth Tatianā, *a celebrated and worthy* man, told us.[51]

---

[49] *V. Petr. Ib.*, 13-14.

[50] *Pleroph.* 2.

[51] *Pleroph.* 20.

Further, we hear about Anianus, 'a worthy scholar, virtuous and orthodox',[52] and of Epiphanius of Aphta, who is described as a 'pure and humble man, permeated with tenderness',[53] and further of the priest Themision of Alexandria, 'a man remarkable because of his purity and earnest manners'.[54] But particularly illustrative is the portrayal of the Palestinian priest Paul who, according to John, was the object of Empress Eudocia's deepest veneration:

> On the north side of the village of Ganta, four miles from Jerusalem, Eudocia found a priest named Paul. This man loved the ascetic life, and was adorned with every evangelical perfection, holiness, virginity, purity, charity towards the poor, and kindness towards strangers. He was revered as a mediator by all the villagers and by the Empress.[55]

This said, the reader will go on reading the main story, fully convinced of its veracity. In fact, it was through such reports of the protagonists' virtues that John Rufus created his holy men, dressing them in easily identifiable attributes of trustworthy witnesses to the divine truth.

Ascetic virtues such as humility, purity, honesty, devotion, and impassivity play a key role in John's portraits of holy men and ascetic masters, and are deeply rooted in early Egyptian asceticism. As recognized in Egyptian ascetic theory the path to ascetic independence of the material world leads through virtues, since virtues are the most efficient defense against the attacks of internal and external enemies. The virtue of humility, which in the sources on the lives and spirituality of the holy men of the East is given a particular status of excellence,[56] is also prevalent in the hagiography of John Rufus.

In the process of peeling off his personal wishes in order to uphold the virtue of humility, the monk is also committed to the activities of manual labor and prayer.[57] The concept of manual labor has always been essential in the Christian monastic tradition. To the fathers of the Egyptian desert it was more than necessary

---

[52] *Pleroph.* 38.

[53] *Pleroph.* 48.

[54] *Pleroph.* 74.

[55] *Pleroph.* 20.

[56] See *i.a. AP* Antony 7; Abba Isaiah, *Asceticon* 15.80.

[57] See *i.a. AP* Antony 1 and 19.

for survival. Above all, they regarded it as a bulwark of the inner watchfulness of the soul against the dangerous passion of idleness.[58] But at the same time manual labor was regarded as secondary in relation to prayer, the inner work of the soul. Manual labor was never to be considered as the main occupation of the monk. Prayer was more important. This notion of the status of manual labor in Eastern asceticism is displayed in an episode in the *Plerophories* where John once more shows that his protagonists consistently follow in the paths of the Egyptian fathers. Here John tells us a story that he had heard from a certain scholastic named Epaenetus, who, while a young student in Alexandria, used to go out in the desert to hear a word from the mouth of the great old Abba Zeno of Enaton.

> One day I found the old man carrying a rope with his eyes directed towards the sky. As I supposed he was praying, I refrained from speaking to him until he had finished his prayer.[59]

Rope-making, a common occupation among the desert fathers, is here shown in a way that presents the manual labor as something of little importance compared with the striving for inner stillness through prayer, and, as appears in the sequel, with the holy man's visions of the disturbance of the immediate future.[60] Through his experience of manual labor the old monk is able to put aside all thoughts of his work, which he carries out automatically, in favor of the inner communication with God. Hence, in the relation between material and spiritual labor, the latter is the most significant.

To present the protagonist as a famous holy man thus becomes a matter of great rhetorical importance. In the *Plerophories* the priest Apollo of Caesarea is said to have been honored and venerated by everybody,[61] and the Egyptian monk Abba Pior is mentioned as 'a man celebrated everywhere',[62] as Abba Leontius, a

---

[58] Abba Isaiah, *Asceticon* 15.87.

[59] *Pleroph.* 13.

[60] In the *Plerophories* the prayer of a holy man is several times connected with a desire to gain knowledge and instruction from God concerning the apostasy of the bishops at Chalcedon, see *Pleroph.* 25, 57, 86.

[61] *Pleroph.* 26.

[62] *Pleroph.* 49.

hermit living in Lycia.[63] But we also know that one of the favorite
themes of early monastic literature was stressing the holy man's
repugnance to the popularity that brought hordes of people to his
monastic retreat, attracted by the wisdom of this teaching. For
instance, Zacharias Scholasticus tells us, in his biography of Isaiah,
that Isaiah's fame forced him from Egypt up to Palestine, where he
withdrew into the desert near Eleutheropolis. But not even there
was he left alone. A considerable number of monks and lay people
in spiritual distress came to the Judaean desert to confer with him.
Isaiah finally found peace in the neighborhood of Gaza, became a
recluse, and had no contact with the outer world except through
Peter the Egyptian, the leader of his disciples.[64] This theme recurs
in a particular form in John's anecdotes about Heliodorus and Basil
of Thebais. Even if a monk managed to live for a very long time in
complete obscurity he would, sooner or later, be discovered,
following the curiosity of the outside world. This 'discovery' seems
to imply recognition of the authority attained by the holy man after
years of isolation, humility and closeness to God, a confirmation
within the community that the holy man was now to be addressed
by the title of Abba. From that point the ascetic was expected to
serve as a spiritual father in his community, guiding his disciples by
his own visible example.

Such charismatic authority, based on the virtues and ascetic
experience of the holy man, was sometimes transformed into a
more institutional authority. In the end, according to John's report,
both Heliodorus and Basil became heads of monasteries. This is
especially evident in the story of Heliodorus, where the
development from charismatic authority to institutional authority
seems divided into three separate stages. The first stage is that of
anachoretic life, in which the ascetic undertakes extreme social
mortification to rid himself of every obstacle in his way to
approach the closeness to God. Then follows the stage of
coenobitic life, where the monk is submitted to obedience in his
relationship with the monastic father. Through the third and final
stage the ascetic himself becomes leader of monks, distinguished in
ascetic experience and commonly regarded as a spiritual authority.

---

[63] *Pleroph.* 83.

[64] Zacharias Scholasticus, *Vita Isaiae Monach*, 1-3. See also John Rufus,
V. Petr. Ib., 100-104.

This form of development in the monastic life must not be considered as a consistent scheme in John Rufus' anti-Chalcedonian hagiography. John does not prefer one type of monastic life to another, nor does he favor archimandrites and heads of monasteries to anachoretic monks. Instead, charismatic and institutional authority seem to co-exist in John's monastic world, as forms of spiritual power based on the same dependence on public responsiveness, trust, and confidence in the holy man's words and examples.

The basis for the monastic tradition was discipleship, the personal relationship of an untrained monk with an experienced ascetic master. Much of the monastic concept of authority rested on the fulfillment of the ideals and expectations prevalent within the monastic community. At the same time the ascetic father, the *abba*, was regarded as a mere mediator, one in a succession of authorities throughout the history of salvation, from the prophets of the Old Testament and by way of the Apostles of the New Testament.[65] This spiritual heritage constituted the authority of faith. Such inherited faith was superior even to the institutionalized authority of sacerdotal offices. The sort of personal salvation that was given through the mediation of the fathers could never be yielded to the authority of ecclesiastical offices. Furthermore, authority conferred by ecclesiastical ordination was believed to be worthless unless the bearer of such authority also had the authority of faith.[66] Not only was it generally known that an ecclesiastical office was a potential source of sin, as it constantly provided opportunities for turning one's mind from God to worldly affairs. Priestly ordination was regarded as null and void if the office was exercised without the spiritual power of transmitted faith. That was why heresy in early monastic literature was depicted as linked with the institutionalized positions of the ecclesiastical dignitaries.[67]

Within the ascetic communities of the East orthodoxy appears to have been intimately dependent on the success of the ascetic labors, while the ecclesiastical authorities in the cities represented doctrinal rigor only as long as the attitudes of true discipleship under the authority of the ascetic fathers were maintained. This is

---

[65] Rousseau, *Ascetics, Authority, and the Church*, 21-25.

[66] Rousseau, 229-231. Cf. John Cassian, *De Incarnatione* 3.2, ed. M. Petschenig, CSEL 17, 277.

[67] This is particularly evident from the *Vita Aphou*.

evident also in the Chalcedonian hagiography of Cyril of Scythopolis. Several times in his *Lives*, Cyril presents a close connection between the spiritual authority of his holy men and the authority of their disciples as future patriarchs, bishops, or archimandrites.[68] There is an obvious tendency in the works of Cyril of Scythopolis to insert the holy men as the foundation of the monastic and ecclesiastic hierarchy in Palestine. Cyril's holy men create authority, while holders of ecclesiastic authority remain in a submissive position towards the great ascetic fathers.[69] To Cyril it is the holy men in the Palestinian deserts who achieve the victory of Chalcedonian orthodoxy in the reign of Emperor Justinian. The patriarchs and bishops, on the contrary, are reduced to instruments in the hands of the holy men, being directed by the virtues of obedience and true discipleship towards their spiritual fathers. It is the holy men, not primarily the patriarchs and bishops, who overcome the heterodoxy of the Origenist and anti-Chalcedonian monks. To Cyril, the monasteries of Euthymius and Sabas were the most important locations for the preservation of this authority, which had originated in the spiritual powers of Antony and the Egyptian fathers. But at the same time Cyril's world was a world of order and discipline, governed by an ecclesiastic hierarchy that derived its authority from the holy fathers of the Palestinian deserts.

We have, then, two hagiographic approaches to authority that co-existed in Eastern Christianity while representing two completely incompatible conceptions of authority. In one of them the truth of orthodoxy was represented by ecclesiastical power and confirmed by the words, deeds, and virtues of holy men,[70] in the other authority entirely depended on the personal charisma of the ascetic fathers. This latter attitude, which more genuinely represented the early monastic tradition in the East, is particularly evident in the writings of John Rufus. The frequent mention of the Councils of Nicaea, Constantinople, Ephesus, and of great ecclesiastical authorities such as Basil of Caesarea and Cyril of Alexandria, must not tempt us to believe that the unifying forces of

---

[68] *V. Euthym.*, 41, 55; *V. Sab.*, 99, 105, 112.

[69] *V. Euthym.*, 52.

[70] See for example Cyril of Scythopolis' reports of Eudocia's encounter with Simeon the Stylite, *V. Euthym.*, 47-49, and Sabas' defence against the accusations of Emperor Anastasius in *V. Sab.*, 144.

the institutionalized Church constituted the basic criteria for orthodoxy.[71] To the contrary, ecclesiastical authority had no primary significance in judging Catholic truth in the early monastic tradition. Institutional establishment was not necessarily a guarantee for freedom from heresy.

Conclusion

In John Rufus' hagiographic works the holy man comes forth as a gladiator of the orthodox faith, an 'athlete', who by ascetical exertion and renunciation of all worldly matters has reached a level of spiritual insight and perfection that places him between God and man as a mediator of the divine truth. As a monastic rhetorician John Rufus certainly knew how to utilize the concept of the holy man to the utmost, creating images of ascetic authority based on expectations and beliefs common in the monastic communities of the Roman East. In his anecdotes he draws pictures of ideal ascetics serving God and the true faith with ascetic perfection, humility, and purity of heart. By using themes and features drawn from the hagiographic imagination and ascetical teaching of the early monastic tradition, he lets his holy men personify the preservation of the Egyptian tradition in the anti-Chalcedonian communities of the Roman East. In this way the authority of well-known and charismatic ascetics promoted the making of a legitimate tradition that would remain firm in the turbulence of religious and political struggles during the following centuries.

However, John was far from the only propagandist of his day to use the concept of monastic authority as a means of legitimizing polemic expressions. Rather, he was a link in a literary tradition in which the borderlines between polemics, hagiography and historiography were fairly fluid. The society of John and his contemporaries was almost entirely built around the notion of the holy man as a living bridge surpassing the boundaries of the divine and human realm. If they could not be trusted, then who could? Who else but the fathers could mediate the divine wisdom of salvation and the true meaning of the orthodox faith to the common man who lived his life in a constant flow of corruptibility? 'Tell us a word', the disciples of the holy fathers used to say, anxious to know how to be saved from the eternal flux of the

---

[71] Cf. *Pleroph.* 25.

material world. And the fathers spoke, giving immediate responses to the needs of their disciples and providing answers to questions on the meaning and ultimate goal of ascetic labors. To their disciples and admirers they were 'servants of God', equipped with true knowledge of God's *oikonomia* and therefore useful as cudgels in the theological controversies that rent the Roman East in the fifth and sixth centuries asunder.

In the preceding discussion about the images of the holy man in the hagiography of John Rufus we have identified three main features. First, that rhetorically essential for John is his concern for placing his holy men in a continuum of transmitted truth. We have seen that Palestinian hagiographers based much of the ascetic and orthodox prominence on the glorious past of Egyptian monasticism. This is true both for John Rufus and Cyril of Scythopolis.

Secondly, a point of radical difference between the hagiography of John Rufus and Cyril of Scythopolis is their use of monastic themes, such as renunciation of the world. While John Rufus emphasizes exile as a way of returning to an original state of uncivilized purity, Cyril stresses the role of his holy men as colonists in the wilderness. We may here identify two opposing poles that rhetorically distinguish the rivaling traditions of Chalcedonian and anti-Chalcedonian hagiography. Especially in John Rufus' *Plerophories* we find a rather pessimistic view of the civilized world as something fundamentally opposed to the spiritually pure state of living in the wilderness. In the works of Cyril of Scythopolis there is, on the contrary, an opposing negative opinion of the wilderness as fundamentally incompatible with the stability and order of the civilized world. Though both of these hagiographic themes are prevalent already in the *Life of Antony*, they have in this later development been isolated as two opposing poles, projecting two radically divergent visions of the world. In our discussion of the second aspect of John Rufus' holy men we have also touched upon the hagiographic role of the holy man in his relationship to God. In the *Plerophories* we encounter a somewhat paradoxical view of the holy man and his relation to God. In spite of the celebrated prominence of the holy men in the text, the protagonist turns out to be God himself. The holy men play a rather insignificant role in relation to God and his verdict on the Council of Chalcedon, which is the main theme of the text. The holy men are reduced to messengers of God's condemnation. They became assured of the orthodox faith only when such confirmation was received directly from God. The holy men know only what God has transmitted to them, since sometimes even the great fathers of the church cannot be trusted, since they are used as evidence by the heretics as well.

Thirdly, as John Rufus bases his idea of ascetic leadership exclusively on monastic virtues, he reveals that his main interest is focused on the holy man as endowed with personal charisma. The fundament of true authority is not the institutional power of ecclesiastical offices but individual progress on the path of asceticism. This is a point were the difference between John Rufus and Cyril of Scythopolis is even more striking. In Cyril's hagiography the foundation of truth rests with the institutionalized Church, while the role of his holy men seems to be merely that of confirming the doctrines established by the incumbents of ecclesiastical offices. Cyril's concern appears to be that of revealing his holy men merely as protectors and defenders of institutionalized stability and order. True faith is less a result of ascetic charisma and monastic discipleship than a sign of the necessity of obedience to the ecclesiastical hierarchy. Once again we find John Rufus and Cyril of Scythopolis opposed through their different uses of hagiographic themes that in the fourth century seems to have existed side by side. Hence John Rufus and Cyril stand before us as representatives of two divergent and competing monastic cultures, developing their own cultural identities on separate sets of hagiographic themes, which in the fourth century had proved easier to unite into a coherent whole.

4   SIGNS AND REVELATIONS

Visions and Signs in Eastern Monasticism

In the Roman garrison town of Talmis in Nubia there was, at least
until the third century, a temple dedicated to the solar deity Merul,
or Mandulis. The temple was visited regularly by the soldiers
stationed there, as well as by pagan pilgrims from afar, and
numerous epitaphs of veneration, so-called *proskynemata*, put up by
them have been preserved on the stones of the temple. One of the
most striking of these brief testimonies of pagan devotion in this
area during the Roman Empire is a short hymn written, perhaps in
the third century, by an anonymous author.

> O rayshooting lord Mandulis, Titan, Makareus, having
> beheld some radiant signs of your power I pondered on
> them and was busied therewith, wishing to know with
> confidence whether you are the sun god. I made myself
> a stranger to all vice and all godlessness, was chaste for
> a considerable period, and offered the due incense-
> offering in holy piety. I had a vision and found rest for
> my soul. For you did grant my prayer and showed
> yourself going through? the heavenly vault: then
> washing yourself in the holy water of immortality you
> appeared again. You came at due season to your shrine,
> making your rising, and giving to your image and shrine
> divine breath and great power. Then I knew you,
> Mandulis, to be the Sun, the all-seeing aster, king of all,
> all-powerful Eternity. O happy folk, that dwell in the
> city beloved by the Sun Mandulis, even holy Talmis,
> which is under the sceptre of fair-dressed Isis of the
> countless names.[1]

There are numerous stories about dreams and visions in the
literature of the Hellenistic and Roman periods. Not only were
dreams commonly treated as significant revelations for the

---

[1] The text is edited, translated and thoroughly discussed by A. D.
Nock in 'A Vision of Mandulis Aion', *HTR* 27 (1934), 53-104.

knowledge of the universe and the future worthy of interpretation.[2] Dreams and visions were also actively sought in order to gain specific guidance for everyday life or knowledge about the supernatural realities. Consequently, dreams and miracles were recognized as devices for getting at the truth.

The report about the vision of Mandulis is a confirmation of beliefs and conventions prevalent in the mental world of the ancients, from the Homeric poets until the end of late antiquity. To many people in antiquity dreams and visions were regarded as a main instrument for developing one's knowledge about a world constantly filled with innumerable supernatural and divine beings. In order to perceive this invisible part of the world with all its mysteries and secrets, people put their trust in what they experienced either when asleep or in a trance.[3] But while most of the ordinary people of antiquity usually limited their interest to nocturnal dreams, there were also those who for purposes of magic, incubation or spiritual knowledge tried to fill their dreams with a specific desired content. In such cases it was commonly regarded as essential to prepare oneself by fasting, purification and incense offering. The anonymous writer of the epitaph in Talmis surely realized the need of preliminary purification in order to receive visionary knowledge directly from Mandulis. To him contact with the supernatural required a period of quarantine from the impurities of the material world, intimately combining the acquisition of a specific supernatural knowledge with a form of asceticism. In other words, ascetic self-discipline was considered a presupposition for anyone seeking specific knowledge about the universe.

The frequent stories and reports of dreams and visions in antiquity reveal a cultural view of the physical universe held by pagans and Christians alike during Late Antiquity. It was a universe governed by invisible beings that men might experience in dreams and visions. In the context of early Christianity reports of dreams and visions have an obvious place—for instance in the New

---

[2] See J. S. Hanson, 'Dreams and Visions in the Graeco-Roman World', in *Aufstieg und Niedergang der römischen Welt* 2.23.2 (Berlin and New York), 1395-1427.

[3] To Hanson, the modern and rather rigid distinction between the terms a dream and a vision finds no correspondence in antiquity, 'Dreams and Visions in the Graeco-Roman World', 1409.

Testament and the Passions of the Martyrs[4]— either for edification or as arguments for God's guidance of the protagonists. But it was through the development of the hagiographic literature that stories of visions and inspired dreams found their most striking expressions in the early Christian literature. The main reason for this may be traced in the intimate connection between truth revealed through visions and ascetic abstinence and purity that was known even in pagan antiquity. It is also in the hagiographic literature of early Christian monasticism that we find the earliest examples of visions used as propagandistic instruments in doctrinal conflicts. In the *Life of Antony*, Athanasius provides a precise account of a vision perceived by Antony about future Arian persecutions.

> Once while he sat working, he went into ecstasy, so to speak, and he groaned a great deal during the spectacle. Then turning to his companions after a while, he moaned as he trembled; and then he prayed and bending his knees he remained that way for a long time. When he rose the old man was weeping. Those with him now began to tremble, and greatly frightened, they begged to learn from him what it was. And they pressed him a great deal until, being forced, he spoke. And so with much groaning he said, 'My children, it is better for you to die before the things in the vision take place'. Again they importuned him, and he said through his tears, 'Wrath is about to overtake the Church, and she is about to be handed over to men who are like irrational beasts. For I saw the table of the Lord's house, and in a circle all around it stood mules kicking the things within, just like the kicking that might occur when beasts lead around rebelliously. Surely you knew,' he said, 'how I groaned, for I heard a voice saying, 'My altar shall be defiled'.[5]

Such visionary stories set in a controversial context find their expression above all in the hagiographic discourse of late antique Christianity. The natural *loci* of these stories were the literary expressions of popular Christian culture, while they seem to be

---

[4] For instance, some of the most vivid accounts of visionary stories in the Passions of the Martyrs are found in the *Passion of Vibia Perpetua and Felicitas*, ed. and tr. by J. Amat, SC 417 (Paris 1996).

[5] *V. Ant.* 82, tr. by Gregg, *The Life of Antony*, 90-91.

absent in the doctrinal controversies in the East during the fourth,
fifth, and sixth centuries. In fact, we know that Severus of Antioch
regarded visions and prophecies as arguments in theological and
canonical controversies with great suspicion. Yet he most likely
shared the conviction of many of his contemporaries in the East
that a Christian holy man, filled with the purity of mind and heart,
could be granted certain gifts of spiritual power, such as the gift of
wisdom, the gift of healing, the gift of foreknowledge, or even the
gift of visionary experience.[6]

Severus' negative sentiments about visionary stories being
used in doctrinal conflicts could be taken as evidence for
ambivalence in attitude within Eastern monasticism towards
dreams, visions, and other miraculous manifestations. This
supposed ambivalence has to some scholars provided proofs for a
dividing-line between the ascetic traditions of Syria and Egypt. In
1960 Vööbus identified a clearly negative or even hostile attitude
towards visions among the Egyptian monks, while he suggested
that the Syrian monks were known all over the East for their
fondness for dreams and visionary experiences.[7] This polarization
between Syrian and Egyptian monasticism as two completely
independent traditions of ascetic practices—regarding the attitude
towards visions as well as all other features of Eastern
monasticism—appears, however, to be founded on a deliberate
selectivity in the approach to the sources.[8] Obviously there was
among the monks in the East an ambivalence regarding visions.
But differences between monks who regarded visions with
suspicion and those who did not cannot be explained simply as a
matter of geography. Rather, there are reasons to call in question
that the differing opinions actually concerned visionary experiences
in the first place.

If we pay attention to one of the examples referred to by
Vööbus and consider what is actually said, a completely different

---

[6] For examples and discussion, see Rousseau, *Ascetics, Authority, and the Church*, 25-32.

[7] See Vööbus, *History of Asceticism in the Syrian Orient* (Louvain 1960), 307-315.

[8] Vööbus completely neglects the many reports of dreams and visions in the most significant witnesses of early Egyptian monasticism, for example Athanasius, *V. Ant.* 66; *HM* 1.45, 8.17, and 10.4; *HL* 14.6, 29.4, 32.1.

picture is revealed. From the *Apophthegmata Patrum* we know the story about the conversation on the monastic way of living between abba Olympus of Scetis and a pagan priest. The pagan priest asked the abba if it ever happened that the monks, as a result of their spiritual labors, had visions of God. The abba said no, and the pagan priest concluded that this lack of visionary experiences was due to the manifest wickedness in the hearts of the monks. The abba went to the fathers and related the words of the pagan priest to them. The fathers were amazed, and said that the priest was right, because polluted minds separate man from God.[9] This anecdote can hardly be taken as a reflection of a general hostility within Egyptian monasticism towards visions. Instead, what the saying implies is not only the readiness to accept the truth about one's own sinfulness, even from pagans, but also the conviction that impure thoughts darken the inner eye of the soul and prevent knowledge about the mysteries of God through visionary experiences. In contrary to Vööbus assumption, this anecdote is an important proof that there was a wariness of visions within Egyptian monasticism.

In the sayings there are also indications of an attitude of mistrust towards visions based on the significance of humility for progress in the ascetic life. Impurity, it was repeated, was caused by lack of humility, which in turn could be explained as an exaggerated trust in one's own spiritual abilities. To expect visions as a fruit of ascetic struggle and prayer was one symptom of this vice, a disclosure of the fact that ascetic purity had far from been achieved.[10] But there seems to have been more to this suspicion of visions than just a shield against the vice of spiritual pride. There was also uncertainty about whether visions were caused by divine revelation or demonic activities. This problem of true and false visions is particularly clear in what John Cassian writes about a Mesopotamian monk in the desert of Scetis on whom the devil practiced deceit through dreams and revelations in order to convert him to Judaism.[11] The same thing also appears in a saying that relates how a number of monks went to Antony to ask him about the veracity of some visions they had seen. Antony, however,

---

[9] *AP* Olympus 1.
[10] See also *AP* Arsenius 27, Zacharias 5 and Silvanus 3.
[11] John Cassian, *Conlationes* 2.8.

convinced them at once that their visions had been caused by demons.[12] Therefore, visionary experiences should always be treated with care, and a monk should never forget the possibility that they might be due to demonic influence. Nevertheless, visions played a significant role, and were frequently used as signal proof of the trustworthiness of the holy fathers, in Egyptian as well as in Syrian and Mesopotamian monasticism. In the *Historia Lausiaca*, for example, we read the story of a dispute among the monks about the commemoration of Paesius and Isaiah, who had represented two different monastic ways of life. Finally, it fell on abba Pambo to pronounce a decision, and he told the monks that the two were equal in perfection, since one had fulfilled the work of Abraham and the other the work of Elijah. But in order to be sure he asked them to wait until God had manifested the truth to him. Some days later the monks returned to abba Pambo, and he told them that he had seen them both standing in paradise.[13]

It is thus clear that the interest in visions and divine manifestations was not limited to Syrian monasticism. Instead, when Theodoret of Cyrrhus, writing about Jacob of Nisibis, tells us that his ascetic practices purified the eye of his thought to such a degree that it became a mirror for the Holy Spirit and a source of foreknowledge and the power to work miracles, this should not be regarded as an evidence for the acceptance of visions among Syrian monks alone, but as a reflection of an attitude towards visions which prevailed also within Egyptian monasticism.[14] All over the East stories of visions and dreams received by ascetic fathers serve an important function in the process of turning these holy men

---

[12] *AP* Antonius 12. For another example of visions as one possible channel of demonic deception, see *HM* 2.9-10.

[13] *HL* 14.

[14] *HR* 1.3. This is one of the passages used by Vööbus to show that visionary experiences, or what he calls 'pneumatism', was a constituent element of Syrian monasticismin contrary to the conditions in Egypt. In Egypt, Vööbus states, there was only Evagrius of Pontus who devoted himself to 'pneumatic speculations', even though his 'mystical writings' would finally be forbidden, *History of Asceticism in the Syrian Orient*, 308-310. However, our knowledge of the early Eastern monasticism has grown considerably since 1960 .

into signs of authority within the monastic community.[15] In late antique society, where the ascetic fathers were supposed to have direct access to God, as well as knowledge of the divine mysteries, their disciples and biographers certainly regarded it as natural to attribute to them the ability to perceive the invisible world. Through this ability it was possible for them to place the holy men of the East as mediators between the realms of heaven and earth. That holy men did obtain visions and manifestations went without saying, just as a monk was expected not to boast about his own visions.[16]

Most of the reports about dreams and visions in the Hellenistic and Late Antique periods are found in narrative contexts, such as novels, biographies or historiographies. In these kinds of narrative material dreams and vision often appear as technical devices to direct the course of events in accordance with their specific message or meaning. Thus it was through a vision that, for instance, Paul and his companions (Acts 16:6–12) decided to end their journeys in Asia Minor, to go instead into Macedonia. From this perspective it is the reaction or response of the receiver that is crucial for many reports about dreams or visionary experiences. Generally, such stories lead to at a resolution of some kind that concludes the plot or, at least, carries it into a new narrative stage.[17] This we recognize not least in early Christian hagiography, where stories about visions are often incorporated as useful narrative tools for the establishment of divine authority, serving as proof of God's express and particular concern for the holy protagonists. A recurrent feature in Christian hagiography is visionary experiences as a means God uses to guide his holy servants on the path towards perfection. A typical example found in John Rufus' *Life of Peter the Iberian* is the report of the vision of Christ in the guise of a monk that Peter, as a young but spiritually advanced man, had at the imperial residence while he was teaching an amazed circle of devotedly Christian courtiers about salvation. As a result of this vision Peter finally decided to leave

---

[15] Rousseau, *Ascetics, Authority, and the Church*, 28-29. For a discussion about the role of dreams and visions in *HM*, see B. Ward, 'Introduction', in *The Lives of the Desert Fathers* (Kalamazoo 1981), 41-42,

[16] For one example of this attitude, see *HM* 8.15.

[17] See Hanson, 'Dreams and Visions in the Graeco-Roman World', 1415.

Constantinople to become a monk.[18] In such cases the visionary experiences may be understood as crucial stages in the holy men's lifelong progress towards ever increasing degrees of holiness, revealing the underlying theological idea of the constant interplay between God's will and the holy man's own initiative.

Reports of visions and dreams are not always followed by accounts of the reaction or response of the receiver. In this type of reports of visions the receiver falls into the narrative periphery as the attention is entirely concentrated on the revealed message in itself.[19] This applies also to those ancient texts that contain only a single dream or report of a vision, for example, the hermetic treatise called *Poimandres* and the *Apocalypse of John*. In these texts, where dreams and visions are employed as vehicles for philosophical and theological arguments, almost in the form of a particular literary genre, the receivers of the visionary experience play no more than a secondary role. In the *Poimandres* the receiver of the visionary dream remains anonymous, and in the *Apocalypse of John* he is clearly defined as merely a messenger of the prophecy to be delivered to the seven communities in Asia Minor. In constant focus, instead, is the truth revealed in the visionary dreams, guiding the reader through a more or less extensive symbolism into knowledge about God, the physical existence or the eschatological realities. As regards early Christian material, there is an abundance of texts, either constituting a single reported vision or a more or less loose conglomerate of reports, that reveal this form of reported visions as a—by no means negligible—part of the rise of Christian theological reflection.[20] It is within this form of elaboration of dream and vision reports that we must place the *Plerophories* of John Rufus.

---

[18] See above, chapter 2, 87-88.

[19] One example, pointed out by Hanson, is Cicero's *The dream of Scipio*. Edited by J. G. F. Powell, *On Friendship; The Dream of Scipio* (Warminster 1990).

[20] Hanson, 'Dreams and Visions in the Graeco-Roman World', 1421-1425. For the concept of prophecy and divine communication and its relation to cosmography in the historical and political thought of the later Byzantine period, see S. MacCormack, 'Christ and Empire, Time and Ceremonial in Sixth Century Byzantium and Beyond', *Byzantion* 52 (1982), 287-309.

Being a collection mainly of vision reports also of stories about miracles and orthodox steadfastness, the *Plerophories* stands somewhat on the literary borderline between hagiography and treatises on visions. The stage for the vast majority of the reports contained in the collection is set in the midst of the anti-Chalcedonian monastic milieu of the Eastern Empire, and in each story the protagonists are the most prominent of the ascetic fathers. Thus John Rufus presents his reports in a package of conventional hagiographic themes and concepts deeply rooted in Eastern monasticism. Yet the work clearly deviates from the narrative schemes of early Christian hagiography present also in anecdotal texts such as the *Historia Lausiaca* and the *Historia Monachorum* as regards the general focus of the work. Since the *Plerophories* is a collection of visions and miracles the attention is constantly focused on the message revealed in these. The content of the message revealed is more or less isolated from the pious receivers, who are only humble channels for God's communication of the orthodox truth.

What makes the *Plerophories* a coherent whole is the rhetorical use of stories about dreams, visions and other kinds of divine manifestations that reveal the truth. But what is it that turns these reports of visionary and miraculous manifestations into an efficient instrument for the creation of anti-Chalcedonian propaganda? On a superficial level, perhaps, it is merely the overuse of short anecdotes based on the same formal elements and presented through an pedagogy of excessive repetition of one single message—preserve the orthodox faith and stay away from the Chalcedonian heretics! Over and over this unambiguous message is dinned into the heads of the readers in order to provoke emotional response, since every single rhetorical figure rests on widespread expectations within Eastern monasticism, held by everyone to be incontrovertible proof of trustworthiness. However, for a more profound comprehension of the rhetoric of the visions reported in the *Plerophories* as representations of an anti-Chalcedonian worldview, it is necessary to observe these accounts from the perspective of their underlying ideological structures.

It should be remembered that reports of visionary experiences and other miraculous manifestations in John Rufus' works are not exclusive to the *Plerophories*. Such reports can be found also in his *Life of Peter the Iberian* and in the *Commemoration of the Death of*

Theodosius, though the only vision reported in the latter work is repeated almost verbatim in the *Plerophories*.[21] But in these texts stories of visions are always included as part of the general hagiographic presentation, forming integrated elements of the narratives about the holy protagonists, their ascetic struggles and their warfare against Chalcedonian heresy. Here vision reports are used mainly as evidence for God's constant presence in the earthly existence of the holy men. Yet it remains clear that the rhetorical use of stories of visions is a particularly important feature in John Rufus' authorship. For John, the main function of vision reports, as in the case of other reported miracles, is to demonstrate God's sovereign power. It is this divine power and some of its various aspects as represented in John Rufus' reports of visions and miracles that will be the focus in the subsequent discussion.

The Power over Time

In the *Plerophories* the most striking form of dreams and visionary experiences is that of prophetic visions that reveal the future. In most cases these clairvoyant experiences are received by distinguished ascetics, recognized by the community of readers as trustworthy witnesses of truth. Typical instances are provided early in the collection in the group of anecdotes dealing with the monk Pelagius of Edessa. From John we learn that this Pelagius had been forced to flee from his hometown as a result of his accusations of heresy made against Ibas of Edessa, and that he settled in Palestine at the time of the episcopate of Juvenal, before the Council of Chalcedon. John tells us further that Pelagius was a good friend of Peter the Iberian at Maiuma. During one of their meetings Pelagius is reported to have told Peter that in a vision he had seen the transgression at Chalcedon and the persecutions of the holy fathers brought about by Emperor Marcian—seven years before these events actually took place.[22]

In the next story we learn that Peter the Iberian, who in the company of some other holy men had gone to meet with Pelagius, found the old man weeping, repeating the name of Pulcheria, the sister of Theodosius II and Marcian's empress. The explanation given to Peter and his companions was that Pulcheria, who had

---

[21] *Narr. de ob. Theod.*, 24. See above, chapter 2, 95.
[22] *Pleroph.* 2.

promised her virginity to God, who engineered the banishment of Nestorius, and whom the monks of the East regarded as a saint, would eventually betray her faith and virginity, and even persecute the holy fathers. This vision was fulfilled later, John writes, when Pulcheria married Marcian and became his accessory, not only in government but also in unfaithfulness and sins.[23]

In the third anecdote we are informed that Pelagius, together with the deacon Pamphilus of Jerusalem, in order to pray used to walk the holy road of Golgotha while it was still night. One night it happened that Pelagius received a vision while he was praying, and as he burst into tears he repeated the name of Juvenal three times. When Pamphilus asked him what he had seen, the old man explained that Juvenal, the bishop of Jerusalem, who was now carried in triumph by the monks and the clergy, would be seen carried in triumph by demons and Roman soldiers.[24]

In the following fourth report of the prophetic visions of Pelagius of Edessa we learn that he also predicted Peter the Iberian's ordination as bishop. When Peter heard this prediction in the presence of his companion John the Eunuch, he was vexed, and reproached Pelagius for what he regarded as the senile driveling of an old man who had himself escaped ordination. Pelagius preserved his calm and assured that he knew what he was saying, adding the profoundly mysterious words: 'May he be troubled who is to be troubled'.[25]

This short series of anecdotes about the visionary experiences of Pelagius of Edessa concludes with a report containing some remarks on his orthodox mind. Here we learn that Pelagius constantly prayed to God that he would never transgress the orthodox faith or communicate with the Chalcedonian bishops, and that he, according to the literal wording of his prayers, died when staying in the house of an innkeeper at Ascalon. We are told that at the very moment of Pelagius' death Peter the Iberian saw him in a dream during his stay in Oxyrhynchus in Egypt, Pelagius asking for Peter's prayers, since he had now entered heaven. Further, we learn that that Pelagius' mother had been fasting for a whole week before giving birth to him, and that she was therefore

---

[23] *Pleroph.* 3.
[24] *Pleroph.* 4.
[25] *Pleroph.* 5.

elevated to holiness. John Rufus finally tells us that when Pelagius had reached mature age he interpreted the death of a certain honorable man in Edessa as a sign of the coming apostasy. From this moment on he decided to undertake a monastic life, eventually becoming a 'chosen vessel'.[26] Focusing on the interrelation between orthodoxy and ascetic life, these concluding notes about Pelagius of Edessa provide further arguments for his credibility as a channel of the spiritual communication through which the divine truth is announced to mankind. Rather than his prophetic gifts in themselves it is Pelagius' credibility as a perfect witness of truth, persistent in the orthodox faith and devoted to the ascetic call, that lends the stories about him their actual rhetorical power. Yet it is God and his divine message, foreboding the deceits to come and imposing unconditional zeal for the truth, that remain the center of the visions reported by Pelagius. Consequently, while the holy man himself is merely a mediator of this divine message, it is God who is the protagonist in the stories, since he possesses the ultimate power over time and grants his foreknowledge to his most beloved servants for the salvation of the faithful.

The section on Pelagius of Edessa is immediately followed by two similar accounts of the clairvoyant predictions of holy men against Chalcedon. In the first, John Rufus relates the words of the Alexandrine priest John of Beth Tatianā concerning one of the meetings he had in his youth with Abba Elladius, a distinguished monk and prophet at Kellia. Driven by an urge to withdraw from the world, he asked the old man whether or not God supported his wish to enter the monastic life. The abba advised him to follow his desire for a life in ascetic tranquility, and to strive for perfection, since the Church would soon be troubled by persecution. The old man then told John that there would arise an emperor named Marcian, who would incite the bishops to establish in writing that he who was crucified was not God. Only the bishop of Alexandria would refuse to subscribe to the opinions of this emperor, and therefore he would be sent into exile and be succeeded by an apostate. Since John was troubled by these words the abba went on to say that the apostate bishop of Alexandria would eventually be killed, whereupon God would send a priest as bishop of the orthodox. This bishop would be forced into exile, but would finally

---

[26] *Pleroph.* 6.

return and after a certain time be perfected in obedience to the orthodox faith. The old man was then silent, and John threw himself at his feet, asking him in vain to continue his report.[27] In the next story John Rufus tells how Abba Zeno of Kefar Se'arta, as he predicted the apostasy of Chalcedon, urged his disciples to go into voluntary exile because of the coming persecution and the rebellion of the heretics, while he locked himself up in his cell in utter solitude. There he stayed in sorrow and grief until he died, one year before the Council.[28]

From Abba Isaiah we hear the following account, received from Abba Paul of Thebais, about the future arrival of the Emperors Marcian and Leo:

> Twenty years from now a transgression will take place on behalf of the bishops that will result in the withdrawal of God, foretold by the Apostle. A wicked man will appear, an emperor named Marcian. This emperor will die after little more than six years. For a time there will be a deceiver in his place, and he will effect a certain degree of peace and calm in the churches. These events will be rolled up until the arrival of the Antichrist.[29]

To the same category of stories in the *Plerophories,* in which the testimonies against Chalcedon find expression through the clairvoyant gifts of holy men, belongs the account of the last words of Heliodorus, the hermit of the mountains of Taurus who for years lived with the brute beasts but spent his last years as the head of a monastery. As Heliodorus was about to depart from the earthly world, he gathered his disciples around him and predicted the transgression of the bishops at Chalcedon, twenty-four years before the Council. At the same time he instructed them to leave for Egypt and Palestine as soon as they experienced the beginnings of these troubles, to find support among the orthodox fathers dwelling there. Many years later the words of Heliodorus were recounted by one of these disciples to Peter the Iberian during his exile in Egypt.[30]

---

27 *Pleroph.* 7.
28 *Pleroph.* 8.
29 *Pleroph.* 12.
30 *Pleroph.* 31.

In some cases we meet with clairvoyant descriptions of specific historical events or individuals. From John Rufus we hear that during his visit in Egypt Peter the Iberian was troubled about Proterius' persecutions of orthodox monks. A holy man at Scetis named Potamon comforted him and said that he should not be worried, since God would put things right and that the 'sodomite and murderer' would finally be slain. John Rufus then ends the story with the remark that Proterius was killed three days later.[31]

In some stories the historical circumstances behind the reports is somewhat obscure. The Egyptian ascetic Abba Pior is said to have experienced a vision where he saw many monks struggling over a large cross, pulling it in opposite directions, a vision that announced the emergence of a controversy between Egyptian and Palestinian monks prevalent in John Rufus own time. The very same controversy was also predicted by Lucius, a monk at Kellia, who told his fellow-monks about a time when two men would claim to bear witness about Christ and the orthodox faith without communicating with one another.[32] What controversy John Rufus refers to is left untold, but possibly it is related to disagreements within the anti-Chalcedonian movement concerning the *Henotikon*. In such cases it is reasonable to suggest that it was this sort of vision reports that Severus of Antioch had in mind when attacking the use of dreams and visions as rhetorical devices for condemning the Egyptian patriarchate because of its acceptance of the *Henotikon*.[33]

As a final instance of the clairvoyant powers of holy men as a rhetorical means for opposing Chalcedon we consider the ironical account of Leontius of Ascalon. Before the Council, when Leontius was still a monk and an archimandrite, Abba Zeno said to him: 'You will become bishop but you will not die as a bishop'. Accordingly Leontius was eventually appointed bishop of Ascalon but proved full of hypocrisy, since he actively supported Nestorius and took part in the transgression of the faith at Chalcedon. At his return from the Council the inhabitants of Ascalon refused to accept him as their bishop and Leontius was forced to settle in Cyprus, where he died. Since his family wished that his earthly

---

[31] *Pleroph.* 34.
[32] *Pleroph.* 50. Cf. 51.
[33] See above, chapter 1, 72-73.

remains should be buried in his hometown, they arranged for his coffin to be loaded on a ship for transportation to Ascalon. However, on the same ship there was another coffin, which contained the remains of a chariot-driver from Constantinople. On the open sea the ship was suddenly struck by a storm, and forced to reduce the cargo the seamen threw into the waves the coffin they believed was the chariot-driver's but which was in fact the expelled bishop's. The mistake was not revealed until the members of Leontius' family opened the coffin to prepare the body for the funeral and dress it in episcopal vestments. Since it was immediately decided that the mistake should be kept secret, it was the chariot-driver who was buried in the tomb of Leontius. Hence the prediction of Abba Zeno was fulfilled, in accordance with God's rightful judgement.[34]

In this story the clairvoyant prediction is pushed into the background, while the story itself is turned into a cautionary tale about a heretic bishop who is justly deprived of his episcopal honors as the result of God's punishment. The vision and its message evidently play a subordinate role in relation to the subsequent events manifesting God's initiative and his punishment of the enemies of faith. In itself Abba Zeno's vision reveals only that God, who has power over time and space, delivers his preliminary judgement on a future apostasy. But the focus in the story about Leontius rests mainly on the execution of God's verdict through his immediate interference in the world that results in a tragicomic redress of divine justice.

Power over Nature

The emphasis on God's power in the *Plerophories* is evident not only in the reports about visions and dreams, but also through natural signs and miracles. Such are the group of signs related to John Rufus by a group of venerable old monks hiding in the monastery of Abba Romanus. At the time of the Council, we learn, the people of Palestine saw the sky darken, and stones that resembled building bricks rained down on earth. Many people gathered them up, but when they were used without judgement they caused blindness. Darkness is also said to have appeared in other parts of the Empire, and in Constantinople the population was so troubled that

---

[34] *Pleroph.* 52.

Marcian ordered the composition of a document where it was written that the darkness, which had originated during the reign of Theodosius (the emperor who condemned Nestorius), had now dispersed as a sign of the light of Marcian's reign. But to those with ears to hear and eyes to see, John writes, this document was nothing but a written confirmation of the fact that, following the transgression of the bishops at Chalcedon, God had left the world.[35] In the *Plerophories* the signs of transgression are particularly notable: in the church of the Holy Sepulcher in Jerusalem the great cross is suddenly consumed by fire and turned into ashes;[36] in Alexandria the host is found corrupted at the communion, and the wine turned into vinegar,[37] and at a baptism in Rhinocoroura the Holy Spirit flies away in the shape of a dove as a sign of the lost grace of the Churches.[38]

In another anecdote John Rufus gives an eyewitness account of what he experienced when, in the company of one of the citizens of Jerusalem who knew the surroundings, he was walking on the road from Jerusalem to Siloe. At the foot of a mountain he noticed a monastery that was dilapidated and overgrown. Since this was a region where there were many monks he was astonished, and asked his companion about the reason for this decay. His companion explained that Juvenal had once lived in this monastery, before the Council of Chalcedon. But as a result of Juvenal's treason against Dioscorus the monastery had been struck by the wrath of God and left to decay.[39] John Rufus also tells us about Theodore of Mopsuestia and his assumed denial of the authenticity of the Acts and the gospel of John. When Peter the Iberian and two Cilician monks protested against his blasphemous statements, Theodore replied that it was not for monks to meddle in such questions. Three days later Theodore died, consumed by a demon.[40]

Another example of signs revealing God's ultimate power over the physical world is found in the story about the monk Epiphanius of Aphta, who was arrested by the Chalcedonian priest

---

[35] *Pleroph.* 10.
[36] *Pleroph.* 11.
[37] *Pleroph.* 65bis.
[38] *Pleroph.* 75.
[39] *Pleroph.* 16.
[40] *Pleroph.* 45.

of that village and sentenced to be flogged the next day if he did not join him in communion. But the holy old man refused, saying: 'It is not possible for me to reject the faith I have received from the holy fathers'. During the night the old man prepared himself for the sufferings which he would endure in God's name, but the next day the priest was found dead, without any signs of disease. The people of the village were struck by fear, and immediately released the blessed Epiphanius.[41]

We also find reports in which Chalcedonians and anti-Chalcedonians as two conflicting parts leave the verdict in the hands of God, in the form of trials by fire. First we hear about a group of Pamphylian monks in dispute about the orthodox faith. To achieve a solution they threw the Encyclical and the *Tome* of Leo into a fire, whereupon it turned out that only the *Tome* was consumed by the flames. John ends with the note that the dyophysite monks then at once converted to orthodoxy.[42] Next there is a story that takes place in a village close to Ptolemais in Palestine. The village priest was once involved in a dispute with one of the villagers, who was not learned but nevertheless orthodox and zealous in his faith. This orthodox man was told by the priest to either change his views or leave the village. Since the sympathies of all the villagers were with this man, the priest suggested that they should both place their right hands over a fire to prove which of them was a combatant of the true faith. The orthodox villager accepted the suggestion, and the test was set up. While the priest's hand was severely burned, the hand of the orthodox villager was preserved without injuries.[43] What is particularly striking in this story is the opposition between a priest, being a heretic, and a simple but pious layman, who triumphantly overcomes the test. Once again we find the idea of ascetic humbleness as the true locus of orthodoxy, whereas the material glory of ecclesiastic offices is represented as the highway to evil passions and heresy.

---

[41] *Pleroph.* 48.

[42] *Pleroph.* 46.

[43] *Pleroph.* 47, 98-100. Cf. the story about Abba Copres and the Manichean in *HM* 10.30-32.

The Power of Judgement

It is thus clear that, for instance, the story about Leontius of Ascalon   not primarily deals with a holy man's clairvoyant knowledge about future apostasy, but with God as the ruler of time and space pronouncing his verdict on heretics long before their transgression of faith. This is the focus of a number of anecdotes in the *Plerophories*. In several cases we find God's preliminary verdict on heresy mediated through the mouths of holy men. For instance, we learn from one story that Juvenal, as he visited the monasteries situated around Jerusalem during Lent, arrived at a settlement of monks where he found an old and distinguished ascetic who immediately shut himself up in his cell when he saw the bishop approach. Accompanied by a number of clerics and townspeople Juvenal approached the cell and knocked on the door. As the door remained closed, Juvenal and his companions kept knocking until the cell was about to collapse. Then the holy man raised his voice and shouted: 'Go away, Antichrist! I will never let Antichrist enter my cell! The traitor Judas will not come in here!' These words embarrassed and enraged Juvenal's companions, while the bishop himself proclaimed loudly and clearly that the old man had obviously gone insane as a result of a too long ascetic life. However, in his own mind he knew that the old ascetic was a holy and godfearing man who was filled with spiritual grace and never spoke an unnecessary word.[44] A similar story is provided in the last anecdote in the *Plerophories*, where John Rufus tells us about the ascetic at the gate of the imperial palace in Antioch and the rage with which he received Johns' friend Nonnus, the bishop of Quennesrin. John was stupefied by the holy man's anger. But later, in the course of events, he understood the motives of the old man, namely that Nonnus would eventually join with Calendion, the Chalcedonian patriarch of Antioch.[45]

God's verdict on Juvenal is in focus also in the following anecdote, which concerns a young lector in the church of the sheep-gate, where Jesus had cured a crowd of invalids.[46] One evening before the Council he saw, on leaving the church after service, Jesus standing in company with the saints. When Jesus saw

---

[44] *Pleroph.* 17.
[45] *Pleroph.* 89.
[46] Matt 21.13.

that the candles in the church had been blown out, and that the sacred vessels had been put back negligently, he was angry and reproached Juvenal for having made his house into a robber's den and filled it with ungodliness. He then inspected the holy vessels in the vestry and instructed the saints who accompanied him to wash the vessels and put everything in its proper place. Seeing the lector draw back in fear, he ordered him harshly to leave at once. The lector then threw himself to the floor and begged for mercy, but Jesus answered: 'Go away! I do not know your deeds'. But as the lector kept begging for mercy, he ordered him to repent and not to repeat his negligence. As soon as Juvenal heard about this visionary experience, he ordered the lector to be dismissed in order to silent the reports of this divine condemnation. John Rufus ends the story with a note that a holy man in the Holy City took the vision as an evident sign that he should not receive communion from Juvenal's hands.[47] In this vision God's verdict on Juvenal, based on the evil state of the church of Jerusalem, is taken as an evident sign of Juvenal's future apostasy at Chalcedon.

The very same motif appears in a story of an immoral deacon in Jerusalem. Having been together with a woman after service in the church of Anastasis he went to sleep in his home on the Holy road. In bed behind closed doors he suddenly heard a voice condemning Juvenal for having filled the church with impurity and corruption. On the following morning the deacon was found at Golgotha, still asleep in his bed, and he became the object of much ridicule. When he woke up he repented, and in tears announced his shame in a way that aroused fear and amazement. Juvenal was filled with shame and excluded the deacon from service, since that man's immoral life was a sign of his own hypocrisy.[48]

As another example we hear that Peter the Iberian when, before the Council, he saw Juvenal's perversity and the heresy of many pilgrims, shut himself up in his cell and fell down before God in tears of mourning. Filled with the spirit of God, he said:

> What have I not done to save mankind? I created heaven and earth. I planted the Paradise, and I made the entire creation for the sake of your happiness. After Adam's sin I gave the law, I sent the patriarchs and the prophets. In order to persuade you I made a great

---

[47] *Pleroph.* 18.
[48] *Pleroph.* 41.

number of signs and wonders and, above all, I sent for
your my son who came among you, preached about the
kingdom of heaven, gave forgiveness for sins, fought
against your sickness, made the blind see and the
paralyzed walk, dispelled demons, was crucified and
died for you. Thereafter he conquered death and
departed from the tomb, confirmed the hope of the
resurrection, ascended to heaven, sending the Holy
Spirit, gave the apostles and evangelists their mission,
and overthrew the idols. In return for all this you have
insulted   me,   overthrown   my   law   and   my
commandments, and transgressed the faith. Look how
your home has become deserted.[49]

John Rufus concludes the story with a remark that for a long time
Peter expressed similar words of lament, until the Council of
Chalcedon.[50] Here we meet with the most evident illustration of
the anti-Chalcedonian holy man as merely a mouthpiece for God's
condemnation of the apostasy established at Chalcedon. Rather
than Peter the Iberian himself, it is God who is the ultimate subject
of this story, pronouncing his verdict on those who bring scandal
and heresy into the churches of Jerusalem. This sort of immediate
judgement upon the followers of Chalcedon from God through the
spiritual minds and eyes of holy men is also found in a story about
Paul of Ganta, who in a sublime vision saw all the people of the
earth gathered around a hill in a large field. On the hill a canopy
was erected with pillars of silver and gold, and beneath the canopy
an altar was placed, adorned with precious stones. In the ineffable
light flowing from the altar the old man saw a great number of the
saints celebrating communion, while from heaven a voice was
heard, condemning the proclaimers of the dyophysite teaching,
those who divided the one and indivisible Christ.[51]

One particularly good example of such judgmental visions is
the already discussed story on how Romanus of Tekoa received full
assurance of the heresy of Chalcedon.[52] As we remember, this story
proceeds from Romanus' refusal to base his judgement about the
validity of an imperial council on hearsay. Instead, the decision to
anathematize Chalcedon must come directly from God, and

---

[49] *Pleroph.* 19.
[50] *Pleroph.* 19.
[51] *Pleroph.* 20.
[52] *Pleroph.* 21.

Romanus therefore goes into the desert to pray to God and be guided by him. Apart from the verdict on Chalcedon delivered directly by God, the most striking feature in this story concerns the question of authority. The holy Council of Nicaea, like the orthodox fathers, could always be interpreted in favor of the wicked. Thus, to gain full assurance concerning the heresy of Chalcedon only a straight and clear verdict received straight from God was to be trusted. Since not even the great fathers of the church could provide certainty regarding the Council of Chalcedon, the only reliable form of confirmation was that which was delivered directly from heaven.

In John Rufus' works God manifests his holy powers especially at the places for Christ's passion, death, and resurrection, which the following story from the *Life of Peter the Iberian* shows. When Peter and John the Eunuch still rested in peace in the Holy City as young ascetics, John was once stricken by a malignant attack of ringworm on his face. Since John suffered from great pain and was ashamed to show himself to others, the two friends went one night to the church of the Holy Sepulcher and fell down at the holy place of Golgotha and prayed to the Lord for deliverance from the terrible disease. Suddenly John perceived something that resembled a hand reaching out from the rock of Golgotha, touching his face and cleaning it. Next morning John found himself cured from the disease.[53]

John then narrates a similar miracle that happened when John again was struck by serious illness that forced Peter to leave him isolated in his cell for the sake of his own health. At one moment as he lived for himself in grief and prayers, Peter heard a voice that announced that John was about to be cured and that he should not be afraid to return to him. At that moment John received his health as thick scales suddenly began to be repelled from all of his body, and his face completely restored. Peter immediately returned to his friend. As he had been cured from his disease, John's body was almost transformed to that of a newborn baby. He spoke with a blurred and unclear voice. Yet Peter asked him to celebrate the liturgy during the Easter, since both at that time had been ordained to the priesthood. When John declined, Peter explained that there was no need for him to speak with a loud voice since God would

---

[53] *V. Petr. Ib.*, 40–41.

hear the liturgical prayers in his heart. John was persuaded, and at the altar he suddenly was able to utter the blessing with a loud and clear voice and completed thus the Holy Communion. After that moment John would never fall into any disease again and remained eloquent for the rest of his earthly life.[54]

John Rufus then proceeds with an account of a vision that John the Eunuch perceived for three days without talking to anyone during that time:

> He saw the second magnificent and glorious coming of our Lord from heaven which suddenly opened, with sounding trumpets, earth quake and transformation, that is, change of the elements, and the universe was filled with lightning, boisterous turbulence, chaos and disorder. First came the angels and the first ranks of the celestial hosts; the angels, archangels, powers, principalities, dignities, the order of the Holy Apostles, the prophets, the martyrs, the righteous, Cherubim and Seraphim. After all these appeared the worshipped and saving cross of the Lord, and then the Lord himself, Savior and Messiah, carried and coming with the glory of the Father and with incomprehensible power, and the prepared thrones and the divine and mighty judgement, which since ages and many times has been proclaimed by the holy prophets and by the Ruler and Savior himself as a testimony to us. He saw only one single altar standing on earth, similar to that which still is preserved among us, and at which they both were serving. A great number of holy monks had gathered around it, each holding his own staff. And behold, suddenly the trumpets sounded and the elements trembled, and the saints were carried away on what appeared to be drifting clouds, away from the altar where they were standing, to meet our Lord. When he had seen this vision for three days and many other mysteries that a man cannot speak about, he was deeply troubled for thirty days after he had returned to himself, and he had no wish to speak to anyone, or rather, he could not. During that time, his thoughts were constantly in heaven and he did not believe that he lived on earth. His face, however, was the face of an

---

[54] *V. Petr. Ib.*, 41-42.

angel, and his appearance was something else than that
of a human being.[55]

This passage speaks, undoubtedly, of a mystical vision that clearly
reminds us about the mystagogy of Dionysius Areopagita. It is a
vision of Christ's triumphant descent from heaven together with
the entire hierarchy of heavenly hosts, centered on the Eucharistic
altar. Here the Christological mystery is gloriously revealed by
means of a theophany of power and light through which God's
presence in Christ is made evident. Through this essentially
Christocentric vision, it is affirmed that knowledge about the
mystery of the Incarnate Word will be obtained only at the altar of
the orthodox.[56]

In the focus of the stories about the visionary experiences of
John the Eunuch remains the emphasis on the ultimate power of
the Father and the glory of the Son. These supreme visions of
God's power and judgement are closely associated with worship
and liturgy, particularly at the very place of the Lord's passion and
death. Behind this we immediately see the theology behind the anti-
Chalcedonian formula: 'one of the Trinity has been crucified'.
Through these manifestations God reveals himself as utterly
transcendent, appearing as the judge of the world who proclaims
his anathema upon those who dare to deprive the Son of his
proper glory at the same time as he maintains his benevolent grace
over those gathered around the one true altar of anti-Chalcedonian
orthodoxy.

The Power of the Marginalized

During the very same night that Peter the Iberian gave up breath,
the Egyptian priest Athanasius perceived the following visions: he
saw a great church, filled with light and splendor, and in which
many saints had gathered around the earthly remains of Peter. At
the ambon stood Peter, the bishop of Alexandria who was
martyred in 311, dressed in a white and shiny stole, and addressed
an eulogy on the blessed Peter, while all the saints praised him with
words of rejoice. From this vision, the disciples of Peter realized
that his death had occurred on the third day of the

---

[55] *V. Petr. Ib.*, 42-43.

[56] Cf. A. Golitzin, "'A Contemplative and a Liturgist': Father Georges
Florovsky on the Corpus Dionysiacum', SVTQ 43 (1999), esp. 155-158.

commemoration of Peter of Alexandria that according to the Alexandrine custom was celebrated for three days.[57] Here John Rufus reveals his preference for linking his protagonists with the great leaders of the Egyptian church, not only by name but also by the day of their deaths.[58] But the connection made to Peter of Alexandria, the seal of the martyrs, also reveals an anti-Chalcedonian identity linked to the struggles of the holy martyrs against the ungodly powers of the world. To preserve the true faith and reject any compromise with unbelievers is to share the glorious call of martyrdom, thus taking part in the heavenly communion of the saints.

A handful of anecdotes in the *Plerophories* concern the problem of authority of the anti-Chalcedonian pioneers and leaders. In the story of the Egyptian monk Andrew, seeing in a vision the Chalcedonian bishops throwing Christ into a blazing furnace, and Dioscorus standing alone as the only one who refused to take part in their wicked deeds, the main argument is evidently that of divine legitimization.[59] While the bishops are described as tainted by the malady of the Jews, since they made an image of the incarnated God, Dioscorus comes forth as a guardian of the truth when, together with his successor Timothy Aelurus, he carries the cross of Christ as Simeon of Cyrene had done.

Sometimes the great protagonists of anti-Chalcedonian orthodoxy are legitimized through visions that announce or confirm their office as a mission received directly from God. One example is the story about how Timothy Aelurus, as a young schoolboy, one day met an old and venerable man who took him into his arms and said: 'Peace be with thee, Timothy, bishop of completion'.[60]

Another divine confirmation of the authority of the heroes of the anti-Chalcedonian resistance appears in a vision that Abba Isaiah received in his cell, and in which he saw the inhabited parts on earth covered with impurity. An angel descended from heaven carrying a spade which he gave to Peter the Iberian, instructing him

---

[57] *V. Petr. Ib.*, 135-136.

[58] *Narr. de ob. Theod.*, 24, 27, where Theodosius by days of commemoration is linked to the Apostle James, and Romanus to Peter the Iberian.

[59] *Pleroph.* 14.

[60] *Pleroph.* 15.

to purify the earth from the great stench, because that was what he had been told to do. Peter at first refused, pointing out the impossibility for any man to undertake such a mission. But the angel insisted, and Peter seized the spade to fulfill his mission as an orthodox bishop.[61] The protagonist is described as equipped with powers superior to those of ordinary men, taking up the part of Hercules cleaning the stable of Augias. But it is also taken for granted that such powers are always dependent on God's will. The mission received from God may be impossible to execute with human hands. Yet, since the spiritual powers of the elect derive from God alone, the fulfillment of the mission will be possible as long as it ultimately rests on God's initiative.

From the *Plerophories* we learn that the episcopal call derives entirely from God, as yet another way for God to communicate the verdict on Chalcedon to mankind, and to provide support to the faithful in times of persecution. In this way anti-Chalcedonian leadership implies the call to be a mirror of God's will, serving the community of believers with what comes from God alone. However, the call of the elect to be a mouthpiece of God is never limited to holders of ecclesiastical offices. Guiding the Christian community on the path of orthodoxy and clear-cut condemnation of the Chalcedonian faith is but one way to fulfill the divine mission on earth. As we have seen in many of the visions related, the mere testimony of a universal apostasy established in the world following Chalcedon is in itself a mission of divine origin. Though the vast majority of the visionary experiences in the *Plerophories*, foretelling or confirming the transgression of faith at the Council, are received by distinguished old men of ascetic prominence, God does not exclusively select holy men as channels for his message to mankind. In many anecdotes in the *Plerophories* it is manifested that God communicates his will through anyone he wants as a channel for his divine wisdom and judgement. He even lets the heretics themselves bring prophetic witnesses against themselves. In fact, we are told that Proterius in front of a saintly woman prophesied against himself, saying that he who would replace Dioscorus would be Antichrist.[62]

---

[61] *Pleroph.* 65.
[62] *Pleroph.* 69.

In another account we find that God does not exclude heretics from his gracious concern—he provides the non-orthodox, too, with visionary experiences that elucidate the true faith. We hear about a certain scholastic named Anianus, who lived with his wife in Constantinople. Anianus himself was a non-Chalcedonian who had received baptism from the hands of Peter the Iberian in Alexandria. His wife, however, still confessed the faith of the Chalcedonians, though she possessed many virtuous qualities. One day she was struck with a serious disease, but when she was about to die she had a vision in which she was led by angels on a dark road where she could hear the despairing voices of the damned. Thereafter she was led on a road of light, joy, and glory, and the angels spoke to her: 'Behold those with whom your husband is joined, while the others were joined with the bishops who approved the Council of Chalcedon'. After this vision she became orthodox, we are told, and died in perfection at the end of the same year.[63]

Several stories in the *Plerophories* concern women who appear as witnesses for the truth. For instance, we hear about Zoë in Pamphylia, who reproached Claudius, the bishop of Attaleia, for having signed the *anti-Encyclical*. When the bishop explained that he had signed with his hand but not with his spirit or with his heart, the holy woman responded: 'In what manner it is possible for the hand to move if the spirit has not already wanted it and caused it to do so. Can a dead man move? In the same way the hand cannot move without the spirit'.[64] Further, John describes a vision received by the Alexandrine woman Agathoclea, who after the withdrawal of Emperor Basiliscus' *Encyclical* did not know what to do regarding the communion. Having prayed to God for certainty, she had a vision in which she saw a large church with two altars. One was large but dark and bare, and in front of it a well-known Chalcedonian bishop was celebrating the Eucharist. The other was small, but adorned with gold and precious stones, and in front of it a little child was celebrating the Eucharist. She recognized the child as the Lord, who said to her: 'Receive communion from this altar'. At once, John explains in the end of the anecdote, she rejected communion with the dyophysites, and in her life as well as in her

---

63 *Pleroph.* 38.
64 *Pleroph.* 82.

faith she manifested herself as a true and brilliant model of orthodoxy.[65] The argument is based on the strongly polarized choice between receiving communion at the dyophysite altar, cold and bare, or at the orthodox altar, shining with the light of divine glory. The dyophysite altar is represented by a well-known bishop whose name is not revealed. This bishop is opposed to the Lord, who appears as a child with all the connotations of purity and sinlessness. In this way it is easy to recognize the opposition between the divine and orthodox untaintedness on the one hand and the sinful attachment to institutionalized forms of power on the other. Again the often-expressed connection between heresy and attachment to the material world is made evident.

We remember the same polarization as a fundamental theme in the story about Abba Andrews' visionary experience of Dioscorus' refusal to participate in the burning of Christ in the Chalcedonian furnace of heresy. Here the errors of the majority of the bishops are set against the Alexandrine patriarch, represented as a humble old man carrying the cross of Christ The heresy of the majority is here placed in immediate opposition to the purity of a minority who are ardently struggling for their faith unto death. The same opposition between ascetic humility and worldly power is also found in the frankness of certain holy men as they confront the heretics. For example, we hear about a certain servant of Christ named John, who was an *officialis comitis* in Alexandria. He was one day involved in a discussion about the Holy Virgin with his *comes*, who had joined the party of the Nestorians in Syria, and he asked the comes: 'Do you believe that the Holy Virgin is the mother of God?' The comes responded that he believed that the Holy Virgin was the mother of God and the mother of Christ as well, whereupon John asked: 'So then, has she given birth to one or two?' The *comes* was left speechless.[66]

These stories highlight what seems to be one of the main themes in the *Plerophories*, namely the vision of the world as profoundly divided between orthodoxy on the one hand, represented with all connotations of humbleness and purity, and heresy on the other, as an inherent part of the world of the wealthy and powerful. In the *Plerophories* we can identify a strong

---

[65] *Pleroph.* 86. For other examples, see 70-71, 73.
[66] *Pleroph.* 62. Cf. 61, 63.

polarization between emperors and patriarchs on the one side, monks, lay people and women on the other, that reflects a view of worldly power as clearly opposed to monastic purity when taken as something more than an instrument for the preservation of the apostolic faith. Ecclesiastical dignitaries such as Juvenal are constantly brought forth as examples of the corruptibility that followed when faith was rejected in favor of material positions. Thus the anti-Chalcedonian world vision appears before us as a story of the constant struggles of a marginalized and humble crowd with the worldly authority that leads the majority into the evils of heresy.

Conclusion

To understand how the use of visions, dreams, and miracles in the Early Byzantine world as legitimate arguments in doctrinal disputes, we must realize that, even in the pre-Christian past, such manifestations were recognized as means by which supernatural powers communicated with man. The Christianity of Late Antiquity had not changed the general view of the relation between the natural and the supernatural, the world of heaven and the world of history. The Christian God had defeated the gods and powers of pre-Christian religion, but the way in which he made his will known among men had not changed. The role of the priests of the old religions in interpreting the messages sent out from the supernatural world to guide ordinary men had been taken over by the late antique holy man, who served as God's ambassador on earth. To the Christians of the Byzantine Middle East the idea of the holy man as a mediator between heaven and earth was an integral part of their cultural consciousness. Through the ascetic fathers, it was believed, God made known his approval or discontent with the affairs of men, particularly in times when the purity of the divine truth was endangered. In such times of apostasy, when the Trinitarian faith was replaced by a blasphemous idea of Christ as merely a man, God did not remain silent but repeated, through signs and visionary experiences given to his most beloved servants, his demand for the ultimate obedience towards the divine truth. This is the fundamental theme of almost every story in John Rufus' *Plerophories*.

The perspective of our discussion of the visions and miracles related in the *Plerophories* has rested on a consideration of the stories in the collection as manifesting different aspects of divine power. From this perspective it has been proved that John Rufus does not use his stories of visions and signs primarily to emphasize the divine power of holy men and their zeal for the orthodox faith. The essential purpose of these stories is the truth itself, as expressed through a divine language of power. Thus the holy men, as receivers of these divine manifestations, fade into the background and join a diverse crowd of protagonists that includes venerable ascetics, simple priests and deacons, intellectuals, and women. These are the protagonists of the *Plerophories*, all vehicles for God's message to man about the necessity of remaining firm in the orthodox faith. However, as every word from the mouths of the protagonists that testifies about the heresy of Chalcedon, is simply God's own word, God remains the ultimate subject of every story in the collection.

5   THE IMAGE OF THE ENEMIES

The Hagiographic role of Heretics

It is sometimes said that a good story needs a villain. The introduction of any kind of danger into a story is one of the most basic narrative devices to attract the reader's attention. This is an aspect that we cannot afford to neglect when considering late antique expressions of Christian hagiography. If there were no villains in the *Life of Antony*—whether demons, wild animals or heretics—the text would never have caused such commotion in the spiritual life of the late antique world as it did. In fact, the text would probably have fallen completely flat.

The descriptions of the demons and their attacks are undoubtedly the best-known feature in the *Life of Antony*, and have enjoyed a splendid reception in art as well as literature. Perhaps it was these descriptions of the demons and their temptations, which form the core of the ascetic theology presented in the *Life*, that led to the rapid spread of the text all over the Empire. But except for the demons there are in the *Life of Antony* another set of villains, i.e. the Arian heretics, whose assaults on and violations of the truth are described in a series of passages in the second part of the work. These passages have even prompted the suggestion that the *Life* was composed as a polemical pamphlet directed against the Arians.[1] However daring such suggestions may be it is true that Antony appears in the biography as a zealous anti-Arian, in his theology as well as in his life. About the Arians we are told that they were the precursors of Antichrist and that their teaching was worse than the venom of serpents. Full with repugnance against

---

[1] This argument was set out by R. C. Gregg and D. E. Groh, *Early Arianism: a View of Salvation* (Philadelphia 1981), 131-159.

143

them the old man exhorted everyone to avoid consorting with them, nor be attracted to their malicious beliefs.[2]

Anti-Arianism is surely a striking feature of the *Life of Antony*. But the anti-Arian harangues in the text cannot alone provide sufficient evidence that the biography was composed exclusively as a polemical weapon against the Arians. It should further be noticed that Arianism, according to Athanasius, was not Antony's sole target in his faith and zeal for orthodoxy:

> He did not have anything to do with the Meletian schismatics, because he knew their original evil and apostasy. Nor did he have any friendly connections with the Manichaeans and some other heretics, except that he exhorted them to convert themselves into the true faith. He thought and taught that friendly association with them was detrimental and pernicious to the soul.[3]

In the light of early monastic hagiography it is clear that the primary intention of introducing heretics in a text was not to denounce a specific heresy of the day but to confirm the personal authority of one or several holy men. The portrayal of a holy man as an adversary of heretics and a defender of orthodoxy was an integral part of the process of transforming him into a myth in the service of the Church. As literary devices, heretics served the same rhetorical purpose as pagans, demons, wild animals, diseases, etc., namely as instruments through which the authority of the holy man was manifested. Faced with these worldly powers, the virtues and charismatic powers of the holy men became signs of the divine presence in a world dominated by corruptibility and evil powers.

Thus, monastic stories about confrontations between heretics and holy men—as well as stories of healings, miracles, and other charismatic activities—were intended primarily to point out how God acts through the hands of men with ascetic authority. Stories dealing with different kinds of heretics and heresies are a constant theme in early hagiographic literature, even if the number of such stories varies considerably from one work to another. In some cases the purpose of the stories is to reveal the sharp-

---

[2] *V. Ant.* 68-69, 81-82. In spite of the differences between the Antony of the Life and the Antony of the Letters, he appears in both works as an ardent anti-Arian. See Rubenson, *The Letters of St. Antony*, 140-141.

[3] *V. Ant.* 68.

wittedness of the holy man and his eloquence. In the *Historia Religiosa*, for example, we are told how the great Aphrahat used the words of God to confront the arguments of the heretics and the syllogistic traps of the philosophers.[4] We also remember that it was with words of divine inspiration directed against the Arians that Antony made such an impression on the people of Alexandria, Christian laymen as well as pagan priests, that people flocked to him to be cured from demons and diseases by this 'man of God'.[5] But heretics are rejected not only through the words spoken by the holy man, but also through miracles serving as signs of God's divine judgement. We have, for instance, the story in the *Historia Monachorum* about Abba Copres, who found himself unable to change the mind of a Manichaean and therefore set out a test. Each of them would walk through a fire, so that it would be proved that the man who was unharmed by the flames also possessed the true faith. When Abba Copres stepped into the fire the flames parted so that the fire did not harm him, while the Manichaean was severely burned and driven away in disgrace by a furious mob.[6] Other miracles also occur as arguments of persuasion. For instance, Palladius relates that rumors circulated in Egypt that the great Macarius had brought a dead person back to life to convince a heretic who rejected the resurrection of the body.[7]

Keeping in mind the narrative structures of early monastic hagiography we find no differences between these examples and other stories dealing with expulsions of demons, cures of the diseased and the taming of wild animals. All of these stories seem to be built on a common, fairly uncomplicated pattern: the Abba is confronted with some kind of danger or crisis directed against himself, against his neighbors, or against the Christian community, and uses his charismatic or spiritual abilities in order to bring about victory. In fact, the holy man is never defeated in the critical moment. Nothing can impede the spiritual powers of the holy man in his struggles. Heretics appear one after the other, in the same way as the demons and other evil powers, extremely vulnerable in contests with holy men. The inevitable result of this vulnerability is the definitive defeat of the heretics, either in the form of disgrace,

---

[4] *HR* 8.2.
[5] *V. Ant.* 70.
[6] *HM* 10.30-2.
[7] *HL* 17.11.

as was the case with the burnt Manichaean, or in gruesome
torments followed by death, the destiny of many notorious
heretics.[8]

The heretic in early hagiographic literature was characterized
as a human representation of demonic powers, determined to
ensnare and deceive the simple and turn them away from the
appropriate aims of life. Only an ascetic master, trained to
withstand the conspiracies of the demons, was able to win the
spiritual battles against the heretics. Hence the maintenance of the
faith of the fathers was profoundly connected with the ascetic
labors of gaining independence of worldly matters and control of
one's thoughts. In other words, resisting external enemies and
resisting those within were simply two different aspects of the same
spiritual struggle. As one of the powers of this world heresy was
considered to cause severe damage to the spiritual health of the
ascetic.[9] Therefore it was repeated, again and again, within the
monastic circles, that contact with heretic in any form was to be
avoided, except in situations of exhortation and reproach. To
maintain associations with heretics was the same as turning to the
world of the material. But sometimes the hagiographers saw the sin
of worldly attention as directly inherent in the beliefs of the
heretics. For example, Arianism was considered blasphemous
because of its alleged degradation of the Son of God into the realm
of the created, and as a result the Arians were regarded as no better
than pagans in their worship of created things.[10]

Within early monastic culture the heretic was characterized by
his fundamental offence against the faith that had been transmitted
to him by the fathers. Behind this characterization of the heretic we
recognize the basic features of the ascetic concept of authority that
had developed in Eastern monasticism. The teaching of the heretic
was teaching without tradition. Heresy was demonic imagination
(*phantasia*), a result of the failure or refusal to maintain the essential
principle of true discipleship under the ascetic fathers. To depart
from their faith was to leave the desert in search of worldly
pleasures, power or wealth. These were the temptations of the
bishops, and many were those monks who on being ordained as

---

[8] See e.g. *V. Ant.* 86.
[9] Cf. *V. Ant.* 82, 348-349, where the teaching of the Arians is
explained to be caused by the plots of the demons and the devil.
[10] See *i.a. HR* 1.10.

bishops found their ascetic strength grow weaker.[11] Some found it better, when urged to receive ordination, to mutilate themselves rather than to leave the desert for worldly affairs.[12] However, to others the temptations of power and wealth were said to have been too great. Many in the Eastern Empire in the fifth century believed that it was through such men, having fallen under the yoke of the world and hence become easy targets for anti-Trinitarian views, that heresy had been established in the world at Chalcedon in 451.

The Heresy of Chalcedon

At the heart of anti-Chalcedonianism was the conviction that the Chalcedonian bishops, by their condemnation of Dioscorus and their approval of the dyophysitic teaching of Pope Leo, had proved themselves true disciples of Nestorius. The fact that the supposed connection between the teachings of Nestorius and the Christological formula set up at Chalcedon formed the main argument of the anti-Chalcedonians against the Council is evident even from the biographies of Cyril of Scythopolis.[13] In John Rufus' works the conviction that Chalcedon basically implied a rehabilitation of Nestorianism, is clearly marked in the very first anecdote of the *Plerophories*. In this story, which clearly sets the tone of the work, we are told about the demoniacal spasms that struck Nestorius when he in a sermon in the Church of Holy Mary had dared to deny the Blessed Mother her position as the Theotokos.[14]

In addition to this opening story, there are three other anecdotes in the *Plerophories* where Nestorius himself plays an essential part. All of them are incorporated in a group of anecdotes enclosed in an account of an auditory revelation on the death of Emperor Theodosius II,[15] during whose reign Nestorius was condemned, and by the report of the Trinitarian vision of Peter the Iberian.[16] The thematic continuity of this group is broken only by a story of a prophecy about the death of Proterius.[17] The first story is an account of the sudden death of Nestorius during his exile in

---

[11] Cf. *AP* Aphy 1.
[12] Cf. *HL* 11.
[13] *V. Euthym.*, 42. *V. Sab.*, 143, 146.
[14] *Pleroph.* 1.
[15] *Pleroph.* 32.
[16] *Pleroph.* 37.
[17] *Pleroph.* 34.

Thebais, as it was experienced by a member of the Alexandrian aristocracy who had heard him confirm his denial of Christ as God and the Holy Virgin as Theotokos. To this story John has added a short note, which is said to be from taken from the lost *Church History* of Timothy Aelurus, that the dead body of Nestorius was rejected three times by the earth before it was at last immured in a wall.[18] Next, after the story about the death of Proterius, John tells about the events leading up to the summoning of the Council of Ephesus and the condemnation of Nestorius. He focuses on the fortunes of the venerable Antiochene deacon Basil. Commanded by God to go to Constantinople to oppose Nestorius' blasphemies, this Basil entered the church where Nestorius was preaching and exclaimed: 'Be orthodox, bishop! Your teaching is bad! Why do you oppose the teaching of the fathers?' When he then publicly protested against the indulgence of the Emperor Theodosius towards Nestorius, the imperial *magister* intervened, arrested Basil and sentenced him to exile. But in the night, the Emperor was almost killed by a stone that fell on him. He then saw a stranger who told him that his sufferings were caused by his disobeying Basil. The very next day the Emperor visited Basil and asked him what he should do to please him, and the holy man urged him to summon a council, in order to anathematize Nestorius.[19] In the next anecdote we hear of Eliana, a holy woman who was told by an angel of the future ordination of Nestorius to the patriarchal throne in Constantinople, and she was exhorted not to receive communion from his hands. The anecdote ends with a long extract from the *Historia ecclesiastica* by Timothy Aelurus on Nestorius' exile and death.[20]

There are also numerous stories in the *Plerophories* in which Nestorius in a more indirect way appears as the mastermind behind the decisions established by the Chalcedonian bishops. One is the story about Leontius of Ascalon, who was expelled from his bishopric by the people of Ascalon because of his support of Nestorius after the latter had been condemned at the Council of Ephesus. In another story Juvenal is revealed as the man through whom Nestorius had gained new life.[21] Further, several times the

---

[18] *Pleroph.* 33.
[19] *Pleroph.* 35.
[20] *Pleroph.* 36.
[21] *Pleroph.* 40.

link between Chalcedon and Nestorius is shown by the use of the term 'Nestorians' as synonymous with the adherents of the Council of Chalcedon.[22] But the connection between Nestorius and Chalcedon is even clearer in one of the homiletic passages, where the decisions at Chalcedon are declared to have been the result of a severe inconsistency regarding the condemnation of Nestorius at Ephesus. With the words of Paul, 'If I build up again the very things that I once tore down, then I demonstrate that I am a transgressor' (Gal 2:18), John argues that the bishops at Chalcedon transgressed not only the orthodox faith but also the canonical decree established by the three hundred and eighteen fathers at Nicaea which prohibited the establishment of any confession and faith which did not accord with previous settled decrees. According to John, therefore, the Council of Chalcedon was not only unorthodox but also uncanonical.[23]

John's fundamental concern was to attack Chalcedon because of its rehabilitation of the enemies of the great Cyril, the defender of the true faith against Nestorius, the new Judas, who beside the Father worshipped two sons. This asserted kinship between Chalcedon and Nestorius was far more than a rhetorical device or an instrument of ideological manipulation; above all it reflected the general conception among the anti-Chalcedonians, that Chalcedon, following the wicked faith of Nestorius, denied the hypostatic unity of the Word, thereby not only failing to acknowledge the full divinity of the Son, but also dividing the Son, as one hypostase of the Godhead, into two sons.

Since it was assumed that the bishops at Chalcedon had accepted Nestorius' division of the Son into two parts, it seemed that the Council had also supported the Nestorian belief in God's impassibility in the person of Christ. The question whether Christ had suffered in the flesh simply as a man or as God had been one of the key elements in the controversy between Cyril and Nestorius. In his opposition against Nestorius, Cyril stressed the inability of God, the Word, to be subjected to human sufferings in his own nature. But since the Word, incapable of suffering, hypostatically united flesh to himself and became man it was,

---

[22] *Pleroph.* 14, 62, and 88. Martyrius, patriarch of Antioch in 458-469, is mentioned by John as 'Nestorian and bishop', *Pleroph.* 89.

[23] *Pleroph.* 59.

according to Cyril, proper to state that he suffered in this flesh. Consequently, through this hypostatical unity the Word was able to undergo all kinds of human suffering, as long as it was stated that this was experienced in human flesh and blood. To Cyril Christ was one and unique, and without the preservation of the hypostatic unity it was inevitable that one would fall into the fallacy of speaking of two sons.[24] Now, as Severus noted,[25] there was no mention of a hypostatic union in the so-called *Tome* of Pope Leo. Instead, Leo emphasized that after the union into one person the two natures preserved their own properties without any defect, the divinity equal and consubstantial to the Father and the humanity subordinated to the Father. In this way it was not in his divine nature that the Word of God was crucified and buried, but in the weakness of his human nature.[26] To anti-Chalcedonian theologians this notion of the distinct and maintained properties of the divine and human natures in the incarnated Word implied a radical break with the hypostatic union in Cyril's theology. Once the indivisible Word of God had been divided into a duality of two sons, one glorified as God and another one who suffered death on the cross. Instead of a Triad of hypostases in the Godhead, Timothy Aelurus complained, a Tetrad had been introduced, in which the body of Christ was consubstantial with the Word but at the same time different from the Word, just as the Son was consubstantial with the Father without being the Father.[27] This was Nestorianism,

---

[24] Cyril of Alexandria, *Ep. ad Nestorium* [second], PG 77, 47-50. Here it is worth noticing that much of Cyril's objections against Nestorius was focused on what he believed to be an importunate materialistic conception of the mystery of incarnation, see S. Wessel, 'Nestorius, Mary and Controversy, in Cyril of Alexandria's Homily IV', *AHC* 31 (1999), 1-49.

[25] Severus of Antioch, *Liber contra impium grammaticum* 3.1.3, ed. and tr. by J. Lebon, CSCO, Script Syri 4.5, 20-22. Cf. V. C. Samuel, *The Council of Chalcedon Re-examined* (Madras 1977), 198-199.

[26] Leo, *Ep. ad Flavianum* (ep. 28), 767-768.

[27] Timothy Aelurus, *Ep. ad Epictetum*, 30[b], 334. For the arguments of Severus of Antioch against the *Tome* of Leo, see *Ep. ad Oecumenium* 1, ed. and tr. by Brooks, in *A Collection of Letters*, PO 12.2, 180-181: 'But we must anathematize those who confine the one Christ in two natures and say that each of the natures performs its own acts'. Here it must be noted, that the anti-Chalcedonians, just as Cyril of Alexandria, used the terms *physis* (*kyānā*), *hypostasis* (*qnūmā*), and *prosopon* (*parṣūpā*) synonymously, see

hence a blasphemous refutation of the orthodox faith of the consubstantial Trinity.

In the early history of non-Chalcedonianism this assumption found a clear expression in the addition of the words 'who was crucified for us' to the *Trisagion* during the patriarchate of Peter the Fuller.[28] In the eyes of the Chalcedonians this addition was evidence of a tendency among the anti-Chalcedonians towards Patripassianism, and the attribution of the death on the cross of the Son to God the Father.[29] In the light of the *Plerophories*, where his own Christological views are given their clearest expression, John Rufus shows himself aware of such accusations of heresy, perhaps also of the risk that his own brothers in faith could interpret this addition in a way that revived the ancient heresy of Sabellius. Christ must, according to the holy fathers, be confessed as the incarnated Word of God, the second hypostasis of the Trinity, consubstantial with the Father and with mankind. This is reflected in a vision received by Peter the Iberian in which the mystery of the holy Trinity was manifested to him by the Apostle Peter. The Apostle had shown him three great spheres of profound and mysterious light, completely inaccessible, incomprehensible, and unintelligible, except for the second sphere where the Savior appeared 'with the traits of a Nazarene'.[30] Together the three spheres were one essence, one nature, one glory, one might, one light, and one divinity, but three hypostases. And since the second hypostasis was represented as concrete manhood, it was evident that he who suffered and died on the cross was neither the Father nor the Holy

---

Lebon, *Le Monophysisme sévérien*, 252: 'Nous pensons donc qu'en donnant aux termes nature, hypostase et même personne, un sens equivalent, les auteurs monophysites restaient en conformité de language avec leurs prédécessurs alexandrins'.

[28] See Severus of Antioch, *Hom.* 125, *Cathedral Homilies*, ed. and tr. by M. Brière, PO 29.1, 248: 'There is a reason for which this has been added to the doxology, which oppose the Jewish madness of Nestorius and which in this way is chanted in the holy churches of God'.

[29] The matters of controversy is reflected by Severus of Antioch, *Hom.* 125, 244. 'It is thus an absolute necessity because of the unfaithful to say that we rise up this doxology to the Son. In fact, the Father and the Holy Spirit are never in humanity, nor in weakness, or in death'. See also Frend, *The Rise of the Monophysite Movement*, 168.

[30] *Pleroph.* 37.

Spirit, but Christ as one of the hypostases of the Trinity. Obviously, this vision reflects the *Trisagion* controversy and the arguments used by anti-Chalcedonians against alleged accusations of heresy. Hence, John defends the anti-Chalcedonian orthodoxy not only by explaining the Word as a distinct constituent of the Godhead, but also by stressing the humanity of Christ without, however, separating him from the one indivisible Godhead.[31]

One of the main objections among the anti-Chalcedonians against Leo's Christology was, as has already been noted, that it seemed to imply that the properties of each nature after the union were preserved in a way that fixed the independence of the two natures, so that a fourth hypostase appeared to have been introduced in the Trinity.[32] But instead of acknowledging the independent status of the humanity and divinity of Christ, the anti-Chalcedonian theologians stressed, in accordance with Cyrillian concepts, that through the hypostatic unity God, the Word, had made the human body his own, and that consequently the human property could only be seen as the property of the Word. Through the human body the Word was made visible in such a way that the body partakes in the divine glory in the same way as the Word partakes in the conditions of human existence. Accordingly, Severus wrote, the Word, in order to manifest his own humanity, experienced hunger, just as he was tired after a journey and was subject to other bodily weaknesses, except that he did not fall under sin.[33] Thus the humanity of Christ is never to be separated as a property independent of his divinity. The humanity and divinity of Christ is not confused but mixed (in the Cyrillian and Cappadocian sense)[34] into an intimate union implying that the suffering and death of the humanity of Christ was hypostatically the suffering and death of the Word. In the *Plerophories* this key element of anti-Chalcedonian doctrine is most obviously reflected

---

[31] The dependence of the tradition from the Cappadocians is here particularly evident. For the importance of the Trinitarian concept of the Cappadocians for the arguments of the anti-Chalcedonians in the *Trishagion* controversy, see Severus of Antioch, *Hom.* 125, 238-40.

[32] The matter is discussed in Lebon, *La Christologie du monophysisme syrien*, 433-442.

[33] Severus of Antioch, *Ep. ad Oecumenium* 1, PO 12.2, 183-185.

[34] Lebon regards the anti-Chalcedonians as terminological traditionalists, see *La Christologie du monophysisme syrien*, 444, 578-579.

in John's report of the words uttered by a holy man to Emperor
Marcian:[35]

> I was close to Christ and I went with him everywhere
> when he made signs, healed, and taught; when he was
> insulted and persecuted; when he was arrested, flogged,
> crucified, and crushed with pains; when he was buried,
> resurrected; when he ascended to heaven and sat down
> on the right side of the Father. I was with him all the
> time, and him whom I have seen teach, heal, and raise
> the dead, I have also seen tired, crying, hungry, thirsty,
> and helping others in their suffering. I never saw two in
> him, one and another, but I saw the incarnated Word
> of God, always one and the same, performing different
> acts, in suffering as well as in glory, to be but one single
> nature.

This forceful passage is perhaps one of the best illustrations of the
faith of ordinary anti-Chalcedonians in the Roman East in the fifth
and sixth centuries. Here the uniqueness of Christ is put forward in
rejection of the doctrine of two independent constituents after the
union, without neglecting the full integrity of his humanity and
without introducing confusion into the hypostatical union.

In John Rufus' works dogmatic statements are rare, and
although it is possible to distinguish a specific doctrinal content
underlying the text it is evident that the main purpose of the work
was not to provide any explicit theological expressions as
arguments directed against the Chalcedonians. But in the last
chapter, which opens with an anecdote about the apostate bishop
Nonnus of Quennesrin and then turns into a lengthy sermon
against Chalcedon, we find another passage that reveals the
foundation of anti-Chalcedonian doctrine. That it is not

---

[35] John Rufus, *Pleroph.* 61. Perhaps the contrastive parallelism with the
words in Leo's *Tome* is intended, see *Ep. ad Flavianum* (ep 28), 769-770:
'To hunger, to thirst, to grow tired, and to sleep: these are evidently
human. But to satisfy five thousand men with five loaves of bread and to
give the Samaritan woman living water, a drink which frees the one
drinking from further thirst, to walk on top of the sea without sinking,
and to calm the waves stirred up by a storm, are doubtless the work of
God'. A corresponding passage is also cited by Severus of Antioch as
words from Cyril, *Ep. ad Oecumenium* 1, PO 12.2, 184-5.

appropriate to confess two sons, two persons, two Christs, or two natures, John says, was stated quite clearly by the holy fathers, who also confirmed the truth and fullness of the Incarnation. Therefore, as they rejected the heretics, they did not allow the acceptance of the two natures after the union, nor that the words uttered by the celebrant at the holy Eucharist were reduced to 'the body of Christ'. Instead, the wording ought to be 'the body of God the Word' or 'the body of Christ and our savior, the Word of God'. To confine oneself, as one of the priests in Antioch did during Martyrius' patriarchate, to the words 'the body of righteousness' when delivering the holy Eucharist, we learn, is the same as spurning the Son of God, profaning the blood of the covenant, and outraging the spirit of Grace (cf. Heb 10:29).[36] Here the well-known elements of anti-Chalcedonian theology are presented not as a demonstration of doctrinal positions but as rhetorical figures wedged in between lengthy harangues of biblical quotations.

John Rufus' discussion in the last chapter of the *Plerophories* on proper and non-proper expressions for confessing the mystery of the Incarnation reveals a further aspect of the anti-Chalcedonian mind that brings us closer to the essential motives behind the controversy. As John here sorts out incorrect expressions of faith, and favors the use of expressions with connections to Trinitarian orthodoxy, his concern is evidently not theological theory but liturgical practice, particularly in reference to the celebration of the holy Eucharist. Against the background of Timothy Aelurus' and Severus acceptance of at least a theoretical distinction between the divine and human properties after the Incarnation, it becomes clear that their condemnation of Chalcedon was in no way based on theological theory. From John Rufus' expositions it is obvious that the Chalcedonian controversy was not a matter of theory but one of practical veneration of the true divinity of the Word in the liturgical celebration of the Eucharist. Celebration of the Eucharist was the true moment of confession, the moment of mystery when believers found themselves placed face to face with the divine truth. The mere veneration of the human properties of the incarnated, for instance by the words 'the body of righteousness', would in that situation be not only senseless but in fact blasphemy against the mystery of the Eucharist.

---

[36] *Pleroph.* 89.

It is the basic assumption of this study, that John Rufus' three hagiographical works, the *Plerophories* not least, confirm the underlying theological concerns behind the resistance against the Council of Chalcedon. They do not present any new aspects on the anti-Chalcedonian theology and the doctrinal motives underlying the resistance against Chalcedon. Theologically the works should not be considered as anything but a mere repetition of the basic elements of early anti-Chalcedonian theology, for instance as they are found in the works of Severus of Antioch. On the contrary it might be said that John Rufus' works are marked by a profound lack of theological creativity, revealed not least in the reduction of the traditional Cyrillian and anti-Nestorian terminology and thought into axioms of persuasive discourse in the form of hagiographic literature. This of course radically separates John Rufus' texts from the works of contemporary and creative theologians such as Severus of Antioch. But at the same time it must be stressed that it was never the purpose of John Rufus to devise theological arguments for the superiority of the orthodox faith. Rather, his works were composed to provide, by means of a series of short hagiographic anecdotes, tangible proofs for God's verdict on Chalcedon as it was mediated through the words and deeds of holy men. Through these stories the holy mediators of God's verdict provided behavioral patterns for a group of anti-Chalcedonians in Palestine who were constantly confronted with the disturbing problem of maintaining orthodoxy while living in a region swarming with Chalcedonian heretics. The message of John Rufus' works are evident and constantly repeated: Be orthodox and do not mix with heretics in any respect, since God has proclaimed his judgement upon them through the testimonies of our holy fathers.

Heresy as a Disease

It is thus not the theological argument that is the driving force in John Rufus' works, but the testimonies, from authoritative ascetic fathers and other venerable persons, of the dangers of Chalcedonian heresy and the fallacy of those who maintain communion with these renegades. John's concern is first and foremost the principle of *imitatio*. The ascetic fathers were to be imitated, and so was their faith, since as true ascetics they loved the truth that was taught in all orthodox churches and by the fathers of the three holy Councils. Hagiographic culture, as we have seen, nursed the interdependency of orthodoxy and asceticism, and in times of controversy developed to its highest pitch. To be a true disciple of an ascetic father implied not only success in one's ascetic struggles but also adherence to the orthodox teaching and rejection of the heretics.

Nowhere in early hagiographic literature is this contiguity of asceticism with orthodoxy more obvious than in the *Plerophories*. As a matter of fact, it is the most striking feature of the work, most evidently expressed in the concept of renunciation. Just as a monk must renounce the world and all associations with impure men and corruptible things, he must also renounce all intercourse with those who reject the orthodox truth.[37] The most common demonstration of this renunciation is the withdrawal from every sacramental communication with heretics. For example, there is an account by John about the holy sister of the venerable Stephanus, who was archdeacon in Jerusalem. On Saturdays she used to take part in the vigils in memory of the saints, especially in the churches dedicated to Stephanus the Protomartyr and John the Baptist. After the Council she found it impossible to visit these churches to pray and take communion with Juvenal and the other transgressors. But, since she was greatly troubled by these evil circumstances, which had forced her to abstain from the company of the saints, the Protomartyr revealed himself to her in her cell and comforted her: 'Where you are, we are too, and we will be with you'.[38] We are immediately reminded of the stories in which certain individuals, who after the Council refrained from communion with the Chalcedonian bishops, miraculously received the Eucharist in their hand when they had withdrawn to pray in solitude. In another story John tells us about God's concern for those who remain firm and who avoid communion with the heretics in every way. In this story

---

[37] For the importance of avoiding heretics in the alphabetic collection of the *Apophthegmata Patrum*, see *AP* Theodore of Pherme 4, Agathon 5, Sisoes 48, and Chomas 1. Particularly striking is the response of Abba Agathon when he was accused to be a fornicator, a pride man, a slanderer, and a heretic: 'The first accusations I take to myself, for that is good for my soul. But heresy is separation from God. Now I have no wish to be separated from God', tr. by B. Ward, *The Sayings of the Desert Fathers: The Alphabetical Collection* (London and Oxford 1975), 18.

[38] *Pleroph.* 79.

we learn that during the patriarchate of Proterius the Alexandrine scholastic Serapion was deeply grieved when he found himself deprived of the Eucharist on Easter Sunday, since the persecuted priests of the faithful did not dare come forward to celebrate the Holy sacrifice. In the night, at the hour when Holy communion was celebrated, Serapion went out, began to cry and raised his hands to heaven in prayer. When he had finished his prayer he found in his hands a piece of Christ's body.[39]

The ultimate virtue is the separation from communion with the renegades. In the end this is that virtue which after death determines the final verdict before the throne of judgement. For one who during his life had associated with the Chalcedonian renegades there was no hope, no matter the degree of his personal devotion in the ascetic life or his loving-kindness towards others. In the monastery of Romanus at Eleutheropolis, many years after the death of Romanus, the old Pelusian monk Timothy departed from this life, and as he was being prepared for burial he suddenly woke up again from the dead. When the astonished monks asked him how this miracle had come about, he assured them that he had really been dead and that he had been led to the place of the judgement. But the reason why he had escaped the torments of Sheol was simply that he had remained true to the orthodox faith and from childhood had stayed away from the Chalcedonian renegades.[40]

Sometimes John reveals his taste for the morbid and horrible: the spasmodic twists of Nestorius, his rotting tongue, his decomposing body, the impurity which fills the *Tome* of Leo, and the despairing cries of the condemned in the darkness of Sheol, where Emperor Marcian is seen hanging from iron hooks over a consuming fire, submitted to eternal pain.[41] With such descriptions of the final miseries of the unfaithful, together with the repeated accusations against the Chalcedonians, it is all too evident that there is no middle way between accepting and rejecting the Council of Chalcedon. Through the rhetorical techniques of thrill and horror, while displaying examples of the cultural archetypes, John's

---

[39] *Pleroph.* 77.
[40] *Pleroph.* 87.
[41] *Pleroph.* 1, 27, 36, 38, 40.

intention is to show that there is no way of compromising with the
enemies without oneself falling into heresy.

But even more striking is the idea of heresy as a contagious
disease that could affect even the most orthodox and holy of God's
servants. Heresy was regarded as a dangerous kind of pollution that
spread into the society of the orthodox through even the slightest
contact. Like a dangerous epidemic Chalcedonianism could be
resisted only by isolation within the social boundaries of anti-
Chalcedonian culture. If the boundaries were crossed, whether
deliberately or accidentally, terrible things would happen. For
instance, we are told the tragic story about a holy woman from
Pamphylia who traveled to Jerusalem in the company of her sons
and settled in peace on the Mount of Olives. Once when she had
gone up to the holy place where the Lord had ascended into
heaven to pray, she found in the church a gathering of
Chalcedonians. But as she turned to get away from this place of
impurity she found that the gates had been closed, so that she
could not leave. Throughout the liturgy she hid behind a pillar,
until she could return to her cell and her sons. In the end she was
taken ill and was on the point of departing from the world of the
living when a loud voice told her sons to go and hear the
accusations which were brought against her—that she could hardly
be regarded as righteous and as one of the flock of the orthodox
when she had remained with a gathering of renegades in the church
of the Ascension, witnessing their perverted celebration of the holy
Mysteries.[42] This story, related to John by a son of the holy woman,
served as a call for extreme cautiousness when visiting the holy
places in Palestine. For a long time the holy places in Palestine, and
especially in Jerusalem, had served as a meeting-place for pilgrims
from the far corners of the Christian world. Given the mixed
crowds that gathered in Palestine it is far from surprising that the
anti-Chalcedonians in the Judaean desert recognized their exposure
to heresy when praying and celebrating the Eucharist at the well-
visited holy places in Jerusalem.

---

[42] *Pleroph.* 80. Cf. M. Douglas' discussion on the sanctions which
diffreent cultures exposes on persons who violate the lines of society:
'Physical crossing of the social barrier is treated as a dangerous pollution,
(...). The pollutor becomes a doubly wicked object of reprobation, first
because he crossed the line and second because he endangered others'.
Purity and Danger (London 1966), 138-139.

This situation undoubtedly contributed to the awareness among John and his friends that the faith they shared in their veneration of the holy doctors of the Church was that of the minority. In the Eastern Empire the anti-Chalcedonians appeared to be in control, since the policy of Emperor Anastasius was to accommodate the pro-Chalcedonians to the faith of the anti-Chalcedonians. But in Jerusalem the ecclesiastical authorities still realized the importance of directing their own religious policy in accordance with the faith of the constantly growing Chalcedonian population.[43] The 'current strength of the orthodox faith' regarding the state of the Empire did not apply to the situation in Palestine, where the Chalcedonians found reason to accuse the anti-Chalcedonians of being schismatics, since they were the smaller party. John therefore added the following words to his anecdotal collection:

> To those who say: 'The whole world is reflected in the churches. But you who are few in numbers, you are schismatics, even though you say that you are orthodox and filled with zeal for the truth'; to them the fathers have instructed you to answer in the following manner: 'Bear in mind the thousands of men who went out from Egypt, and the manifold signs and manifestations they saw. But with the exception of two, they all proved to be rebels and transgressors, and they perished in the desert. Not only did they perish without attaining eternal bliss, but following their unfaithfulness they were also refused to enter the Promised Land. Moses, the greatest lawgiver and prophet of all, gave the commandments and said: 'You shall not follow the majority in doing wrong' '.[44]

Later in the text, the use of Biblical allusions such as 'Many shepherds have destroyed my vineyard, they have trampled down my portion' and 'for one is better than a thousand',[45] helps to demonstrate a strong isolationism that locates the truth in the

---

[43] It did not take long for John, who replaced the deposed Patriarch Elias, on the patriarchal throne in Jerusalem, to realize that the people of Palestine only would accept a Chalcedonian patriarch in Jerusalem. See Frend, *The Rise of the Monophysite Movement*, 230.

[44] *Pleroph.* 55; Ex. 23.2.

[45] Jer 12.10; Sir. 16.3.

marginalized community of believers, whereas every kind of evils is linked to the majority.

With an emphasis on the ascetic cautiousness towards things belonging to the world of corruption and evil, John Rufus constantly proclaims that with the transgressors of the orthodox ways no compromise is possible. This severe attitude is even more clearly illustrated in the story of how Peter the Iberian one day was forced to say a few words to a former friend, who had fallen away from the true faith when he was entrusted with the administration of the economy of the Church in Alexandria during the patriarchate of Proterius. In the night he saw the Lord in the middle of a large field where a multitude of saints and angels had gathered to praise God, and when he saw the Lord he went towards him in order to worship him. But when the Lord saw him he turned his face away from him. Soon Peter understood that the reason for this behavior was that he had met a renegade.[46] Intercourse with impure matters and persons was not only dangerous because of the risk of being tainted by impurity, as a matter of fact it was considered a sin in itself. There is no doubt that this idea of the radical withdrawal from every form of association with heretics originated in the ascetic renunciation from the inhabited world.

Conclusion

As the last pieces of John Rufus' anti-Chalcedonian world vision are about to fall into place, we find right in front of us an image of a universe sharply divided between what belongs to the divine realm and what belongs to the world. In previous chapters we have focused our attention to the great heroes of this universe, men and women zealously dedicated to the service of the divine truth, as God had proclaimed it through the holy fathers of the orthodox Church. In this last chapter we have finally been concerned with the great villains of anti-Chalcedonian mythology, i.e. the heretics. Everywhere in early Christian hagiography heretics appear to us as demons dressed in human flesh, wicked characters who, following their attraction towards worldly things, have become utterly polluted by their obstinacy against the divine truth. They provide a real threat to the communities of believers, since they are

---

[46] *Pleroph.* 76. Cf; *V. Petr. Ib.*, 75-76.

constantly looking for opportunities to snare the orthodox in the net of heresy. As a character in any hagiographic drama the heretic is usually represented as a force of irresistible danger, capable of disturbing and distorting the faith of the common man. It is only when confronted with the hagiographic hero, the holy man, that the heretic finds his match. Whether converting him with inspired words, driving him away in disgrace as a result of a divine trial, or submitting himself to physical death to become a martyr to his faith, the holy man will never be defeated when confronting the heretic. The holy man always appears as a champion of Trinitarian orthodoxy, quite unaffected by the assaults of the heretic. Yet the heretic is always needed as a narrative device for emphasizing the holiness of the protagonist.

As a fundamental element of the anti-Chalcedonian world vision of John Rufus, heretics have an almost cosmological importance as the chief culprits of a world permeated with corruptibility and demonic powers. This is indicated not only through the idea of Chalcedon as implying something that comes close to a second Fall of mankind. Through the apostasy at Chalcedon the entire world, even the holy places in Jerusalem, suffered from the pollution of heresy. The truth, on the other hand, was maintained only by a minority of believers, scattered over the wilderness of the Eastern Empire as they renounced the world and every contact with heretics. But this dualistic representation of the entire universe in two opposite realms, the one guided by divine truth, the other by earthly heresy, may be regarded as a way of looking upon the world that determined almost every aspect of anti-Chalcedonian mentality. The idea of radical renunciation of all contact with heretics that constantly recurs in the authorship of John Rufus seems to be based on a corresponding idea of renunciation of the material world as a fundamental presupposition for an ascetic conduct of life in the presence of God. At the same time John Rufus provides us with a quite specific view of the difference between the world and the blessed life of ascetics and holy men. John's vision of the world implies a radicalized view of the ascetic notion of the cosmological opposition between this world and the divine realm. The world is the habitat of material impurity, demons and heretics, and it is only by remaining untainted that man can be saved.

With such a cosmology, which strongly emphasizes the dualistic opposition between worldly and spiritual matters as essentially an opposition between good and evil, it would be close at hand to impute a Christology to anti-Chalcedonians such as John Rufus that disregarded or utterly denied the human element in the person of Christ. For how would it be possible for mankind to be saved if the Savior himself is by nature part of a world tainted with impurity? However, if we return to the addition of the Trisagion hymn, 'who was crucified for us', or if we remember John Rufus' report of the frank words uttered by the unnamed holy man to Emperor Marcian about the uniqueness of Christ, appearing in both divine glory and utter humility, we find such conclusions altogether too hasty. In fact, what was attacked by the anti-Chalcedonians was not the humanity of Christ but the alleged Chalcedonian bipartition of the one Son into two independent constituents. Such a bipartition, from an anti-Chalcedonian viewpoint, would be absolutely meaningless and even blasphemous, especially in the context of the celebration of the Eucharist mystery. The concern of pope Leo and the Chalcedonian bishops to divide the activities of Christ into two separate boxes, one divine and the other human, was thus forcefully rejected. The anti-Chalcedonians, in contrary, put tremendous importance on the position that every one of the earthly activities of Christ was the activities of one of the Trinity in the Person of the Son, and thus the activities of God himself. With such a heavy accent on the uniqueness of the Son, the anti-Chalcedonians preserved a particularly powerful theology of incarnation, devoting themselves to a God who did not hesitate to take upon Himself the miseries of the material world and through his suffering and death submitted Himself under the utter consequences of the profound incompatibility between spiritual and worldly matters.

CONCLUSION

The Council of Chalcedon of 451 is generally held to have been summoned to prevent a schism within the Eastern Empire between two rivaling systems of Christological doctrine caused by discrepancies in theological terminology. In western-oriented theology the Council has long been seen as the final, theologically balanced conclusion of a process defining the true meaning of the mystery of the Incarnation. Chalcedon has always been praised for providing a philosophically sophisticated formula that managed to settle once and for all the logical implications of the great paradox of the Incarnation. Since the idea of Christ as a union of two natures, one divine and one human, was proclaimed through four negative adverbs, the Chalcedonian formula of faith has been recognized as one of the most elaborate and aesthetically superlative instances of the intellectual contribution of the fathers of the Church to the development of Christian doctrine. But despite the alleged subtlety of the theological expression the Chalcedonian fathers used in formulating their doctrine, the Council only added fuel to the controversy that raged between the orthodox Churches in the East. In the eyes of the majority of the population in the eastern provinces of the Empire Chalcedon was nothing but a refutation of the Trinitarian faith established by the Nicaean fathers. The bishops summoned to Chalcedon were believed to have asserted the Christological view of Nestorius, thus downgrading the second person of the Godhead to the rank of a created being and re-establishing the heresy of Arius. In this way Chalcedon entailed a new stage in Christian history—the beginning of a general apostasy from the true Trinitarian faith, an apostasy that would prevail until the end of time.

In southern Palestine, particularly in the monastic settlements around Gaza, the charismatic character of Peter the Iberian had attracted a close-knit circle of monks and intellectuals that seems to have become, in the early sixth century, one of the recruiting centers for anti-Chalcedonian leaders. To this circle belonged three of the best-known anti-Chalcedonian characters at the turn of the

sixth century. The first, Severus of Antioch, has gone to history as
the greatest theologian of the period, with an immense production
of doctrinal writings, homiletics and letters. In affirming a
moderate non-Chalcedonian position firmly rooted in Cyrillian
thought, he acknowledged a dynamic continuity of the two natures
in Christ's person, thus distancing himself from the more extreme
forms of anti-Chalcedonian Christology. As a compassionate
Church leader, imbued with a genuine pastoral charity, he opposed
the fanatical and sectarian tendencies in the anti-Chalcedonian
movement, notably by rejecting the re-anointing of converted
Chalcedonians. At the same time he insisted on an explicit
anathema against Chalcedon and rejected the compromise of the
Henotikon since, although it seemed to him to be essentially
orthodox, it failed to pronounce a categorical condemnation of
Chalcedon.

Severus' life is fairly well known to us, thanks to the biography
written by Zacharias Scholasticus, the other important
representative of the 'school of Peter the Iberian'. Born in a well-
to-do family at Maiuma, Zacharias was sent to study in Alexandria,
where he made friends with Severus. After completing his law
studies in Beirut he submitted himself for a short time to the
spiritual guidance of Peter the Iberian's successors at Maiuma,
before entering on a legal career in the imperial capital. Extant
works by him are, besides the *Life of Severus*, a short hagiography
dealing with Abba Isaiah, a treatise on the Creation, and a
refutation of the Manichaean heresy. To him is also attributed a
Church History, rightly recognized as one of our most important
sources for the historical development from Chalcedon to the reign
of Anastasius. It is incorporated in an anonymous Syriac *Chronicle*
covering the period from Emperor Arcadius to A.D. 569.

In Zacharias' *Life of Severus* we find the only external reference
to the third great representative of the circle of Peter the Iberian.
His name was John Rufus, a former priest in Antioch who
probably originated from the province of Arabia, and who in the
days of Emperor Zeno became a monk under the spiritual
authority of Peter the Iberian. His three extant hagiographical
works—the *Life of Peter the Iberian*, the *Commemoration of the death of
Theodosius*, and the *Plerophories*—have long been neglected, for
linguistic and doctrinal reasons. However, these works do not only
provide us with the most explicit propagandistic hagiography in

late antiquity, they are also of considerable value for our knowledge of the early development of the non-Chalcedonian movement in the eastern parts of the Byzantine Empire.

The question Pope Leo put to Julian of Kios about the motives behind the monastic insurrection in Palestine after the Council of Chalcedon has remained unsolved for a millennium and a half. Despite a number of attempts made during the last hundred years we are still ignorant of the fundamental motives that drove a significant portion of the population in the eastern provinces to resist Chalcedon. It has proved difficult to explain why many Christians in the Eastern Empire, particularly in Egypt and Syria, fiercely resisted the Chalcedonian statement that Christ was to be confessed as being 'in two natures' (human and divine) instead of 'out of two natures'. While a wide range of motives have been suggested—founded in theology, semantics, asceticism, spirituality, ecclesiastical politics and even nationalism—no scholar has yet been able to present a fully satisfying explanation, outlining the historical and ideological reasons behind the rise of the so-called 'monophysite movement'.

That the resistance against Chalcedon emanated primarily from monks was already known to Pope Leo when he received the disturbing news of the monastic mutiny against Juvenal of Jerusalem immediately after the Council closed. Worried about the motives for this rebellion among the Palestinian monks, he eventually suggested in a letter to them that their wrath against the *Tome* and the Christological formula established at Chalcedon was induced by fatal misunderstandings, caused by an inaccurate translation of the *Tome* from Latin into Greek. If only those misunderstandings were removed, and the monks humbly accepted the Catholic authority, he hoped that they would no longer find the Incarnation of the Word a stumbling block. Explaining the monastic resistance against Chalcedon as the result of a misinterpretation is still the most frequent approach to the schism between the Chalcedonian and the non-Chalcedonian Churches in the fifth and sixth centuries. It is true that twentieth-century investigations into the doctrinal divergence between these two traditions have revealed that there was no real difference in their views on the human and divine natures in Christ. But explaining the background of the Christological debate merely in terms of differing usages of the concepts of *physis* and *hypostasis* is not an adequate approach to shedding light on the controversy that raged in the Eastern Empire in the fifth and sixth centuries. The Chalcedonian controversy was not merely a conflict about semantic connections between certain words and concepts, but rather about conflicting ways of looking upon reality.

A great deal of the difficulties that have hampered previous approaches to the problem seems to be caused by what Bernard Flusin called an 'error of perspective,' that is, the tendency to disregard our most valuable sources for a balanced approach to the motives for the monastic resistance against Chalcedon, i.e. the anti-Chalcedonian hagiographic works. As a result of confessional preferences, or quite simply a reluctance to take into account texts not preserved in Latin or Greek, attention has been drawn chiefly to the Chalcedonian hagiography. Cyril of Scythopolis' *Lives* have erroneously been seen as mainstream representatives of Palestinian hagiography. But such a view presupposes an understanding of Palestinian hagiography as the fruit of a historical continuity, a view that does not correspond with our present knowledge of this hagiography during the fifth and sixth centuries.

In the present investigation we have tried to challenge this 'error of perspective' not only by focusing on the anti-Chalcedonian writings of John Rufus, but also by, in so doing, approaching the problem of the foundations of anti-Chalcedonianism by fitting his writings into the framework of a specific anti-Chalcedonian 'culture'. We have specified a definition of culture as intimately connected with representation and meaning. In this way culture may be described as the mirror through which the community considers reality and sorts out what is true from what is false. Since culture is the medium through which a community perceives reality, it covers the notion of *mentalité* taken as the collective worldview or world vision of a certain local group of people. It is one of the most basic assumptions of this study that a comprehensive understanding of the motives behind the anti-Chalcedonian movement must proceed from the ways in which the anti-Chalcedonians themselves viewed reality. This approach to the problem of culture calls for a certain degree of comparative awareness, emerging in the present study in the attempt to identify certain rivaling sets of meaning and representation in the anti-Chalcedonian culture of John Rufus and the Chalcedonian culture set forth in the hagiography of Cyril of Scythopolis.

Following this theoretical framework we have sorted out a number of characteristic features in John Rufus' hagiography that reflect certain aspects of the symbolic world behind the fierce resistance against the Council of Chalcedon in the fourth and fifth centuries.

First, John Rufus' hagiographic writings present a cosmology based on a strong opposition between God and the evil powers dominating the world following the apostasy at Chalcedon. John Rufus reveals a vision of the world as a drama between good and evil, where the holy men and women stand before us as instruments of God's concern for those faithful servants who in times of apostasy preserve the faith of their fathers. Through their virtues and their perseverance in the true faith, the holy men are particularly worthy of being channels for God's messages to mankind. The holy men emerge as the true friends of God, as they maintain their intimacy with the divine by constant prayers and humble obedience, readily accepting the call to be agents of God's will. But against the background of his conception of the universe as deeply divided, the holy men in the cosmological drama are remarkably downplayed. The focus of John Rufus' hagiography is not on the holy men themselves but on God and his verdict on Chalcedon. Though essential as models for ascetic life and for appropriate professions of the orthodox faith, the holy men are merely symbols of God's workings in the world to promote the truth and condemn the Chalcedonian heretics.

The role that John Rufus, in his hagiographic representation of the cosmological battle between orthodoxy and heresy, attaches to the ultimate power of God is evident from the rhetorical use in his texts of visionary experiences and miraculous manifestations. In contrast to the ascetic heroes of Cyril of Scythopolis, John Rufus' holy men do not perform any miracles of their own. In fact, there is in his texts not a single report of miracles performed by the holy men themselves. Where miraculous events are reported the emphasis is always on the divine origin of these manifestations. Likewise, the frequent reports of dreams and visions received by John's protagonists are to be regarded primarily as the vehicle through which God communicates his verdict on the heretics, rather than as tokens of the holiness of individual ascetics. This pattern is evident not only in the *Plerophories* but also in the *Life of Peter the Iberian*, where Peter is presented as simply an instrument of God's loving concern for those who preserve the orthodox faith. This downplaying of the hagiographic role of the holy men corresponds with God's revelations of the truth through anyone he chooses as a channel for his divine message. Among these channels for the divine verdict on the Chalcedonian heresy we find not only holy men but sometimes ordinary men as well, not distinguished as strict ascetics. When we read in the *Plerophories* about the report given by an officer named Zeno, the visionary experience of the Chalcedonian wife of Anianus the Scholastic, or the remarkable things seen by the immoral deacon in the Church of Anastasis in Jerusalem, John Rufus reveals that ascetic prominence and observance of the orthodox faith is not a necessary prerequisite for bearing witness to the truth. Instead, he moves the focus to God, who through his own incontestable will chooses whomever he pleases as a mouthpiece for the divine truth. That God is the only reliable source of truth is made clear when the believers are faced with different interpretations. Not even the venerable doctors of the orthodox Church can be trusted, since their expositions of the true faith are distorted by the deceitful interpretations of the heretics. The faithful must put their trust in God's verdict, delivered straight from heaven. The truth is with God, and in his benevolent concern for his faithful servants he manifests it, proclaiming his authority as the Supreme Being of the visible and invisible universe.

Secondly, unlike the image of the holy man that is presented e.g. in Athanasius' account of Antony, the emphasis in John Rufus' stories about holy men is the concept of virtue received, rather than the return to a natural state of holiness. To John, the foundation of ascetic holiness is intimately linked with the idea of history as the revelation of virtue and truth. Thus the powers of the holy man may be considered as powers derived from the past. The holy man maintains the link with the past by remaining a disciple under the spiritual authority of the old masters of ascetic life, men adorned with every imaginable virtue. The importance of continued discipleship is closely connected with preserving orthodoxy. Staying close to the ascetic masters is the safest way to remain in communion with the orthodox fathers. Hence we meet with an idea of ascetic holiness that is based on a sense of tradition, and on the essential position of ascetic authority as a stronghold against the perversions of the material world. When, in his preface to the *Life of Peter the Iberian*, John Rufus calls for a continued discipleship under the spiritual leader even when this leader has departed from the world, he reveals what to him is the true meaning of ascetic life. To John the ascetic life is essentially a living memorial to the holy fathers of the past who, since they are paragons of virtue and evangelical conduct and supported and nurtured by the grace of God, provide excellent models for steadfast imitation, in their virtues as well as in their orthodox faith.

Thirdly, against the background of the explicit conflict between God and the evil powers of the material world, John Rufus outlines a corresponding opposition between the orthodox truth, represented by humble and virtuous holy men, and falsity represented by worldly authorities such as emperors, and by ecclesiastical dignitaries. The authority of orthodox holy men is set against that of men of wealth, power, and worldly glory as an essential element in the cosmological battle between good and evil. By adhering to the blasphemy of Chalcedonianism, emperors, patriarchs and bishops have turned away from the true meaning of ecclesiastical authority, which entails a proper balance between administrative responsibilities and the constant readiness to stand up for the faith. Abandoning their duty to defend the faith against heresy, and giving themselves up to the heretics, they have themselves become part of the evil forces that are warring against God. Holders of worldly authority thus take the shapes of demons, incessantly harassing those who remain firm in their orthodox faith. Through Chalcedon the world has become an evil empire, and to provide his faithful with comfort and sustenance God sends his most beloved servants, such as Dioscorus, Timothy Aelurus, and Theodosius of Jerusalem. John Rufus' notion of orthodox episcopacy is clearly dependent on the virtue of ascetic renunciation, as he often emphasizes the unwillingness of God's chosen leaders to receive ordination, until at last they shoulder their episcopal burden with devotion, self-effacement and a lifelong love of the ascetic life. The ideal bishop, in John Rufus' hagiography is represented by Peter the Iberian, who confirms the concept of ecclesiastical leadership that Athanasius of Alexandria had established that of an ascetic entrusted with sustaining the community of the faithful. According to John the true bishop fulfills a mission which is given immediately from God and which he cannot escape. Though the mission of cleansing the world from the impurity of heresy may seem impossible, it is still imposed by God on the orthodox bishop. In this way John Rufus presents the orthodox bishop in terms of a Messianic figure selected by God to save the world from the evils of heresy. But the accomplishment of this episcopal mission always rests upon God himself, the bishop being merely the obedient instrument of God in His work for man's salvation.

As a fourth element of the anti-Chalcedonianism of John Rufus we have touched upon the concept of Egypt as the homeland of ascetic life. The Egyptian ascetic heritage with the radical contrast between the purity of the desert and the perversions of the world of men is throughout the works of John Rufus a permanent image and model for the resistance against Chalcedon. The idea of renunciation from the material world and its temptations is a recurring theme in the anti-Chalcedonian propaganda of John Rufus. Here we find Chalcedonianism presented above all as a religion of the world of men, associated with all the evils of human civilization such as power, wealth and splendor, while anti-Chalcedonian orthodoxy is clearly associated with the purity of the uncorrupted nature. The virtues of the ascetic life in the wilderness are closely linked with the virtue of orthodoxy, making the complete separation from the civilized world a prerequisite for the continued adherence to the orthodox fathers. This is one of the most obvious points on which John Rufus dissociates himself from the Chalcedonian hagiography of Cyril of Scythopolis. In contrast to the orthodox purity of the wilderness emphasized by John, Cyril brings forth his holy men as pioneers of civilization—*Chalcedonian* civilization. As Euthymius, Cyril's hero, penetrates the Judaean desert he opens the way for the Chalcedonian faith by subduing the evils of the wilderness, such as wild animals, Saracen barbarians, and heretics. Cyril presents us with a Chalcedonianism in which civilization and obedience under the ecclesiastical hierarchy are inherent. In the hagiography of John Rufus and Cyril of Scythopolis we thus encounter two monastic cultures—both Palestinian in origin and emanating within a time span of a few decades—which are diametrically opposed and represent two completely different ways of looking upon reality.

The fifth aspect of John Rufus' cultural world vision deals with the idea of Egypt as the homeland of Trinitarian and anti-Nestorian orthodoxy. The doctrinal heritage from Athanasius and Cyril of Alexandria forms the theological framework within which John Rufus regards the anti-Chalcedonian struggle as a continuation of the anti-Arian struggles of Athanasius, the anti-Nestorian struggles of Cyril, and Dioscorus' struggle against the *Tome* of Leo. John remains loyal to the legacy of the great Alexandrine patriarchs, and to their defense of the full divinity and Oneness of Christ. John sees the link between Nestorius, Leo and Chalcedon as self-evident, and consequently never ceases to rage against the uncanonical activities of the bishops at Chalcedon. Apparently they revived the very same blasphemous doctrine that the pious Emperor Theodosius had condemned through the Council of Ephesus twenty years earlier. A great deal of evidence in the works of John Rufus points at the heresy of Chalcedon being understood as basically anti-Trinitarian. Against the teaching of Chalcedon John emphasizes the transcendental and ineffable mystery of the Holy Trinity, implying that any attempt to the divide the second hypostasis of the Godhead into two would contradict the worship of Christ as essentially one with the Father, and turn him into a mere man—as the Jews had argued he was. John thus anticipates John of Ephesus' accusation against Chalcedon of adding a fourth *hypostasis* to the Godhead. However, it is important to notice that John Rufus never denies the full humanity of the incarnated Christ but rather seems to share Severus' concept of the human element of Christ as a property of its own.

The sixth aspect of John Rufus' anti-Chalcedonian culture is the heavy emphasis on preserved purity and the dangers of being tainted by heresy by the slightest association with heretics. This aspect, which forms the background to the manifest features of sectarianism in John Rufus' hagiography, may partly be explained through the particular situation that the anti-Chalcedonians in Palestine faced as the whole region was overrun by Chalcedonian pilgrims from all parts of the Empire. The call for a complete rejection of any compromise with heretics that is an inherent part of John Rufus' anti-Chalcedonianism may also be explained against the background of the ambivalent feelings among the anti-Chalcedonians towards Emperor Zeno's *Henotikon* and its failure to deliver an explicit condemnation of Chalcedon. To John, orthodox purity is basically freedom from compromise and association with heretics. This view originates in the concept of heresy as a contagious disease endangering the unconditional adherence to the orthodox faith. Associating with heretics, in whatever way, is to John in itself a fatal transgression. This idea is evidently based on John's persistent emphasis on the ascetic virtue of renunciation, since he considers the orthodox life as essentially an ascetic way of living. Once more we find John Rufus' conception of orthodoxy closely linked with themes derived immediately from a monastic context, in a manner that confirms Eduard Schwartz' observation that anti-Chalcedonianism is 'in eminentem Sinne eine Mönchsreligion'.

Finally, we have found from our investigation of the world of John Rufus an articulated identity of being in a state of marginalization. To John this is a natural condition that follows with the general apostasy of Chalcedon. Following the Council the whole world is tainted with the disease of heresy, placing the visible universe under the immediate command of the demons. To belong to the few is in itself a state of grace, since truth does not belong to the many. The world of the many is a world of compromise and distortion of the truth, whereas God constantly manifests his concern for the small community of believers. To be part of the many is to be part of the corruptibility of the material world, whereas adhering to the faith of the few implies full assurance of the truth—that Chalcedon was a revival of Nestorianism and that God's condemnation weighs heavy on anyone who proclaims the dyophysite teaching of the Chalcedonian bishops. It was against this background that the boundaries of the anti-Chalcedonian culture were drawn up. Outside these boundaries prevailed heresy, wickedness and pollution, inside orthodoxy, goodness, and purity. The worldview of John Rufus and his readers is thus revealed as a self-contained and self-sufficient model of a culture that found its internal identification in the confident claim of walking in the footsteps of the holy fathers. Its external borders were defined in terms of opposition against a dominant culture that beset the communion of saints and was utterly polluted by the sins of worldliness. As part of the Eastern monastic culture it regarded itself as a counter-culture preserving orthodoxy and pure conduct from being defiled by the perverseness of the many.

There remain at least three important questions that have been touched upon in the present study but require further considerations elsewhere. The first deals with the intimate connection between the anti-Chalcedonian movement and the intellectual centers of the Eastern Empire—Alexandria, Beirut and Gaza. As pointed out in Chapter 1 (sect. 2) it is evident from the social network around Peter the Iberian that anti-Chalcedonianism may be regarded as an intellectual movement. Particularly striking are the constant references to the group of law students in Beirut who were eventually drawn into the ascetic circle around Peter the Iberian and his successors. The implications of the strong presence of philosophers and rhetoricians in the anti-Chalcedonian circles remain open for further investigations, especially the question of the relations between the academic centers, the imperial authorities, and the Church. This would give an important contribution to our understanding of the rise and development of the anti-Chalcedonianism in the fifth and sixth centuries.

This opens up for a much larger question about the social setting of the Chalcedonian controversy and the social, political, and economic position of the people who involved in the resistance against the Council of Chalcedon. More research on the structures of power in the Eastern provinces and the political background of anti-Chalcedonianism that may explain the explosions of civic rage in the aftermath of Chalcedon. The often-repeated suggestion about nationalism and cultural conflicts ought to be discussed in a much broader setting. A careful analysis of these matters would add much to our present knowledge about the social and political aspects of the anti-Chalcedonian movement.[1]

Moreover, it would be profitable to pursue the question about the liturgical and ecclesiological views of the anti-Chalcedonian movement, especially in relation to the works of Dionysius Areopagita. We have seen in chapter 5 how the anti-Chalcedonians

---

[1] Preliminary remarks about the relation between anti-Chalcedonianism and the economic and social differences within the Eastern Empire is presented in Frend, 'The Monophysites and the Transition between the Ancient World and the Middle Ages', in *Convegno internazionale: Passaggio dal mondo antico al medio evo da Teodosio a San Gregorio Magno (Roma, 25-28 maggio 1977)*, Atti dei convegni Lincei 45 (Rome 1980), 339-365. See also Jones, Where Ancient Heresies National or Social Movements in Disguise?', *JTS* 10.2 (1959), 280-298.

seem to have based their opposition against the dyophysite teaching of Chalcedon on worship and liturgy rather than on doctrinal speculation. The main concern for their struggle was the fear that the Chalcedonian dogma distorted the veneration of the Son as truly God, expressed through the liturgical formula: 'one of the Trinity has been crucified'. For the anti-Chalcedonians, orthodoxy was linked to an appropriate liturgical worship that may be related to the liturgical spirituality of Dionysius with its emphasis on the transcendent Word. Attempts have already been made to put the Dionysian Corpus into the context of the anti-Chalcedonian movement, but many challenges still remain as regards the connections between Dionysius and anti-Chalcedonianism.[2]

---

[2] For attempts to identify Peter the Iberian with Dionysius Aeropagita, see Honigmann, *Pierre L'Ibérien et les écrits du pseudo-Denys l'Aréopagite*, Bruxelles 1952; H. Engberding, 'Kann Petrus der iberer mit Dionysius Areopagita identifiziert werden?' *OC* 38 (1954), 68-95; I. Hausherr, 'Le pseudo-Denys est-il Pierre L'Ibérien?', *OCP* 19 (1953), 247-260; R. Roques, 'Pierre l'Ibérien et le 'Corpus' dionysien', *RHR* 145 (1954), 69-98; Van Esbroeck, 'Peter the Iberian and Dionysius the Areopagite', 217-227.

BIBLIOGRAPHY

Primary Sources

Acta conciliorum oecumenicorum, ed. by E. Schwartz (Strasbourg, Berlin and Leipzig 1914-1940).

Aeneas of Gaza, *Theophrastus*, PG 85, 872-1003.

Akten der Ephesinischen Synode vom Jahre 449, ed. by J. Flemming, in *AKWG* 15, (Göttingen 1917), 1-159.

Apophthegmata patrum. PG 65, 71-440; tr. by B. Ward, *The Sayings of the Desert Fathers: The Alphabetical Collection* (London and Oxford 1975).

Athanasius of Alexandria, *Epistulae ad monachos* [first and second], PG 25, 691-693, and PG 26, 1185-1188; tr. by L. W. Barnard, *The Monastic Letters of Saint Athanasius the Great* (Oxford 1994), 10-13.

   Epistula ad Dracontium, PG 25, 523-534; tr. by L. W. Barnard, *The Monastic Letters of Saint Athanasius the Great* (Oxford 1994), 4-9.

   Vita Antonii, ed. and tr. by G. J. M. Bartelink, *Vie d'Antoine*, SC 400, Paris 1994; eng. tr. by R. C. Gregg, *Athanasius: The Life of Antony and the Letter to Marcellinus*, The Classics of Western Spirituality, (New York, Ramsey and Toronto 1980).

Benedict of Nursia, *Regula Monasteriorum*, ed. and tr. by A. de Vogüé and J. Neufville, *La règle de Saint Benoît*, SC 181-186 (Paris 1971-1972).

Cicero, *The dream of Scipio*, ed. and tr. by J. G. F. Powell, *On Friendship; The Dream of Scipio* (Warminster 1990).

Codex Theodosianus, ed. by T. Mommsen and P. M. Meyer (Berlin 1905).

Coptic Texts in the University of Michigan Collection, ed. by W. H. Worrell (London 1942).

Cyril of Alexandria, *Epistula ad Nestorium* [second], PG 77, 43-50.

175

Cyril of Scythopolis, *Vitae*, ed. by E. Schwartz, TU 49.2 (1939 Leipzig); tr. by R. M. Rice, *Cyril of Scythopolis: The Lives of the Monks of Palestine*, CS 114, (Kalamazoo 1991).

Decrees of the Ecumenical Councils: Volume One: Nicaea I to Lateran V, ed. and tr. by Norman P. Tanner (London and Washington 1990).

Pseudo-Dionysius of Tel-Maḥrē, *Chronicon*, ed. and tr. by J.-B. Chabot, *Incerti auctoris chronicon anonymum pseudo-Dionysianum vulgo dictum*, CSCO, Script. syri, 3.1 (Paris 1927-1949).

Evagrius Scholasticus, *Historia Ecclesiastica*, ed. by J. Bidez and L. Parmentier (London 1898); tr. by A.-J. Festugière, *Byzantion* 45 (1975), 187-488.

Gregory Thaumaturgus, *Origenem oratio panegyrica*, ed. and tr. by P. Guyot, *Oratio prosphonetica ac panegyrica in Origenem* (Freiburg 1996); eng. tr. by M. Slusser, *Gregorius Thaumaturgus: Life and Works*, in The Fathers of the Church 98 (Washington 1998).

Historia monachorum in Aegypto, ed. and tr. by A.-J. Festugière, Sub. Hag. 53 (1971); eng. tr. by N. Russel, *The Lives of the Desert fathers: The Historia Monachorum in Aegypto* (Kalamazoo 1981).

Abba Isaiah, *Asceticon*, ed. and tr. by R. Draguet, *Asceticon: Les cinq recensions de l'Asceticon syriaque d'abba Isaïe*, CSCO, Script. Syri 120-123 (Louvain 1968).

Isodore of Pelusium, *Epistulae*, PG 78, 177-1645.

Jerome, *Vita Hilarionis*, PL 23, 28-54.

> *Vita Pauli*, PL 23, 17-28; tr. by W. H. Fremantle, in *The Principal Works of St. Jerome*, A Select Library of the Nicene and Post-Nicene Fathers of the Christian Church, ser. 2, vol. 12 (Grand Rapids 1983), 299-303
>
> *Vita Malchi*, PL 23, 54-60.

John Cassian, *Conlationes*, ed. and tr. by E. Pichery, *Conférences*, CS 64 (Paris 1959).

> *De Incarnatione*, ed. and tr. by M. Petschenig, CSEL 17 (Prague 1888).

John of Ephesus, *Vitae*, ed. and tr. by E. W. Brooks, PO 17-19 (Paris 1923-25).

John Malalas, *Chronographia*, ed. by L. Dindorf, CSHB 32 (Bonn 1831).

John Moschus, *Spititual Meadow*, ed. and tr. by M.-J Rouët de Journel, *Jean Moschus: Le pré spirituel*, SC 12 (Paris 1946).

John Rufus, *Narratio de obitu Theodosii Hierosolymorum et Romani monachi*, ed. and tr. by E. W. Brooks, CSCO, Script. syri, 3.25 (Paris 1907), 21-27.

Vita Petri Iberi, ed. and tr. by R. Raabe, *Petrus der Iberer. Ein Charakterbild zur Kirchen- und Sittengeschichte des fünften Jahrhunderts* (Leipzig 1895).

Plerophories, ed. and tr. by F. Nau, *Jean Rufus. Plérophories, témoignages et révélations contre le concile de Chalcédoine*, PO 8.1 (Paris 1912).

Leo, *Epistulae*, PL 54; tr. by E. Hunt, *St. Leo the Great: Letters*, in The Fathers of the Church, vol. 34 (Washington 1964); and C. L. Feltoe, *Letters and Sermons of Leo the Great*, in A Select Library of the Nicene and Post-Nicene Fathers of the Christian Church, ser. 2, vol. 12 (Grand Rapids 1983 [repr]).

Lucian, *Opera*, ed. and tr. by A. M. Harmon, LCL (London and Cambridge/Mass. 1913-1967).

Marc the Deacon, *Vita Porphyrii*, ed. and tr. by H. Grégoire and M.-A. Kugener, *Vie de Porphyre, évêque de Gaza*, in Collection Byzantine publiée sous le patronage de l'Association Guillaume Budé (Paris 1930); eng. tr. by C. Rapp, in T. Head (ed.), *Medieval hagiography: An Antology* (New York 2000), 59-75.

Michael the Syrian, *Chronicon*, ed. J.-B. Chabot, *Chronique de Michel de Syrien patriarche jacobite d' Antioche (1166-1199)*, 4 vols. (Paris 1905-1907).

Nestorius, *Liber Heraclidis*, ed. and tr. by F. Nau, *Le Livre d'Héraclide*, Paris 1910; eng tr. by G. R. Driver and L. Hodgson, *The Bazaar of Heraclides* (Oxford 1925).

Palladius, *Dialogus de vita Iohanni Chrysostomi*, ed. and tr. by A.-M. Malingrey, *Dialogue sur la vie de Jean Chrysostome*, SC 341 (Paris 1988).

Historia Lausiaca, ed. by C. Butler, *The Lausiac History of Palladius*, Text and Studies 6, 2. vols. (Cambridge 1898-1904);

tr. by R. T. Meyer, *The Lausiac History*, in ACW 34 (London 1965).

Passio Perpetuae et Felicitatis, ed. and tr. by J. Amat, *Passion de Perpétue et de Félicité*, SC 417 (Paris 1996).

Plutarch, *Vitae*, ed. and tr. by B. Perrin, *Plutarch's Lives*, LCL (London and Cambridge/Mass. 1914-26).

Sacrorum conciliorum nova et amplissima collectio, ed J. D. Mansi (Florence and Venice 1759-98).

Serapion of Thmuis, *Epistula ad discipulos Antonii*, ed and tr. by R. Draguet, 'Un lettre de Sérapion de Thmuis aux disciples d'Antoine (A.D. 356) en version syriaque et arménienne', *Le Muséon* 64 (1951), 4-17.

Severus of Antioch, *Homiliae cathedrales*, ed. and tr. by M. Brière, *Les homiliae cathedrales de Sévère d'Antioche (Homélies CXX à CXXV)*, PO 29.1 (Paris 1932).

A Collection of Letters, ed. and tr. by E. W. Brooks, *A Collection of Letters of Severus of Antioch, from Numerous Syriac Manuscripts (Letters I to LXI)*, PO 12.2, Paris 1919.

Liber contra impium grammaticum, ed. and tr. by J. Lebon, CSCO, Script. syri 4.4-6 (Paris 1929-1938).

Select Letters, ed. and tr. by E. W. Brooks, *The Sixth Book of the Select Letters of Severus, Patriarch of Antioch*, 4 vols. (Oxford 1902-1904).

Socrates, *Historia ecclesiastica*, ed. and tr. by G. C. Hansen, GCS N.F. 1 (Berlin 1994); eng. tr. by A. C. Zenos, *Church History from A.D. 305-439*, in A Select Library of the Nicene and Post-Nicene Fathers of the Christian Church, ser. 2, vol. 11 (Grand Rapids 1983 [repr.]).

Sozomen, *Historia ecclesiastica*, ed. and tr. by J. Bidez and G. C. Hansen, GCS 50 (Berlin 1960).

Theodoret of Cyrrhus, *Historia religiosa*, ed. and tr. by P. Canivet and A. Leroy-Molinghen, *Historie des moines de syrie*, SC 234, 257, Paris 1977-79; eng. tr. by R. M. Rice, *Theodoret of Cyrrhus: A History of the Monks of Syria*, CS 88 (Kalamazoo 1985).

Theopistus of Alexandria, *Vita Dioscori, ed. by F.* Nau, *Histoire de Dioscore, patriarche d'Alexandrie, écrite par son disciple Théopiste,* JA, ser. 10, vol. 1-2 (Paris 1903), 5-108, 241-310.

Thomas av Marga, *Historia monastica,* ed. and tr. by E. A. Wallis Budge, *The Book of Governors. The Historia Monastica of Thomas Bishop of Marga* (London 1893).

Timothy Aelurus, *Epistula ad Epictetum,* ed. and tr. by R. Y. Ebied and L. R. Wickham, 'A Collection of Unpublished Syriac Letters of Timothy Aelurus', *JTS N.S.* 21 (1970), pp. 321-369.

Vita Aphou, ed. and tr. by E. Drioton, *La discussion d'un moine anthropomorphite audien avec le patriarche Théophile d'Alexandrie en l'année 399,* ROC 10 (= 20), (1915-1917), 92-110, 113-128.

Zacharias Scholasticus, *Ammonius sive de mundi opificio disputatio,* PG 85, 1012-1144.

Antirrhesis, PG 85, 1143-1144.

Historia ecclesiastica, ed. and tr. by E. W. Brooks, CSCO, Script. syri, 3..5-6 (Paris 1919-24); eng. tr. by F. J. Hamilton and E. W. Brooks, *The Syriac Chronicle Known as that of Zachariah of Mitylene* (London 1899).

Vita Isaiae Monachi, ed. and tr. by E. W. Brooks, CSCO, Script. syri, 3.25 (Paris 1907), pp. 1-16.

Historia de Petro Ibero [fragment], ed. and tr. by E. W. Brooks, CSCO, Script. syri, 3.25 (Paris 1907), 17-18.

Vita Severi, ed. and tr. by M.-A. Kugener, *Vie de Sévère par Zacharie le Scholastique,* PO 2.1 (Paris 1907).

Pseudo-Zacharias, *Historia ecclesiastica,* ed. and tr. by E. W. Brooks, *Historia ecclesiastica Zachariae Rhetori vulgo adscripta,* CSCO, Script. syri, 3.5-6, (Paris 1919-24). [books 1-2, 7-12].

Secondary Sources

Allen, P., 'Zacharias Scholasticus and the *Historia Ecclesiastica* of Evagrius Scholasticus', *JTS N.S.* 31.2 (1980), 471-488.

Assemani, S. E. and J. S., *Bibliothecae apostolicae Vaticanae codicum manuscriptorum catalogus,* vol. 3 (Rom 1759).

Bacht, H., 'Die Rolle des orientalische Mönchtums in den kirchenpolitischen Auseinandersetzungen um Chalcedon (431-

519)', in A. Grillmeier and H. Bacht (eds.), *KvCh*, vol. 2 (Würzburg 1953), 193-314.

Binns, J., *Ascetics and Ambassadors of Christ: The Monasteries of Palestine, 314-631* (Oxford 1994).

Brakke, D., *Athanasius and the Politics of Asceticism* (Oxford 1995).

Brown, P., *Authority and the Sacred: Aspects of the Christianisation of the Roman World* (Cambridge 1995).

'The Rise and Function of the Holy Man in Late Antiquity', *JRS* 61, (1971), 80-101

'The Saint as Exemplar in Late Antiquity', *Representations* 1.2 (1983), 1-25.

Børtnes, J., *Visions of Glory: Studies in Early Russian Hagiography* (Oslo 1988).

Cameron, A., *Christianity and the Rhetoric of Empire* (Berkeley and Los Angeles 1991).

Charanis, P., *Church and State in the Later Roman Empire: The Religious Policy of Anastasius the First, 491-518* (Thessaloniki 1974).

Chesnut, G. F., *The First Christian Histories: Eusebius, Socrates, Sozomen, Theodoret and Evagrius*. TH 46 (Paris 1977).

Chitty, D. J., 'Abba Isaiah', *JEH* 22 (1971), 47-72.

The Desert a City: An Introduction to the Study of Egyptian and Palestinian Monasticism under the Christian Empire (Oxford 1995 [repr.])

Clark, E. A., *The Origenist Controversy: The Cultural Construction of an Early Christian Debate* (Princeton 1992).

Cox, P., *Biography in Late Antiquity*, Berkeley 1983.

Crum, W. E., *Theological Texts from Coptic papyri* (Oxford 1912).

Darnton, R., *The Great Cat Massacre and Other Episodes in French Cultural History* (New York 1984).

Delehaye, H., *Cinq leçons sur la méthode hagiographique*, Sub. Hag. 21 (Bruxelles 1934).

Does Chalcedon Divide or Unite: Towards convergence in Orthodox Christology, edited by P. Gregorios, W. H. Lazareth, and N. A. Nissiotis (Geneva 1981).

Douglas, M., *Purity and Danger: An Analysis of the Concepts of Pollution and Taboo* (London 1966).

Downey, G., *Gaza in the Early Sixth Century* (Norman 1963).

Eco, U., *La struttura assente: introduzione alla ricerca semiologica* (Milano 1971).

Engberding, H., 'Kann Petrus der iberer mit Dionysius Areopagita identifiziert werden?', *OC* 38 (1954), 68-95.

Evelyn W. H. G., *New Coptic Texts from the Monastery of St. Macarius* (New York 1926).

Flusin, B., 'L'hagiographie palestinienne et la réception du concile de Chalcédoine', in J.-O. Rosenqvist, ΛΕΙΜΩΝ: *Studies Presented to Lennart Rydén on His Sixthy-Fifth Birthday*, (Uppsala 1996), 25-47.

Miracle et Histoire dans l'œuvre de Cyrille de Scythopolis (Paris 1983).

'Naissance d'une Ville sainte: autour de la Vie de Pierre l'Ibère', in *Annuaire de l'Ecole Pratique des Hautes Etudes, Section des Sciences Religieuses* 100 (1991-92), 365-368.

Frend, W. H. C., 'The Monophysites and the Transition between the Ancient World and the Middle Ages', *Convegno internazionale: Passaggio dal mondo antico al medio evo da Teodosio a San Gregorio Magno (Roma, 25-28 maggio 1977)*, in *Atti dei convegni Lincei* 45 (Rome 1980), 339-365.

The Rise of the Monophysite Movement: Chapters in the History of the Church in the Fifth and Sixth Centuries (Cambridge 1979).

Glucker, C. A. M., *The City of Gaza in the Roman and Byzantine Periods* (Oxford 1987).

Goehring, J. E., 'Monastic Diversity and Ideological Boundaries in Fourth-Century Christian Egypt', *JECS* 5 (1997), 61-84.

Golitzin, A., ' 'A Contemplative and a Liturgist': Father Georges Florovsky on the Corpus Dionysiacum', *SVTQ* 43 (1999), 131-162.

Gray, P. T. R., *The Defense of Chalcedon in the East (451-553)* (Leiden 1979).

Gregg, R. C., and Groh, D. E., *Early Arianism: a View of Salvation* (Philadelphia 1981).

Grillmeier, A., *Jesus der Christus im Glauben der Kirche: Band 2/1, Das Konzil von Chalcedon (451), Rezeption und Widerspruch (451-518)* (Freiburg, Basel und Wien 1986).

Haas, C., 'Patriarch and People: Peter Mongus of Alexandria and episcopal Leadership in the Late Fifth Century', *JECS* 1.3 (1993) 297-316.

Hanson, J. S., 'Dreams and Visions in the Graeco-Roman World', in *Aufstieg und Niedergang der römischen Welt* 2.23.2 (Berlin and New York, 1395-1427).

Harnack, A. von, *Lehrbuch der Dogmengeschichte*, vol. 2 (Tübingen 1909).

Harvey, S. A., *Asceticism and Society in Crisis : John of Ephesus and the Lives of the Eastern Saints* (Berkeley, Los Angeles, London 1990).

Hausherr, I., 'Le pseudo-Denys est-il Pierre L'Ibérien?', *Orientalia Christiana Periodica* 19 (1953), 247-260.

Head, T., *Hagiography and the Cult of Saints: The Diocese of Orléans, 800-1200*, (Cambridge 1990).

Honigmann, E., *Évêques et évêchés monophysites d'Asie antérieure au VIe siècle*, (Louvain 1951).

'Juvenal of Jerusalem', *Dumbarton Oaks Papers* 5 (1959), 209-279.

Pierre L'Ibérien et les écrits du pseudo-Denys l'Aréopagite, in *ARB* 47, Classe des lettres (Brussels 1952).

'Zacharias of Mitylene (534 A.D)', in *Patristic Studies*, Studi e testi 173 (Vatican City 1953), 194-204.

Hunt, E. D., *Holy Land Pilgrimage in the Later Roman Empire AD 312-460* (Oxford 1982).

Jalland, T., *The Life and Times of St. Leo the Great* (London 1941).

Jones, A. H. M., *The Later Roman Empire: A Social Economic and Administrative Survey, 284-602*, vol. 1-3 (Oxford 1964).

'Where Ancient Heresies National or Social Movements in Disguise?', *JTS* 10.2 (1959), 280-298.

Karmiris, J. N., 'The Problem of the Unification of the Non-Chalcedonian Churches of the East with the Orthodox on the

Basis of Cyril's Formula: Mia Physis tou Theou Logou Sesarkomene', in P. Gregorios, W. H. Lazareth, and N. A. Nissiotis (eds.), *Does Chalcedon Divide or Unite: Towards convergence in Orthodox Christology* (Geneva 1981), 29-49.

Klein, R., 'Die frühe Kirche und die heidnische Bildung', in P. Guyot (ed.), *Gregorius Thaumaturgus: Oratio prosphonetica ac panegyrica in Origenem* (Freiburg 1996), 83-116.

Kofsky, A., 'Peter the Iberian: Pilgrimage, Monasticism and Ecclesiastical Politics in Byzantine Palestine', *LA* 47 (1997), 209-222.

Lang, D. M., 'Peter the Iberian and his Biographers', *JEH* 2 (Oxford 1951), 158-168.

Lebon, J., 'La Christologie du monophysisme syrien', in A. Grillmeier und H. Bacht (eds.), *KvCh*, vol. 1, 425-580.

Le monophysisme sévérien: Étude historique, littéraire et théologique sur la résistance monophysite au concile de Chalcédoine (Louvain 1909).

MacCormack, S., 'Christ and Empire, Time and Ceremonial in Sixth Century Byzantium and Beyond', *Byzantion* 52 (1982), 287-309.

Meyer, M. A., *History of the City of Gaza: from the Earliest Times to the Present Day* (New York 1907).

Moeller, C., 'Le Type de l'empereur Anastase I', *SP* 3 (=TU 78) (Berlin 1961), 240-247.

Murphy, F. X., and Sherwood, P., *Konstantinopel II und III*, in G. Dumeige and H. Bacht (eds.), *Geschichte der ökumenischen Konzilien*, vol. 3 (Mainz 1990).

Mönnich, C. W., *Geding der Vrijheid, De betrekkingen der oosterse en westerse kerken tot de val van Constantinopel (1453)*, (Zwolle 1976).

Nau, F., 'Introduction', *Jean Rufus: Plérophories, témoignages et révélations contre le concile de Chalcédoine*, PO 8.1 (Paris 1912), 5-10.

Nock, A. D., 'A Vision of Mandulis Aion', *HTR* 27 (Baltimore 1934), 53-104.

Orlandi, T., 'Un frammento delle Pleroforie in Copto', *StRiOC* 2, (Rome 1979), 3-11.

Koptische Papyri theologischen Inhalts (Vienna 1974).

Perrone, L., *La Chiesa di Palestina e le controversie cristologiche* (Brescia 1980).

'Dissenso dottrinale e propaganda visionaria: Le Pleroforie di Giovanni di Maiuma', *Augustinianum* 29 (1989), 451-495.

'Monasticism in the Holy Land: From the Beginnings to the Crusaders', *POC* 45 (1955), 31-63.

Regnault, L., 'Isaïe de Scété ou de Gaza? Notes critiques en marge d'une Introcuction au problème isaïen', *RAM* 46 (1970), 33-44.

Roldanus, J., 'Stützen und Störenfriede: Mönchische Einmischung in die doktrinäre und kirchenpolitische Rezeption von Chalkedon', in van Oort and Roldanus (eds.), *Chalkedon: Geschichte und Aktualität: Studien zur Rezeption der christologischen Formel von Chalkedon,* (Louvain 1997), 123-189.

Roques, R., 'Pierre l'Ibérien et le 'Corpus' dionysien', *RHR* 145 (1954), 69-98.

Rousseau, P., *Ascetics, Authority and the Church: In the Age of Jerome and Cassian* (Oxford 1978).

Pachomius: The Making of a Community in Fourth-Century Egypt (Berkeley 1985).

Rubenson, S., 'The Egyptian Relations of Early Palestinian Monasticism', in O'Mahoney, A., G. Gunner, G. and Hintlian, K (eds.), *The Christian Heritage in the Holy Land* (London 1995), 35-46.

The Letters of St. Antony: Monastic Tradition and the Making of a Saint (Minneapolis 1995).

'Philosophy and Simplicity: The Problem of Classical Education in Early Christian biography', in T. Hägg and P. Rousseau (eds.), *Greek Biography and Panegyric in Late Antiquity* (Berkeley, Los Angeles and London 2000), 110-139.

Sachau, E., *Die Handschriften-Verzeichnisse der Königlichen Bibliothek zu Berlin,* vol. 32: *Verzeichniss der syrischen Handschriften,* vol. 2 (Berlin 1899).

Samuel, V. C., *The Council of Chalcedon Re-examined* (Madras 1977).

Schwartz, E., 'Johannes Rufus: ein monophysitischer Schriftsteller', in *SHAW* 3.16 (Heidelberg 1912), 1-28

'Publizistische Sammlungen zum acacianischen Schisma', in *ABAW* 10.4 (München 1934).

Stein, E., *Histoire du Bas-Empire* (Paris 1949).

Toews, J.E., 'The Historian in the Labyrinth of Signs: Reconstructing Cultures and Reading Texts in the Practice of Intellectual History', *Semiotica* 83.3 (1991), 351-384.

Towards unity: The theological dialogue between the Orthodox Church and the Oriental Orthodox churches, ed. by C. Chaillot and A. Belopopsky (Geneva 1998).

Trombley, F. R., *Hellenic Religion and Christianization c. 370-529*, vol. 2 (Leiden 1994).

Valantasis, R., *Spiritual Guides of the Third Century Guide-Disciple Relationship in Christianity, Neoplatonism, Hermetism, and Gnosticism* (Minneapolis 1991).

Van Dam, R., *Saints and their Miracles in Late Antique Gaul* (Princeton 1993).

Van Esbroeck, M., 'Peter the Iberian and Dionysius the Areopagite: Honigmann's thesis revisited', *OCP* 59 (1993), 217-227.

Van Parys, M., 'Abba Silvain et ses disciples', *Irénikon* 61 (1988), 313-30, 451-480.

Van Uytfanghe, M., 'L'Hagiographie: un 'genre' chrétien ou antique tardif', *AB* 111 (1993), 135-188.

Vööbus, A., *History of Asceticism in the Syrian Orient*, vol. 2. CSCO, Subsidia 17 (Louvain 1960).

Ward, B., 'Introduction', in *The Lives of the Desert Fathers*, CS 34, (Kalamazoo 1981), 3-46,

' 'Signs and Wonders': Miracles in the Desert Tradition', *SP* 18, (Oxford, New York 1982), 539-542

Wessel, S., 'Nestorius, Mary and Controversy, in Cyril of Alexandria's Homily IV, (De Maria deipara in Nestorium, CPG 5248)', *AHC* 31 (1999), 1-49.

Wilken, R. L., *The Land Called Holy: Palestine in Christian History and Thought*. (New Haven and London 1992).

Witakowski, W., *The Syriac Chronicle of Pseudo-Dionysius of Tel-Maḥrē*, (Uppsala 1987).

'Syrian Monophysite Propaganda in the Fifth to Seventh Centuries', in L. Ryden and J. O. Rosenqvist (eds.), *Aspects of late Antiquity and early Byzantium: Papers read at a Colloquium held at the Swedish Research Institute in Istanbul, 31 May-5 June 1992* (Stockholm 1993).

Wright, W., *Catalogue of Syriac Manuscripts in the British Museum acquired since the year 1838*, vol. 3, (London 1872).

Zotenberg, H., *Catalogues des manuscrits syriaques et sabéens de la Bibliothèque Nationale. Catalogue des manuscrits orientaux de la B. N.*, 2, (Paris 1874).

INDEX